First published in Great Britain in 2023 by

Policy Press, an imprint of
Bristol University Press
University of Bristol
1–9 Old Park Hill
Bristol
BS2 8BB
UK
t: +44 (0)117 374 6645
e: bup-info@bristol.ac.uk

Details of international sales and distribution partners are available at
policy.bristoluniversitypress.co.uk

British Library Cataloguing in Publication Data
A catalogue record for this book is available from the British Library

ISBN 978-1-4473-6918-9 hardcover
ISBN 978-1-4473-6919-6 paperback SPA members' edition (not on general release)
ISBN 978-1-4473-6920-2 ePub
ISBN 978-1-4473-6921-9 OA PDF

Cover design: Bristol University Press
Front cover image: iStock/sebastian-julian

SOCIAL POLICY REVIEW 35

Analysis and Debate
in Social Policy, 2023

Edited by
Ruggero Cefalo, Marcia Rose and Andy Jolly

Contents

List of figures and tables

Notes on contributors

Marco Arlotti is Lecturer in Economic Sociology at the Department of Economics and Social Sciences at the Marche Polytechnic University (Italy). His research interests are in long-term care policies, minimum income schemes and multilevel governance.

Matthew Barber-Rowell completed his PhD at Goldsmiths, University of London and is currently an independent scholar, who also holds an Honorary Postdoctoral Fellowship with Liverpool Hope University, and a Research Fellowship with the William Temple Foundation. His work is considering applications for the Curating Spaces of Hope paradigm and consultative methodology. This is taking place through exploration of dialogue, leadership and shared values in uncertain times, and the interdisciplinary implications for social policy, urban geography, sociology of religion, Faith Based Organisation and public theology, in the UK and internationally.

Andrea Blasini is a contract Professor in Administrative Law at the Department of Political Sciences at the University of Pisa. He received his PhD in '*Persona e tutele giuridiche*' from School of Advanced Studies Sant'Anna of Pisa. His research interests are in administrative procedure, public procurement, public-private partnership, public organisation and welfare policies.

Federico Bruno is Postdoctoral Researcher at the University of Milan, where he obtained his PhD in Political Studies in 2020. His research interests include the role of ideas in politics, EU politics and social policies.

Ruggero Cefalo is Postdoctoral Researcher in Sociology and Comparative Welfare Policies at the Department of Sociology at the University of Vienna. His research interests are in school-to-work transitions, social policies, multilevel governance, spatial disparities and youth studies.

Stephanie Fleischer is Principal Lecturer at the School of Humanities and Social Science at the University of Brighton. Her research interests are in the financial circumstances of students, first year student experiences, absenteeism, mindsets and resilience as well as intergenerational matters.

Aimee Grant is Senior Lecturer in public health at the Centre for Lactation, Infant Feeding and Translational Research, Swansea University, and a Wellcome Trust Career Development Fellow leading the Autism: from menstruation to menopause project. Her interests are in health, inequality and qualitative methods, particularly participatory approaches and documentary analysis.

Stephanie Green is a PhD student and Research Coordinator for Care Homes in Wales at Swansea University. Her research interests include intergenerational care, ageing, and health and social care policy.

Joe Greener is Lecturer in Sociology, Social Policy and Criminology at the University of Liverpool. His research interests lie in critical policy and political economy analysis in a range of substantive areas including mental distress, neo-colonialism, urban studies and migration.

Kate Howson is an early career researcher and Senior Partnership lead for Research at Social Care Wales. Her research interests include ageing, knowledge mobilisation, relationship-centred care and the impact of intergenerational activities on social care outcomes.

Andy Jolly is Lecturer in Social Work at the University of Plymouth, and Honorary Research Fellow at the Institute for Community Research and Development, University of Wolverhampton. His research interests are in household food security in the UK and bordering practices in children's social care.

Penelope Laycock is Tutor in Social and Public Policy at the University of Glasgow and a PhD student in Social Policy at the University of Strathclyde. Her research interests are in substance use policy, trauma and health inequalities.

Jiaxin Liu is Lecturer in Gerontology at the University of Southampton. Her research focuses on ageing and social policy, with a particular interest in intergenerational family support, public pensions and social policy in China/East Asian societies.

Mirain Llwyd Roberts is Gwynedd Age-friendly Coordinator in a Welsh local authority, having previously been appointed the first Bridging the Generations Coordinator in Wales. She has also undertaken a Master of Research in intergenerational practice with Dr Catrin Hedd Jones at Bangor University.

Stefano Neri is Associate Professor in Comparative Welfare Systems and Sociology of Organization at the Department of Social and Political Sciences at the University of Milan. His research interests are in health, social and childcare policies, labour regulation in public services, health and social professions.

Lois Peach is a PhD student, Research Associate and Graduate Teacher at the School for Policy Studies, University of Bristol. Her research interests include non-familial intergenerational relationships, childhoods, ageing and dementia, and post-humanism.

Marcia Rose contributed to this process as a Youth Practitioner. Her undergraduate thesis dealt with young people's bereavement support, and her master's degree addressed student mental health. Marcia is undertaking research for her PhD on social prescribing and men's mental health with the supervision of Professor Paul Montgomery and Dr Jason Schaub at The University of Birmingham. Her research interests include mental health, education and social policy.

Lena Sakure is a speech and language therapist, PhD student and demonstrator at University College London. Her research interests include social interaction, relationships and experiences in early years and long-term care settings, qualitative methods of inquiry and intergenerational programmes.

Amy Sanders is a Postdoctoral Research Associate in the Wales Institute of Social and Economic Research and Data (WISERD) at Aberystwyth University. Her research interests are in civil society and the third sector, governance, representation, equality and intersectionality.

Akanksha Sanil is a PhD scholar in the Department of Political Science at the University of Delhi. She has a particular interest to critically engage with social policy issues in India, especially those that include the dynamics of inequality, marginality, and exclusion, of individuals and communities.

Matthew Barber-Rowell completed his PhD at Goldsmiths, University of London and is currently an independent scholar, who also holds an Honorary Postdoctoral Fellowship with Liverpool Hope University, and a Research Fellowship with the William Temple Foundation. His work is considering applications for the Curating Spaces of Hope paradigm and consultative methodology. This is taking place through exploration of dialogue, leadership and shared values in uncertain times, and the interdisciplinary implications for social policy, urban geography, sociology of religion, Faith Based Organisation and public theology, in the UK and internationally.

Hilary Silver is Professor in Sociology, International Affairs, and Public Policy & Public Administration at George Washington University and Professor emerita of Sociology and Urban Studies at Brown University. Her research interests include social exclusion, urban poverty, and homelessness and policies that address them

Elena Vivaldi is Associate Professor in Constitutional Law at Sant'Anna School of Advanced Studies in Pisa. She is the scientific director of the Advanced Training course 'IDA – Inclusion, Disability, Accessibility: the social model of disability tested by the pandemic' and the coordinator of the Politics, Welfare, Rules (POWER) research area of the Sant'Anna School. She teaches Rights and Social Policies in the History of the Italian Republic. Since July 2020, she has been Italy's national expert in the European Disability Expertise (EDE) network, funded by the European Commission.

Lizzie Ward is Principal Research Fellow in the School of Humanities and Social Science at the University of Brighton. Her interests include ageing, care ethics, intergenerational relationships and experiential knowledge.

Gemma Williams is an Economic and Social Research Council (ESRC) Postdoctoral Research Fellow in Social Policy at the University of Brighton. Her research interests include linguistics, communication, social policy and neurodivergence. Gemma is also an associate with the National Development Team for Inclusion.

Kathryn Williams is an Autistic ESRC funded PhD student at Cardiff University's School of Social Science and is also a voluntary non-executive director at Autistic UK Community Interest Company (CIC), an organisation run by Autistic people for Autistic people. Her PhD is examining the role of communication in access to healthcare for Autistic adults. Her other research interests include epistemic injustices faced by Autistic people, neoliberal-ableism and neuronormativity within social policies.

Richard Woods is a PhD student at London South Bank University's Critical Autism/Disabilities Studies research group and an active member of the Participatory Autism Research Collective. His PhD is investigating the proposed mental disorder 'Pathological Demand-Avoidance' (PDA). His other academic interests include Monotropism theory and Autism and the social model of disability.

Eve Yeo is a Sociology PhD candidate at the University of Liverpool. Her research interests are in welfare governance and subjectivities, with a specialisation in Singaporean social policy.

Global developments in social policy research

Ruggero Cefalo, Marcia Rose and Andy Jolly

The long-reaching shadows of the COVID-19 pandemic continue to affect multiple areas of our societies around the world, challenging social policy responses and research in 2023. The consequences of COVID-19 are still a recurring thread across several chapters of this year's Social Policy Review. With respect to Social Policy Review 34 in 2022, a main thematic focus is intergenerational equity and solidarity, thoroughly discussed during the yearly Social Policy Association (SPA) conference. Two further trends can be identified across the contributions collected in this Social Policy Review. First, some chapters extend their view towards less-explored policy fields, looking for instance at the use of substances or at policies for Autistic adults. Second, chapters continue to expand the geographical reach of the review providing evidence on the United States, China, India and Singapore. Thus, they contribute towards a global view on social policy research and developments.

Thematically, we have divided the volume into three sections. Part I contains contributions from the new Social Policy Association policy groups, with chapters covering diverse facets of intergenerational equity and solidarity. Part II delves into research developments in social policy analysis, with a wide thematic range that explores elderly care, Faith Based Organisations, employment services and third sector-government partnerships. Part III continues the international theme of last two years, with contributions covering social policy developments in the USA, in Singapore, in England and Wales.

In Chapter 1, Peach, Sakure, Llwyd Roberts, Green and Howson explore the relationship between research, policy and practice within programmes of intergenerational practice, that involve different generations being together in organised initiatives, sharing experiences, knowledge and resources. The chapter shares research insights and reflects on the future sustainability and yet-to-be fulfilled potential of intergenerational practice within social care. Chapter 2 by Ward and Fleischer discusses the impact of the COVID-19 pandemic on intergenerational relationships, drawing on empirical research carried out in 2020, which explored older and younger people's perspectives on generational differences generated by the pandemic and the policy responses to it. The study findings suggest cross-generational understandings of the social, economic and political issues that face all generations. In Chapter 3, Laycock investigates current circumstances surrounding alcohol and drug use and their intergenerational transmission in Glasgow, where this issue causes disproportionate health impacts on those from more deprived areas. The author uses the theory of locus of control to better understand how childhood experiences impact adult behaviour, outcomes, and health inequalities, in particular substance abuse. Chapter 4 by Akanksha reflects on castes as a form of systemic structural inequality in the context of India, arguing that castes have aggravated historic inequities among disadvantaged groups in access to basic services such as healthcare or education, equitable opportunity and even human dignity. In Chapter 5, the final contribution to the intergenerational research section, Liu explores how older Chinese, and their families arrange and negotiate for intergenerational support. In China, rapidly ageing population and changes in family structure, labour market, and cultural and social norms have brought unprecedented challenges to older individuals and their families. Chapter 6, by Arlotti and Neri, opens Part II by investigating the impact of the COVID-19 crisis on the residential care sector during the first wave of the pandemic in seven European countries. The authors frame their analysis by considering the pre-existing structural and institutional conditions predominant in each country selected. In Chapter 7, Barber-Rowell reflects on and explores the potential for contributions of Faith Based Organisations in the context of increased uncertainty brought by the COVID-19 pandemic, arguing for a new paradigm of Faith Based Organisations to enable mapping and coproduction of responses to uncertainties in social policy. Chapter 8, by Vivaldi, Blasini and Bruno, adopts a social innovation perspective to analyse an experimental social policy project implemented in Pisa (Italy), that allowed participants to access a series of personalised services aimed at social inclusion and job placement. In Chapter 9, Sanders applies a feminist institutionalist lens to explore the impact on equalities groups of an innovation of third sector engagement in policy making, specifically looking at the Third Sector–Welsh Government partnership. In this chapter, policy actor accounts are examined to consider which equalities organisations are advantaged or disadvantaged by the formal and informal facets of the institution of this partnership.

Chapter 10 by Silver opens Part III by examining the introduction of special policies to prevent COVID-19 infections among people experiencing or at-risk of homelessness, in the USA and in Europe. The author observes that, while the crisis enabled progressive reforms to break through the path-dependent status quo, the enduring legacy of the pandemic on Housing First, eviction prevention, rental subsidies and other emergency policies remains an open question. In Chapter 11, Yeo and Greener take a critical stance on East Asian social policy provision, by showing its role in reproducing hierarchies. The chapter uses a cultural political economy approach, to illustrate the semiotic reproduction of accumulation strategies through Singapore's Central Provident Fund (CPF). Finally, in Chapter 12, Grant, Williams, Williams and Woods, a group of Autistic academics, deal with the epistemic injustice behind the exclusion of the Autistic input from the policy making process, which they consider to be a core part of Autistic disablement. The authors also propose changes to the policy making process to ensure that it reflects Autistic needs and realities.

Part I

Intergenerational research

Intergenerational research, policy and practice for sustaining social care in the UK: current challenges and future aspirations

Lois Peach, Lena Sakure, Mirain Llwyd Roberts, Stephanie Green and Kate Howson

Introduction

The concept of intergenerationality is gaining momentum among policy researchers and policy makers. In 2022, the annual Social Policy Association (SPA) conference was themed *Intergenerationality: Challenges and Prospects* to respond to increasing interest in the implications of past and present policy making upon different generations, including future generations. The SPA conference brought together experts by experience and researchers of intergenerationality in a range of intersecting areas, including family relations, poverty, education, social care, health, civil society, climate, migration, digital economies and more. At this event, we, as a group of early career researchers and a local authority practitioner explored current challenges facing intergenerational research, policy and practice in social care in the UK and discussed our future aspirations for how these challenges may be overcome. This chapter serves as a summary and a continuation of our conversations.

Intergenerational programmes, policy and practice intend to increase interaction, understanding and support between members of different generations, with the principle aim of fostering meaningful relationships (Sanchez et al, 2018). A common definition provided by the Beth Johnston Foundation is:

> Intergenerational practice aims to bring people together in purposeful, mutually beneficial activities which promote greater understanding and respect between generations and contribute to building more cohesive communities. Intergenerational practice is inclusive, building on the positive resources that the young and old have to offer each other and those around

them. (Beth Johnson Foundation, 2001 cited in Hatton-Yeo, 2015, p 284)

In this chapter, we draw upon intergenerational research which we each individually conducted either in the few years before, during, or after the COVID-19 pandemic across the UK, largely concentrated in England and Wales. Intergenerational practice is gaining momentum in these two nations, although arguably is developing at a slower pace than in the rest of the UK, partly due to formalised country-specific support principally offered by Generations Working Together in Scotland and Linking Generations, Northern Ireland. For instance, at the SPA conference we heard the Older People's and Future Generations' Commissioners in Wales vocalising their support for intergenerational work, but no national policies are yet put in place. We have seen a Welsh local authority appoint Mirain Llwyd Roberts, one of the co-authors of this chapter, as the first 'Bridging the Generations' coordinator, but we are aware of no similar vision for local authority provision across the UK. In England, as will be discussed later in the chapter, a recent national programme called the Care Home Friends and Neighbours Intergenerational Linking Project represents, to our knowledge, one of the largest coordinated attempts to link young people in schools and youth groups with care home residents across local communities. Additionally, reports such as 'Healing the Generational Divide' (Dalton et al, 2019) and 'Key Mechanisms of Intergenerational Work' (Bryer and Owens, 2019) have been presented to the government both in England and Wales. These developments represent notable steps forward, however, progress remains disparate and incremental. Although we recognise that there are no simple, quick or 'magic' answers to the issues surrounding sustainable social care and intergenerational practice, we share insights from our research to argue that research, policy and practice should be guided by the principles of relationality – placing relationships at the centre; non-reductionism – not oversimplifying at the risk of devaluing important information; and reflexivity – actively engaging in critical reflection for continued learning and development. This chapter is organised around these three themes to contemplate the yet-to-be fulfilled potential of intergenerational practice involving adult social care. First, we give context to the notion of intergenerationality and the relationship between intergenerational practice and social care.

Intergenerationality: an opening riff

It would be rare today to find a gerontological article, media report, or policy paper on aging whose opening riff was not the crashing chords of facts about *population* growth, size, risks, and costs. (Katz, 2022, p.1, emphasis in original)

The most logical place to start in a discussion about intergenerational practice and social care is concern over shifting relations of, and requirements for, care resulting from demographic change and population ageing. This is because intergenerational practice in the UK has been justified on these grounds since the 1990s; considered in policy spheres as a vital mechanism for reconnecting divided and disaffected generational groups, and promoting active ageing (Hatton-Yeo, 2010). It is not uncommon then, for the 'opening riff' of an intergenerational policy or practice article to highlight the larger number of older individuals requiring care; the impact of urbanisation and shifting labour market participation; and the reduced spaces for intergenerational mixing in communities. These effects are often aligned with weakening social and political relations between different age groups, both within and outside the family. This has encouraged studies of intergenerationality which explore relations and interactions between generational groups, and the factors which may enhance or constrain experiences of age, difference, conflict and connection (Hopkins and Pain, 2007). The increased interest in this topic within policy research is, therefore, perhaps unsurprising given, as Walker (2002, p 297) contends, 'what society does by way of social policy has a critical bearing on the nature and experience of intergenerational relations'.

Not only does policy influence generational relations but generational relations are arguably having a greater impact on effective public policy. Priority policy areas increasingly differ among age groups, exemplified by generational divisions in voting behaviours at the Brexit referendum and 2017 general election (Dalton et al, 2019). Debates around intergenerational (in)equity and (in)justice intersect with multiple areas of policy making as the redistributive policies and relations of (familial) care foundational to the welfare state inevitably rely upon intergenerational solidarity (Carney and Nash, 2020). The alleged deterioration of generational relations and the 'social contract' of interdependency across the life course between working and non-working citizens upon which the welfare state is premised (Walker and Fong, 2010), has been used by some, ideologically committed to neoliberalism, as justification for dismantling welfare provision (Carney and Nash, 2020). For others, this provides an opportunity for re-imagining it (Shafik, 2021). Regardless of the approach, discussion over the state of generational relations has spurred increased interest in intergenerational policy making.

The notion of intergenerational policy making promotes solidarity among generations, both now and in the future (Lüscher, 2013). This is attempted either by acknowledging the interdependence between generational groups for basic needs such as care, shelter, education and economic support, or, more commonly in the UK, by promoting specific programmes and activities which increase age integration and facilitate interaction (Klimczuk, 2015). Carney and Nash (2020, p 97) argue that solidarity between the generations is key in the process of securing and maintaining social, political and economic security. However, although the 'transformative potential' of intergenerational practice in policy spaces has not gone unnoticed (Hopkins et al, 2011, p 315) as yet there is no specific intergenerational policy in the UK. Therefore, despite agreeing with Steven Katz's aforementioned critique of the oversimplified use of a population ageing narrative, which reproduces the notion of a burdensome older cohort and runs counter to the anti-ageist agenda of intergenerational work, there is no getting away from the increasing relevance of age, ageing and (inter)generational relations in contemporary policy debates.

Background: intergenerational practice in social care

Intergenerational programmes involving adult social care can take different forms, from time-limited and open-ended visitation programmes within residential facilities or day centres to co-located schemes such as childcare and care home facilities on shared sites. Despite variation in their design, in these programmes, older adults and children or young people spend time together, take part in shared activities and interact socially. While there is nothing new about the concept of connecting generations, or indeed humans, in society, it is recognised that there may be an added benefit and nuance of doing so in formal care settings (Steward et al, 2021).

The social care system in the UK, and in England in particular, is considered unsustainable in its current state (Glasby et al, 2021). Factors affecting the sustainability of adult social care are summarised by three D's: (1) Demand – increased need, longer life expectancy and limitations to informal unpaid care for an increasing number of childless older people are raising demand; (2) Delivery – a lack of paid care workers being recruited and high turnover in the sector has been compounded by the impact of Brexit and the COVID-19 pandemic; and (3) Deficiency – the legacy of austerity policies since 2010 has meant less spending on social care from local authorities as well as local disparities in meeting care needs adequately (Hamblin, 2022). In this chapter, we discuss intergenerational work within adult social care provision and refer to care homes, both residential and nursing, as specific sites providing care to older adults and those living with additional physical or cognitive needs. A key challenge for this sector is providing adequate care, while also ensuring that provision is meaningful, supportive of quality of life and connected to local communities. Research evaluating intergenerational programmes within care homes has suggested intergenerational practice may help to address these priorities. For example, Di Bona et al's (2019) mixed methods study of the Adopt a Care Home Scheme, aimed at contributing to dementia friendly communities, suggested that 'Intergenerational initiatives may increase the social inclusion of care home residents, thus offering a positive, sustainable way of drawing on the community to achieve benefits for people living with dementia, children and wider society, at very little additional cost' (Di Bona et al, 2019, p 1680).

Indeed, meta-analysis of recent systematic reviews investigating intergenerational programme outcomes demonstrates that older adults may experience improvements in quality of life, enhanced physical and mental wellbeing, a sense of purpose and reduced depressive symptoms (Peterson, 2022). Additionally, research has suggested children may gain improved understanding and attitudes toward older generations, increased motivation and social skills, as well as learning competencies such as reading, language and artistic skills (Martins et al, 2019). International research has also indicated organisational benefits including staff satisfaction and retention (Weeks et al, 2016). In terms of policy, intergenerational initiatives, especially co-located schemes, may go some way in addressing the segregation of aged care and childcare policies and provision (Radford et al, 2022). This may be particularly beneficial within a UK policy context characterised as fragmented (Hatton-Yeo, 2011) and may also contribute to rising costs associated with both child and adult care. Together, these factors have encouraged organised non-governmental advocacy and greater implementation of intergenerational programmes within care institutions within the UK. Nonetheless, the task of implementing and sustaining intergenerational practice in adult social care, within the current context of provision, remains a challenge for the field.

The potential future sustainability of an intergenerational approach within social care in the UK is a relatively unexplored area in the literature. Although grass-roots organisation of intergenerational practice within social care is gaining momentum, those of us involved in policy research are concerned with the current framing of intergenerational practice within social care as reflecting a neoliberal ethic toward individual and localised responsibility, often with limited or a lack of attached resource, thus avoiding major public sector reform in social care. The lack of a specific intergenerational policy or established mechanisms for support, resource and secure funding for intergenerational work within social care points to the need for a closer relationship between research, policy and practice. As Melville and Bernard (2011) suggest: 'We need to understand better the relationships between intergenerational practice, theory and policy if we are to fully realise the potential of this developing field' (Melville and Bernard, 2011 p 238). We agree that something is missing in enabling intergenerational practice within social care to flourish.

Insights from the symposium

Our symposium and subsequent discussion as part of this chapter represent several different angles or domains of knowledge in relation to intergenerationality in social care. Three of them are provided by researchers of intergenerational programmes. Peach's research uses post-qualitative methodologies and relational theoretical perspectives to take account of human and nonhuman actors in the 'middle', between young and old, such as staff, objects and practices, often excluded from analysis (Peach, 2022). Similarly, Howson's quasi-experimental longitudinal study explored the development of relationships between staff, residents and younger people, commenting on the impact of organisational procedures and policies upon the implementation of intergenerational programmes within social care settings. Sakure investigates what happens in the very moment of social interaction between residents, preschoolers and facilitators of intergenerational sessions using conversation analysis (CA). Sharing our interest in what happens within intergenerational programmes, during the symposium we reflected upon how processes of intergenerationality are somewhat more difficult to measure than outcomes. The consequence being the nature of intergenerational relations is often overlooked and yet, the key to intergenerational practice lies in relationships (Sánchez et al, 2010). To address the challenge of this contradiction, we suggest relational and non-reductionist perspectives have merit for unpacking the mechanisms through which intergenerational relationships generate outcomes. This will be discussed in more detail later.

Two remaining angles on intergenerationality offer further nuance to our discussion. Green applies a poststructuralist approach and the method of critical discourse analysis to investigate the use of the intergenerational concept within seven UK policy and/or strategy documents and stakeholder interviews. She reflects upon how insights about where the field as a whole has come from in terms of language and development can help inform where it may go. In this way, reflexivity should be considered a key aspect of future intergenerational policy making. Llwyd Roberts provides a vital practitioner perspective confirming this. Presenting during the symposium, Llwyd Roberts combined her experience as the first local authority 'Bridging the Generations' coordinator in the UK with findings from her postgraduate research exploring how generations could be better connected within a Welsh local context. Crucially, Green and Llwyd Roberts' insights affirm the relative adolescence of intergenerational research, policy and practice within the UK and reveal how the relationships between individual, community and national approaches toward intergenerational practice contribute to sustainability.

Despite adopting different methodological and ontological positions, the perspectives we each offer have areas of overlap and complementarity. The following discussion is consequently a mosaic of contributions with three common threads: relationality, non-reductionism and reflexivity. We are acutely aware that our experience and expertise lies in the realms of research and practice. As a response, the following section elaborates on what we feel is missing from current knowledge of intergenerational practice within social care; namely, relationality and non-reductionism. The subsequent section on reflexivity explores our future aspirations for intergenerational policy and practice by drawing upon policy analysis and practitioner experiences.

Current challenges

It has been suggested that research accounts for the most significant aspect of the relationship between intergenerational research, policy and practice as it links policy and practice together (Bernard, 2006). However, intergenerational scholars have critiqued the current state of knowledge in the field. Intergenerational practice research is often considered limited in terms of its quality by small sample sizes and the type and duration of interventions means it may be inappropriate or difficult for research methods considered high quality, such as meta-analyses or randomised control trials (RCTs), to be used (Jarrott, 2011). From a theoretical perspective, current research can be seen to demonstrate limited theoretical underpinning, and where theory is used, is conceptually narrow (Kuehne and Melville, 2014). Such research is also largely concerned with demonstrating outcomes (Melville and Hatton-Yeo, 2015), which are often age-specific, addressing one generational group in particular (Vanderbeck, 2007) and, as a result, has a tendency to be subject-oriented rather than relationships-focused (Sánchez et al, 2010). This may be explained by the desire to legitimise intergenerational work to a policy audience with evidence of beneficial outcomes. Yet, academics within the intergenerational field have upheld that relationships are central to intergenerational work (Kaplan, 2004; Sánchez et al, 2010). To address these challenges, we affirm intergenerational research should adopt a relational, non-reductionist and reflexive approach.

Relationality

Relationality refers to the idea that at the centre of intergenerational relations lies a relationship between interconnected individuals (Sánchez et al, 2010). A relational approach, therefore, acknowledges that relationships should be given precedence in the ways we seek to understand interaction between generations. This principle of relationality, although obvious, is not always reflected in the way we design, analyse and report our findings about intergenerational practices. Peach, Howson and Sakure's research, for instance, attempts to understand micro-level relations within interventions in a relational way. Rather than solely concentrating on individual participants and their outcomes, we are interested in the aspects that contribute to the relationships facilitating these outcomes. In short, we are interested in processes of intergenerationality.

Elsewhere, Peach has written about the potential for posthuman/feminist new materialist perspectives to diversify the theoretical and conceptual tools we use to understand intergenerational relations between non-family members (Peach, 2022). She argues that current approaches to intergenerational research which aim to demonstrate age-specific outcomes uphold the generational divide of young/old and enact a separation which limits relational understandings of these initiatives. This is counter to the intention of intergenerational practice which seeks to bring people together. Focusing on participants misses the impact and experiences of practitioners and carers, as well as the influences of material and discursive factors in the intergenerational environment. The relational perspective offered by feminist new materialism, however, provides a different way of considering who *and* what is involved in intergenerational practice within social care and seeks a de-individualised approach toward researching intergenerational relationships.

Peach recently put this approach to work in research of an intergenerational music programme, Rebuilding Bridges, which took place in three care home gardens in the Southwest of England as we emerged from COVID-19 restrictions during the autumn of 2021. Peach considered how interactions between preschool children, musicians, artists and researchers outside, and care home staff and residents inside, were facilitated not only by the practitioners involved but also by the music itself, lyrics, instruments, picnic blankets, pens, paper and paint, and the regulated spaces of the garden and care home lounge on either side of patio doors. This provided a nuanced perspective of the 'socially distanced' intergenerational initiative by focusing on the interconnected nature of human and nonhuman relations. Alongside a more normative mixed methods evaluation undertaken with Kathrin Paal from the University of Plymouth, Peach used a narrative evaluation approach adapted from the Learning Stories assessment tool used within early childhood education (Carr, 2001). This approach produced a book, designed by Harry Flook, of *intergenerational stories*, combining photographs of the sessions, practitioners and participants' reflective accounts and observational vignettes to explore multiple perspectives of the encounters.[1]

Storying intergenerational relations aimed to gain a richer insight into how interactions were enabled and constrained by the activities of practitioners, other people, and things within the intergenerational space. This may also have practical uses in providing an accessible approach toward programme evaluation, responding to the current challenge practitioners face in demonstrating impact (Jarrott et al, 2019). Although representing only an initial step toward alternative evaluation practices, the collaborative approach toward intergenerational storytelling replicated the relational way in which a variety of actors contribute to intergenerational relationships. Additionally, the multivocal nature of the stories told resonates with a non-reductionist perspective toward understanding intergenerational relationships.

Non-reductionism

Non-reductionism is a principle which broadly refers to an appreciation of diversity and multi-dimensionality in our approach to understanding problems, solutions and associated practices. Principally, this term foregrounds the value of rich detail, localised knowledge and nuance as a counter to oversimplification. In this way, acknowledging the different actors involved in intergenerational interaction recognises the multi-dimensionality of relations within these spaces. Like Peach's approach, Howson's research purposefully engages with the range of actors to consider what is involved in delivering intergenerational practice within social care in Wales. Exploring the potential for intergenerational work to help promote care home spaces as age-friendly communities, Howson's quasi-experimental and longitudinal study reported older people's quality of life and young people's attitudes toward residents were enhanced. Qualitative data also suggested an increased sense of purpose for activity coordinators.

The importance of staff attitudes toward the intergenerational activities and care work routines enabling the residents to take part was also highlighted by Howson's research. Aligning with results from other studies (Gigliotti et al, 2005), intergenerational activities were viewed as separate to the care provided to residents, and therefore, considered less significant when staff capacity was limited. In essence, this reflects the contradiction that intergenerational practice can be seen as an approach to a range of complex and overlapping policy priorities, such as age-friendly communities, while simultaneously lacking any mandated support. This contradiction presents barriers for the development of these initiatives and reduces them to an 'added extra' in much social care provision. However, Howson's research suggested that intergenerational practice holds promise for creating spaces where care staff were permitted to reflect and recognise the importance of social connections to residents, carers and the care home community. The use of intergenerational initiatives created dedicated space, time and resources for establishing relationships between staff, residents and individuals from the local community. Relationships, facilitated by objects associated with or made during activities, were central to successful delivery. This aligns with the principles of relationship-centred care (Nolan et al, 2006) and the key aim of the Social Services and Wellbeing Act (2014) in Wales to move the emphasis of social care work toward wellbeing outcomes and away from a task-based approach (Verity et al, 2020). This again highlights the relationality between practitioners, participants, objects, and care home and national policies in the delivery of intergenerational practice within social care.

Sakure argues that to enable meaningful intergenerational policy and practice, we need to contribute different research methodologies which can capture nuanced and relational aspects of intergenerationality. Sakure has found that CA (Hutchby and Wooffitt, 1998) can offer tools and procedures to achieve this goal. In this method, the researcher analyses social interaction between participants second-by-second, turn-by-turn to see how they co-construct talk, meanings and social action in the time and space they share (ten Have, 2007). The method also enables us to take stock of both verbal and non-verbal (for example, eye gaze, facial expression, gesture) participant contributions. Appreciating these features of CA, Sakure collected video recordings of intergenerational and non-intergenerational activities in a care home co-located with a nursery. With CA, she will be investigating the process of talk in intergenerational activity, comparing it with recreational activities where children are not present.

Despite this focus on observing the finer detail of the intergenerational process, Sakure argues that it is important to complement this data with perspectives gathered from the participants themselves. In her case, this involves analysing interviews conducted with residents, facilitators and children with a view to relate CA insights with how participants themselves make sense of their experience. Complementing detailed observational findings with interview data brings participant voices and sense-making into the picture and allows for a richer representation of intergenerational processes. Such mixed qualitative methodology studies can offer useful non-reductionist insights for policy makers, new practitioners and future researchers into what actually happens in social care settings moment-by-moment and what matters to the people involved.

In summary, given Sánchez et al (2010) suggest that relational approaches toward policy and research may sustain intergenerational practice, we agree that the principle of relationality should be embedded in approaches studying intergenerational programmes. For policy makers, this may offer an insight into how their support and enablement of one social group will inevitably have knock-on effects for others, including practitioners. Drawing attention to the crucial, but often under-acknowledged, role of practitioners and nonhuman factors such as objects, care home policies, and caring practices demonstrated that a non-reductionist approach may explore the multi-dimensional nature of intergenerational interaction. Reducing intergenerational practice to an 'added extra' within social care provision is not enough in our opinion and may be countered by formalised intergenerational policy or care home practices which provide infrastructure and support for fostering meaningful relationships. Although we do not want to (in a reductionist manner) suggest there is a simple policy solution to these challenges, we have aspirations for a policy, practice and research landscape which can embrace the complexity of intergenerational relationships. This, we propose, is part of a sustainable approach to intergenerational practice within social care.

Reflexivity

Researchers, especially those engaging with qualitative methodologies, will be especially familiar with the concept of reflexivity as describing an ethical awareness of how researchers influence the conditions of knowledge generation. The reflexivity we refer to here incorporates this, but also refers to how the intergenerational field can critically contemplate intergenerational work. To be reflective, therefore, for us means to be aware not only of our methodological choices and approaches to day-to-day intergenerational practice but also to the very words we use to discuss with peers and report on our findings or policy. We suggest that reflexivity can help us to sharpen and deepen our critical understanding of intergenerationality and its place in social care.

Green's research contends language is a key but still underexplored aspect of the intergenerational research–policy–practice relationship. Intergenerational relations are often negatively framed in policy discourse around competing resources and tensions (Vanderbeck and Worth, 2015). Taking a post-structuralist approach toward the uninterrupted use of the intergenerational concept as a legitimating notion in the field of social policy and practice, Green's critical discourse analysis of seven UK policy/strategy documents revealed important ideological undertones in how intergenerational practices are framed as solutions to long-standing issues within the social care system in the UK. Her approach was informed by Carol Bacchii's (2009) framework, '*What is the problem represented to be?*' to address key influences in the development of intergenerational practices. The findings showed that the socially and politically constructed nature of the intergenerational concept is used to support evolving political narratives around social isolation and loneliness, as well as divisions between generations, being attributed to the individual. This framing or 'problematisation' aligns with a neoliberal approach, wherein the third sector, public sector and individuals in communities are encouraged in policy to take an intergenerational approach, despite this risking the perpetuation of short-term, under-resourced initiatives. Her research suggests that a reflexive understanding of how intergenerational practice has developed in policy, may help to inform future, more sustainable, approaches toward intergenerational work within social care.

Another example of the value of reflexivity comes from Green's work on the use of the intergenerational concept itself. Green's research additionally revealed the selective use of the intergenerational concept, meaning it may become meaningless and act as a barrier to future policy and practice developments. This was supported by semi-structured interviews (n = 22) with key stakeholders from policy and practice across the four UK nations, showing that there is already some shifting away from the notion of intergenerationality, towards a more inclusive approach which includes more than the two generations. This research acknowledges the wider meso, macro and exo-system influences upon our understanding and development of intergenerational practice which Green critiques as having been neglected in a field specifically focused on micro-level intergenerational relations within interventions. More nuanced approaches that acknowledge the complexity of intersecting relations between population, community and individual level forms of intergenerationality are needed (Walker and Fong, 2010; Yarker, 2021). For Green, this means the field of intergenerational research has become 'un-interesting' (Alvesson and Sandberg, 2013). This may seem like an odd argument for a group of intergenerational researchers but what we mean by this is that the narrowness of the field limits diversity in the knowledge we can produce of intergenerationality in these spaces. Addressing this development may open up more reflexive and honest conversations between researchers, with different epistemic and ontological positions (as we are doing here), and practitioners and policy makers, about the suitability of intergenerational practice for social care provision.

An additional challenge presented by a lack of reflexivity is that, in trying to demonstrate that intergenerational practice works, there is little room for highlighting what is not working. Llwyd Roberts's research and practice within a local authority in Wales suggests that a crucial missing piece in how we understand and implement intergenerational practice is the barriers it may face. Llwyd Roberts's research addressed the challenges facing intergenerational practice and, over the past few years, she has had the opportunity to implement her findings in her day-to-day role as a 'Bridging the Generations' co-ordinator for Gwynedd Council, a local authority in North Wales. Llwyd Roberts's research involved conducting a scoping review, four case studies and surveys completed by individuals from various areas across Wales. Across these methods there was consistency in the reasons why intergenerational activities in the local authority were unsustainable and coming to an end. Principally, that the true impact and numerous possibilities for intergenerational practice in the community were yet to be fully understood.

For Llwyd Roberts, the potential of intergenerational practice may be realised when it is viewed not only as a project that works with the young and older members of society but a matter of bringing individuals of all ages together for the benefits of all involved. The popularity of the Channel 4 T.V. programme' Old People's Home for Four-Year-Olds, for instance, has resulted in many underappreciating the diverse forms which intergenerational practice can take. Llwyd Roberts is keen to point out that from a practitioner perspective, planning for intergenerational connection should encompass a variety of approaches, such as naturally occurring relations in shared community spaces (e.g., such as that currently being trialled and built by Grŵp Cynefin in Penygroes, Gwynedd) or carefully considered housing developments, as well as education and care-based interventions. Within these models, we can expect a number of variations, for instance, in terms of organisation, participants and location. It has also been documented that intergenerational programmes can have different types of designs, including structured, explicit interventions, where all objectives and participants are clearly defined before the start, and those set up with an emergent approach, where the activities, participants and facilitation strategies may evolve with the programme (Kaplan & Larkin, 2003). This variability suggests that if we want our approaches to studying, running and promoting intergenerational programmes to be realistic and meaningful for the setting, in other words critically reflexive, they are likely to require local adaptations and responsiveness to a variety of factors including safeguarding, staffing, organisational priorities, funding, and spaces. This, however, does not remove the need for national support and infrastructure.

One example of national support comes from Peach's recent involvement in research, led by Dr Briony Jain and formerly Dr Ali Somers, of the Care Home Friends and Neighbours (CHFaNs) intergenerational linking project in England. This project is the first national intergenerational project in England supporting links between care homes, schools and youth organisations through the work of local community brokers. This project is delivered via collaboration between My Home Life England, part of City, University of London, and the Linking Network, funded by #iwill fund and Dunhill Medical Trust. Demonstrating a reflexive approach, this appreciative inquiry aims to learn valuable lessons about sustaining intergenerational practice involving care homes from the development of intergenerational links across 11 funded areas in England. Although at the time of writing analysis is still in progress, initial findings suggest community brokers, the support of a national team, a collaborative sharing network, advisory groups, and a flexible funding approach are vital mechanisms supporting the connection between education and social care providers in each locality. Similar to Llywd Robert's observation that following the implementation of the new curriculum in Wales (Donaldson, 2015) there has been an increase in interest for intergenerational projects within schools, the CHFaNs local community brokers were able to legitimise intergenerational work by linking it to the curriculum or regulatory criteria, such as those outlined by Ofsted and the Care Quality Commission (CQC). Additionally, like Llwyd Robert's work[2] as a 'Bridging the Generations' coordinator, the CHFaNs community brokers demonstrated creativity in their approaches to intergenerational linking, particularly as a response to COVID-19 pandemic restrictions. As a result, this project demonstrates the importance of coordinated planning, leadership, and ample time needed to implement and sustain intergenerational work within communities.

Together, these perspectives suggest intergenerational programming is hampered by little planning around long-term strategies for sustainability and a lack, or limited duration, of support by funders and promoting organisations (Vieria and Sousa, 2016). From Llwyd Roberts' practitioner perspective this has raised numerous ethical concerns around the impact of projects ending for participants that may benefit from this form of social connection. If we are to avoid the potential harms of short-term programmes and therefore, short-lived benefits, we need greater reflexivity into how the policy-practice-research relationship may be limiting the attention given to the processes involved in sustaining programmes and relations. As Azevedo and Sánchez (2019) suggest this may involve going beyond the sustainability-as-continuity model of intergenerational practice to question not just whether intergenerational practice works, but how it works and whether continuation is even desirable. What Green and Llwyd Roberts' insight, as well as the CHFaNs research, shows then, is that reflexivity about where we have come from and where we are, both in terms of challenges and positive developments, is crucial.

Conclusion

We formed the symposium at the SPA conference to open-up discussion about what is potentially missing within intergenerational practice, research and social policy development involving social care services for older adults in the UK. Being aware of the important links between policy, research and practice, which require greater attention within the intergenerational field (Melville and Bernard, 2011), we have written this piece as a way of dialoguing with policy makers and scholars.

Drawing upon the differing methodological and ontological perspectives and vantage points of our work to converge upon complementary insights, we have highlighted several key messages. We have brought to attention that there is currently no policy in the UK which would guide and promote intergenerational practice within social care; despite non-governmental organisations and charities continuing to engage policy makers and growing momentum around the concept of intergenerationality in policy, research and practice spaces. Our message has been that research into intergenerational interventions within social care should be solidly grounded in the principles of relationality and non-reductionism if it is to offer a truly meaningful contribution to intergenerational policy making. This is research that is able to place intergenerational relationships at its centre and account for the complexities of practice.

We have suggested that relationships are the fuel of sustainable intergenerational practice (Azevedo and Sánchez, 2019). In this way, intergenerational research, policy and practice should also aim to animate the vitality of intergenerational relations by being open to different ways of knowing, doing and developing intergenerationality. We propose practitioners can be key informants, contributing valuable insight for understanding what has been done so far in this field and what could be done in the future. In this chapter and our symposium, we have enacted this value by integrating Llwyd Roberts's practitioner perspective. This kind of dialogue, we argue, is indicative of the broader reflexive process we advocate. As a result, we invite policy makers and scholars to engage with practice-based research which critically contemplates intergenerational work.

Overall, we suggest that meaningful routes to sustainability in this context will require shifts away from the individualistic, outcome-specific nature of much intergenerational research, as well as the hegemonic neoliberal discourse influencing the use of the intergenerational concept in policy and practice, toward more relational, non-reductionist and reflexive discussions about the potential value of intergenerational practice within social care. Although we are cautious of overstating the possibilities for intergenerational practice to provide simple, quick or 'magic' answers to complex policy problems, including the sustainability of adult social care, we support the intention for intergenerational practice to be part of building socially just and connected communities (Hatton-Yeo, 2011).

Notes

[1] See https://generationsworkingtogether.org/case-studies/rebuilding-bridges for more information about the Rebuilding Bridges programme evaluation, including the storybook output 'Rebuilding Bridges: Storying moments of intergenerational connection through music' designed by Harry Flook (https://harryflook.com).

[2] In their role as a Bridging the Generations Coordinator, among other things, Mirain initiated a pen pal scheme during the COVID-19 pandemic linking 153 pairs of younger and older individuals in Gwynedd.

References

Alvesson, M. and Sandberg, J. (2013) 'Has management studies lost its way? Ideas for more imaginative and innovative research', *Journal of Management Studies*, 50: 128–52. Available from: https://doi.org/10.1111/j.1467-6486.2012.01070.x [Accessed 04 December 2022].

Azevedo, C. and Sánchez, M. (2019) 'Pathways to sustainable intergenerational programs: lessons learned from Portugal', *Sustainability*, 11(23): 6626. Available from: https://doi.org/10.3390/su11236626 [Accessed 04 July 2022].

Bacchi, C. (2009) *Analysing Policy: What's the Problem Represented to be?*, French Forest, NSW: Pearson Higher Education AU.

Bernard, M. (2006) 'Keynote 1. Research, policy, practice and theory: interrelated dimensions of a developing field', *Journal of Intergenerational Relationships*, 4(1): 5–21. Available from: Doi: 10.1300/J194v04n01_03 [Accessed 23 August 2022].

Bryer, N. and Owens, J. (2019) 'Review of Key Mechanisms in Intergenerational Practices, and their Effectiveness at Reducing Loneliness/ Social Isolation', [online] 30 September. Available from: https://www.gov. wales/sites/default/files/statistics-and-research/2019-05/review-key-mec hanisms-intergenerational-practices-their-effectiveness-reducing-lonelin ess-social-isolation.pdf [Accessed 30 September 2022].

Carney, G. and Nash, P. (2020) *Critical Questions for Ageing Societies* (1st edn), Bristol: Policy Press.

Carr, M. (2001) *Assessment in Early Childhood Settings: Learning Stories*, London: Paul Chapman.

Dalton, S., Dixon, A., Bell, R. and Kimani, A. (2019) 'Healing The Generational Divide Interim Report on Intergenerational Connection', All Party Parlimentary Group on Social Integration, [online]. Available from: https://socialintegrationappg.org.uk/wp-content/uploads/sites/2/ 2019/05/Healing-the-Generational-Divide.pdf [Accessed 20 June 2021].

Di Bona, L., Kennedy, S. and Mountain, G. (2019) 'Adopt a care home: an intergenerational initiative bringing children into care homes', *Dementia*, 18(5): 1679–94. Available from: Doi:10.1177/1471301217725420 [Accessed 05 December 2022].

Donaldson. (2015) 'A Curriculum for Wales: A Curriculum for Life', [online] 21 November. Available from: https://dera.ioe.ac.uk/24680/1/ 151021-a-curriculum-for-wales-a-curriculum-for-life-en_Redacted.pdf [Accessed 21 November 2020].

Gigliotti, C., Morris, M., Smock, S., Jarrott, S.E. and Graham, B. (2005) 'An intergenerational summer program involving persons with dementia and preschool children', *Educational Gerontology*, 31(6): 425–41.

Glasby, J., Zhang, Y., Bennett, M. and Hall, P. (2021) 'A lost decade? A renewed case for adult social care reform in England', *Journal of Social Policy*, 50(2): 406–37. Available from: Doi:10.1017/S0047279420000288 [Accessed 05 December 2021].

Hamblin, K. (2022) 'Sustainable social care: the potential of mainstream "smart" technologies', *Sustainability*, 14(5):2754. Available from: https:// doi.org/10.3390/su14052754 [Accessed 27 September 2022].

Have, P. (2007) *Doing Conversation Analysis*, London: Sage.

Hatton-Yeo, A. (2010) 'An introduction to intergenerational practice', *Working with Older People*, 14(2): 4–11. Available from: https://doi.org/ 10.5042/wwop.2010.0261 [Accessed 05 December 2022].

Hatton-Yeo, A. (2011) 'Looking back, looking forward: reflections on the 10th anniversary of Beth Johnson Foundation Centre for Intergenerational Practice, United Kingdom', *Journal of Intergenerational Relationships*, 9(3): 318–21. Available from: https://doi.org/10.1080/15350770.2011.593 444 [Accessed 05 December 2022].

Hatton-Yeo, A. (2015) 'A personal reflection on the definitions of inter-generational practice', *Journal of Intergenerational Relationships*, 13(3): 283–4.

Hopkins, P., Olson, E., Pain, R. and Vincett, G. (2011) 'Mapping intergenerationalities: the formation of youthful religiosities', *Transactions of the Institute of British Geographers*, 36(2): 314–27. Available from: https://doi.org/10.1111/j.1475-5661.2010.00419.x [Accessed 27 September 2022].

Hopkins, P. and Pain, R. (2007) 'Geographies of age: thinking relationally', *Area*, 39(3): 287–94. Available from: https://doi.org/https://doi.org/10.1111/j.1475-4762.2007.00750.x [Accessed 27 September 2022].

Hutchby, I. and Wooffitt, R. (2008) *Conversation Analysis*, Cambridge, UK: Policy Press.

Jarrott, S.E. (2011) 'Where have we been and where are we going? Content analysis of evaluation research of intergenerational programs', *Journal of Intergenerational relationships*, 9(1): 37–52.

Jarrott, S.E., Stremmel, A.J. and Naar, J.J. (2019) 'Practice that transforms intergenerational programs: a model of theory- and evidence informed principles', *Journal of Intergenerational Relationships*, 17(4): 488–504. Available from https://doi.org/10.1080/15350770.2019.1579154 [05 December 2020]

Kaplan, M, (2004) 'Toward an intergenerational way of life', *Journal of Family and Consumer Sciences*, 96(2): 5–9.

Kaplan, M. and Larkin, E. (2003) 'Launching intergenerational programs in early childhood settings: a comparison of explicit intervention with an emergent approach', *Early Childhood Education Journal*, 31(3): 157–63.

Katz, S. (2022) 'Population: is it time to revisit this term in aging research?.' *Age, Culture, Humanities: An Interdisciplinary Journal*, 6. Available from: https://doi.org/10.7146/ageculturehumanities.v6i.133332 [Accessed 27 December 2022].

Kuehne, V.S. and Melville, J. (2014) 'The state of our art: a review of theories used in intergenerational program research (2003–2014) and ways forward', *Journal of Intergenerational Relationships*, 12(4): 317–46.

Klimczuk, A. (2015) *Economic Foundations for Creative Ageing Policy: Volume I Context and Considerations.* New York: Palgrave Macmillan

Lüscher, K. (2013) 'Intergenerational policy and the study of intergenerational relationships: a tentative proposal', in I. Albert and D. Ferring (eds) *Intergenerational Relations: European Perspectives in Family and Society*, Bristol: Bristol University Press, pp 65–82.

Martins, T., Midão, L., Martínez Veiga, S., Dequech, L., Busse, G., Bertram, M., et al (2019) 'Intergenerational programs review: study design and characteristics of intervention, outcomes, and effectiveness', *Journal of Intergenerational Relationships*, 17(1): 93–109.

Melville, J. and Bernard, M. (2011) 'Intergenerational shared sites: policy and practice developments in the UK.' *Journal of Intergenerational Relationships*, 9(3): 237–49. Available from: https://doi.org/10.1080/15350770.2011.593 431 [Accessed 30 December 2022].

Melville, J. and Hatton-Yeo, A. (2015) 'Intergenerational shared spaces in the UK context', in R. Vanderbeck and N. Worth (eds) *Intergenerational Space*, London: Routledge, pp 50–64.

Nolan, M., Davies, S. and Brown, J. (2006) 'Transitions in care homes: towards relationship-centred care using the "Senses Framework"', *Quality in Ageing and Older Adults*, 7(3): 5–14. Available from: https://doi.org/10.1108/ 14717794200600015 [Accessed 04 December 2022].

Peach, L. (2022) 'Missing middles: toward a feminist new materialist approach for understanding intergenerational inter/intra-action', *Journal of Intergenerational Relationships*, 1–16. Available from: https://doi.org/ 10.1080/15350770.2022.2126914. [Access 17 October 2022]

Petersen, J. (2022) 'A meta-analytic review of the effects of intergenerational programs for youth and older adults', *Educational Gerontology*, 1–15. Available from: https://doi.org/10.1080/03601277.2022.2102340

Radford, K., Fitzgerald, J.A., Vecchio, N., Cartmel, J., Gould, R. B. and Kosiol, J. (2022) 'Key considerations to the introduction of intergenerational practice to Australian policy', *International Journal of Environmental Research and Public Health*, 19(18): 11254. Available from: https://www.mdpi.com/ 1660-4601/19/18/11254 [Accessed 20 December 2022].

Sánchez, M., Sáez, J., Díaz. P. and Campillo, M. (2018) 'Intergenerational education in Spanish primary schools: making the policy case', *Journal of Intergenerational Relationships*, 16(1–2): 166–83.

Sánchez, M., Sáez, J. and Pinazo, S. (2010) 'Intergenerational solidarity, programs and policy development.', in E.M.A. Cruz-Saco, and S. Zelenev (eds.) *Intergenerational Solidarity. Strengthening Economic and Social Ties*, New York: Palgrave Macmillan, pp 129–46.

Shafik, M. (2021) *What We Owe Each Other: A New Social Contract for a Better Society*, Princeton: Princeton University Press.

Social Services and Well-being (Wales) Act. (2014) [Online] Available from: https://www.legislation.gov.uk/anaw/2014/4/contents [Accessed 03 March 2023].

Steward, A., Hasche, L., Greenfield, J.C., Ingle, M. P., De Fries, C., Fix, R., et al (2021) 'A Review of participant, agency, and community outcomes of non-familial intergenerational programs', *Journal of Social Work*. 23(1): 122–142 Available from: https://doi.org/10.1177/146801 73211057436 [Accessed 04 October 2022].

Vanderbeck, R.M. (2007) 'Intergenerational geographies: age relations, segregation and re-engagements', *Geography Compass*, 1(2): 200–21.

Vanderbeck, R.M. and Worth, N. (2015) *Intergenerational Space*, London: Routledge.

Verity, F., Andrews, N., Calder, G., Anderson, P., Llewellyn, M., Wallace, S., et al (2020) 'Evaluation of the Social Services and Well-being (Wales) Act 2014 Literature Review', Cardiff: Welsh Government.

Vieira, S. and Sousa, L. (2016) 'Intergenerational practice: contributing to a conceptual framework', *International Journal of Lifelong Education*, 35(4): 396–412.

Walker, A. (2002) 'The politics of intergenerational relations', *Zeitschrift für Gerontologie und Geriatrie*, 35(4): 297–303. Available from: https://doi.org/10.1007/s00391-002-0104-7 [Accessed 20 December 2022].

Walker, A. and Fong, F. (2010) 'Relations between the generations: uniting the macro and the micro', *Journal of Intergenerational Relationships*, 8(4): 425–30. Available from: https://doi.org/10.1080/15350770.2010.521096 [Accessed 20 December 2022].

Weeks, L.E., MacQuarrie, C., Begley, L., Nilsson, T., and MacDougall, A. (2016) 'Planning an intergenerational shared site: nursing-home staff perspectives', *Journal of Intergenerational Relationships*, 14(4): 288–300. Available from: https://doi.org/10.1080/15350770.2016.1229550 [Accessed 24 October 2022].

Yarker, S. (2021) 'A research agenda for geographies of everyday intergenerational encounter', *Area*, 53: 264–71. Available from: https://doi.org/10.1111/area.12716 [Accessed 30 December 2022].

2

An intergenerational divide in the context of COVID-19?

Lizzie Ward and Stephanie Fleischer

Introduction

The idea that older and younger generations are fundamentally at odds with each other is not new. The 'generation gap' emerged in the 1960s and has provided ample material for comedy and popular culture. But a less light-hearted assessment of generational division has taken shape over the last decade (Bristow, 2019; Pickard, 2019). Debates, mainly in the media, have focused attention on generational justice and fairness with some social commentators arguing that older generations enjoy privileges and benefits while younger people face hardship and an uncertain future. In this chapter, we focus on intergenerational relationships during the COVID-19 pandemic in the summer of 2020, as a context in which both the virus and policy responses to it reflected generational difference.

Firstly, this chapter offers an overview of media and political discourses around intergenerational divisions since the financial crises of 2008–09 based on a review of scholarly literature from the UK. It discusses the rise of these discourses in relation the EU referendum 2016 and within the context of the COVID-19 pandemic. It then focuses on survey research carried out in July 2020, which explored older and younger peoples' perspectives on generational differences generated by the pandemic and policy responses to it. The potential conflict between protecting older people, deemed more at risk of the virus, or ensuring an economic future for younger people, deemed more at risk from the economic impacts of lockdowns, added another layer to existing discourses about an intergenerational divide. Finally, we consider the implications of the 'generational wars' discourses and the use of age ideology to define social, economic and political issues in the context of the post-pandemic recovery.

The rise of age ideology and generational grievances

Ideas about generational inequalities and conflict can be linked to wider concerns over population ageing and increased longevity. While these are evidence of the advances in living standards and public health over the twentieth century, they have also been viewed as a problem by policy makers concerned about the 'burden' these place on health and care resources, feeding into negative discourses about the unaffordable costs of an ageing population (Walker, 1990). The negative framing of population ageing intensified during the financial crises of 2008–09 when it was mobilised to justify government austerity responses (Walker, 2013; Phillipson, 2015). Walker argued that the UK 2010 coalition government's austerity agenda heralded a new political narrative that 'Britain cannot afford its ageing population' (Walker, 2013, p 812). The resultant 'new ageism' fuelled ideas about intergenerational conflict and inequity and paralleled moves in the US that have seen the scapegoating of older people since the 1980s (Macnicol, 2015). These have been linked to cuts in welfare support for older people, understood by Macnicol as part of the neoliberalisation of old age which shifts attention from 'the widening socio-economic inequalities that have occurred over the last forty years' (Macnicol, 2015, p 140). The politically motivated demonisation of older people attributes growing inequality to older people gaining benefits at the expense of younger people, while ignoring evidence that demonstrates greater inequalities *within* generations (Phillipson, 2015).

In the UK, this narrative has grown to encompass the perceived advantages of the older population in relation to housing, education, pensions and unfair political influence (Pickard, 2019). The UK debates reflect, to some extent, those taking place within Europe amidst concerns that the current younger generation will not achieve the same levels of economic wellbeing enjoyed by previous generations. Various generational differences coalesce under the concept of intergenerational fairness, which as Alexander Shaw (2018) notes in EU debates, has become 'the great new frontier in economic and social policy making, in which age-group cleavages are perceived as having new and perhaps primary significance in the European political economy' (Alexander Shaw, 2018, p 1). However, the European policy debates include an explicit recognition of 'intergenerational solidarity' understood as key in responding to demographic change (for example the European Commission, 2009). Initiatives such as the European Day of Solidarity between Generations, aimed to mitigate the potential breakdown in social cohesion across generations as the uneven impacts of financial crises played out.

What distinguishes the UK context are the political divisions which intensified generational grievances following the BREXIT referendum when age differences emerged between those who voted to leave the EU and those who voted to remain (Coren, 2016; Paxman, 2015; Bristow, 2021; Wildman et al, 2022). The mobilisation of blaming 'baby boomers' for the referendum result, reflected particularly in media discourses, was enabled by earlier claims that the older generation were acting selfishly to protect their own interests to the detriment of younger generations (see, for example, Willetts, 2010).

The polarised framing of different generations 'at war' is troubling and problematic. At a conceptual level it relies on the over-simplistic categorisation of people by 'generation'. Yet as sociological work has shown, 'generation' it is a multi-faceted, complex concept which can be used to refer to generations within family structures, to people belonging to same age cohort, or to people living at a particular historical period (Popescu, 2019). It requires definition according to the context in which it is being used. Moreover using 'age' as the exclusive lens without taking account of other social locations, such as, class, race, gender, limits its analytical value. As Martin and Roberts (2021) argue, blanket statements about particular generations, whether 'baby boomers' or 'millennials' create homogenised stereotypes and leads to 'generationalism'. The denial of intragenerational heterogeneity reduces complex issues into a singular narrative and ignores intersectional factors which shape the different experiences and outcomes of older and younger people. In an analysis of media representations of intergenerational justice, Pickard (2019) finds this use of 'generation' operates to justify neoliberal economic welfare retrenchment as part of 'age ideology':

> the portrayal of social problems in terms of generational war emerges from age ideology and an age system that, among other things, intersects with and naturalises other forms of stratification. … That the age system has been overlooked and underplayed in sociological terms is an important oversight since the former materially and ideologically facilitates the ever-growing socio-economic inequality that is a feature of our times. (Pickard, 2019, p 369)

Pickard's analysis is supported by Cooper's (2021) review of similar debates in the US where intergenerational injustice arguments have been used against state funding for social welfare as 'an important tool in the fight against class redistribution' (Cooper, 2021, p 743). This suggests that intergenerational injustice claims are not neutral but part of a wider ideological agenda. In a study of UK media discourses Bristow (2021) traces the use of intergenerational injustice to 'claimsmaking organisations' that are engaged in promoting such an agenda. Bristow argues that the Brexit vote was an opportunity for these claimsmaking organisations to escalate the rhetoric in which they 'sought to consolidate and extend a sentiment of generational grievance, which informs wider claims about a political divide between old and young' (Bristow, 2021, p 759).

COVID-19 and generational differences

The wider political divisions that the EU referendum reflected were part of the landscape in which the pandemic emerged in early 2020. The indications that the virus impacted older people more severely than other groups in society informed the UK government responses with the initial advice directed towards all people over 70 to self-isolate for 12 weeks (Fletcher, 2021). This drew criticism from the British Society of Gerontology (BSG, 2020) who strongly objected to the inaccurate assumptions that all people over 70 are, by virtue of their age, vulnerable and need to be protected. Moreover, it ignored the actual contributions older people make towards supporting others: 'Quarantining the more than 8.5 million people over 70 years of age will deprive society of many people who are productive and active and who can be a key part of the solution by supporting the economy, families and communities' (BSG, 2020, p 1).

In assessing the BSG's claims that the policy was ageist, Fletcher argues that the policy response was a form of pragmatic discrimination based on epidemiological data, albeit reflecting 'unequivocal examples of ageism ... and institutionally enacted cultural attitudes' (Fletcher, 2021, p 487). Without doubt, the pandemic provided yet another context for social problems to be considered in generational terms. This included the potential rationing of health resources based on age criteria, the indiscriminate use of 'Do Not Resuscitate Notices'[1] in residential care homes and adherence to social distancing restrictions, all of which impacted older and younger people differently (Coker, 2020; Hill, 2020; Proctor, 2020).

However, the pandemic also exposed human vulnerability more widely, and at least in the early stages, our interdependencies and the need for collective responses to the crisis were clear. Arguably, this led to a more considered debate about older and younger peoples' needs within some media discourses (see, for example, Blanchflower and Bell, 2020; Harris, 2020; Sodha, 2020; Williams, 2020). But in some areas of social media the generation 'wars' were inflamed by restrictions perceived as disproportionally impacting younger people for the benefit of older people. For example, in an analysis of Twitter Elliott (2022) found generational ideas linking COVID-19 to older and younger generations' beliefs and behaviour about the climate crisis. Elliott describes this as an 'intergenerational discounting' narrative frame which encompasses a 'breakdown in reciprocal obligations of care' and expressing: resentment and rage, and the suggestion that COVID-19's disproportionate effects on older people is a kind of karmic retribution for their failure to address climate change, which will more negatively affect younger people, making the virus the 'Boomer remover' (Elliott, 2022, p 75). Like earlier 'boomer blaming' discourses, Elliott's analysis of tweets demonstrates the potency of a homogenised characterisation of generation which fails to engage in significant inequalities that situate individual people differently in relation to the social issues they claim to address.

The 'age'-related impacts of both the virus and the responses to it, such as lockdown restrictions and the roll out of vaccinations, have thrown up new dimensions to debates about age and generational relations. It was within this context that we set about exploring how older and younger people experience questions of generational differences. We were interested in how they perceived or experienced the challenges or benefits being assumed on their behalf as a generation and how much insight each had into the world of the other. Next, we turn to our research that explored these questions of generational differences.

Exploring generational differences and shared concerns with older and younger people

We conducted a study during the summer of 2020 as the lockdown restrictions from the first wave of COVID-19 were beginning to be lifted in England. From the end of March, people had to stay at home (apart from essential purposes such as food shopping or medical appointments) and all non-essential shops and businesses were closed. People were permitted to leave home for outdoor recreation in May and by June groups of six were permitted to meet outside and most restrictions had been lifted by July. This context inevitably shaped the responses to our questions as there was still considerable uncertainty about the pandemic and people struggled to make sense of the unprecedented circumstances facing everyone.

Our study was co-designed with members of the South East England Forum on Ageing (SEEFA) and comprised a cross-sectional online survey with two different age groups: people over the age of 70 and students aged between 18 and 24. The survey of mainly closed questions asked for responses to a series of statements which examined the extent to which younger and older participants were experiencing the challenges or benefits being assumed on their behalf as a generation and how much insight they had into each other's worlds. We included open-ended questions which asked participants to give reasons for their responses and this provided some qualitative contextual data.

We used convenience sampling methods (Matthews and Ross, 2010) to recruit participants with a total of 214 people taking part: 134 younger student participants and 80 older participants. Our sample was diverse in some respects, but in both groups most participants identified as female and White and sample characteristics are shown in Table 2.1. The majority of older participants (72) had children or grandchildren.

We analysed the closed survey questions using Statistical Package for the Social Sciences (SPSS) initially to count and describe the responses in each

Table 2.1: Survey sample characteristics

	Student participants	Older participants	Total
N	62.6% (134)	37.4% (80)	100% (214)
Men	29.9% (40)	27.5% (22)	29.0% (62)
Women	67.2% (90)	72.5% (58)	69.2% (148)
Non-binary	2.2% (3)		1.0% (3)
Prefer not to say	0.7% (1)		0.0% (1)
White	68.7% (92)	96.3% (77)	79.0% (169)
Mixed	7.5% (10)		4.7% (10)
Asian	11.9% (16)	1.2% (1)	7.9% (17)
Black	3.7% (5)		2.3% (5)
Other	6.0% (8)	2.5% (2)	4.7% (10)
Prefer not to say	2.2% (3)		1.4% (3)
Shielding from COVID-19	49.3% (66)	35.0% (28)	43.9% (94)
Have a job	51.5% (69)	17.5% (14)	38.8% (83)

Source: Online survey 'Understanding fairness between different generations' carried out by authors July 2020

age group. We then carried out Chi square tests to establish the statistical significance between the younger and older age group for yes/no questions. For ranking questions, such as level of concern/agreement, Mann Whitney U tests were performed with recording median responses for the relevant ranking scale to compare these for each age group to determine statistical significance. The free text answers given to the open questions were coded and analysed thematically to identify emergent themes. Next, we offer selected findings, for the full research report see Ward, Fleischer and Towers (2021).

Age discrimination and disadvantage across different generations

We started by exploring perceptions of age discrimination and disadvantage. All participants were asked to agree or disagree to the general statement 'young people can face discrimination and disadvantage' (Figure 2.1). A higher proportion, 75.6%, of younger participants agreed with this statement compared to 61.2% of older participants.

All participants who answered 'yes' to the statement were asked to provide up to three examples. Both groups referred to negative assumptions that younger people lack life experience and knowledge:

> Often older generations belittle the newer generations experiences. (older participant)

They are seen as wanting more materially than previous generations. (student)

But more concrete examples of discrimination through disability, ethnic background, skin colour, sexuality, gender and social class were given by both groups. Both groups also cited the economic disadvantages younger people face, such as the lack of opportunities, social mobility, low wages and work conditions:

Wages in the workplace are often situated unfairly towards young people. (older participant)

Zero hours contracts. (student)

The generation between 18 and 24 have experienced two economic downturns of severe nature. (older participant)

Unable to leave home financially. (student)

We asked all participants the same question in relation to older people. The majority of both groups (74.6% of younger participants and 78.8% of older participants) agreed that 'older people face discrimination and disadvantage' showing no difference in responses by age.

Similar examples of negative stereotypes of older people were offered by both groups. These concerned older people's assumed lack of ability and value to society, a lack of political voice and negative portrayals of physical appearance:

Figure 2.1: Agreement or disagreement with the statement 'young people can face discrimination and disadvantage'; answers by age group

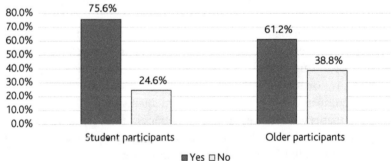

Source: Online survey 'Understanding fairness between different generations' carried out by authors July 2020

Views are ignored or undermined. (student)

Social care provision for older people is poor and underfunded and reflects the extent to which older people are not seen as a priority. (older participant)

Noticeable examples of disadvantage were offered such as: less access to health services, transport and public spaces and digital exclusion. The financial hardships some older people face, including poverty and lack of pensions and barriers to accessing paid work were also recognised:

They are not provided with a pension suitable for them. (student)

Older people are consistently discriminated against in the job market, even though the pension age is regularly raised. (older participant)

Overall, both participant groups appeared to have shared understanding of the discrimination and disadvantages each age group faces.

Generational advantage and disadvantage

We then explored perceptions of generational advantage and disadvantage and asked all participants to respond to a series of statements. In response to the statement 'older people are often seen as well off and privileged' (Figure 2.2) younger participants (81.1%) were more likely to disagree compared to

Figure 2.2: Agreement or disagreement with the statement 'older people (over 70) are often seen as well off and over privileged'; answers by age group

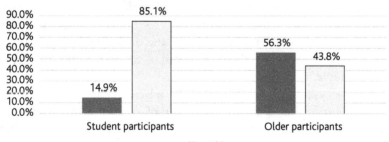

Source: Online survey 'Understanding fairness between different generations' carried out by authors July 2020

Figure 2.3: Agreement or disagreement with the statement 'things were easier for the current generation of older people when they were young'; answers by age group

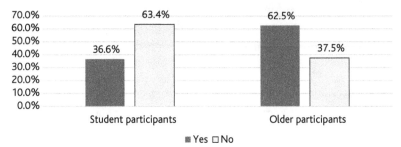

Source: Online survey 'Understanding fairness between different generations' carried out by authors July 2020

43% older respondents. This was a statistically significant difference by age group with half of older participants in agreement that their own age group is 'often seen' as privileged.

Similar examples of perceived privileges were cited by both groups in relation to financial security, home ownership, greater educational and employment opportunities bestowed upon the 'baby boomer' generation:

> Good pension provision due to good job opportunities during working life. (older participant)

> Those who bought houses many years ago have made a fortune in that time. (student)

A higher proportion of older participants (62.5% compared to 36.6% of younger participants) also agreed with the statement 'things were easier for the current generation of older people when they were young' (Figure 2.3). This was a statistically significant difference and possibly suggests younger participants are less convinced by the idea that older people 'had it easier' that circulates through the 'generational wars' discourses. In response to other questions, they demonstrate awareness of the difficulties past generations faced, acknowledging that these are different to their own challenges as younger people.

Again, the examples given by both groups related to employment, housing and education, such as a greater availability of jobs, with better terms and conditions and greater job security, more affordable housing and 'free' higher education:

> Housing was easier – either from council housing or cheap rentals, or even saving to get a deposit to buy a house. (older participant)

No housing crisis. (student)

Education was free. (student)

Both groups thought that previous generations had not faced the social pressures that have come from increased consumerism and, more recently from social media, which may have made their lives easier:

> We had very little choice of material things so there was no pressure to have expensive trainers or be ostracised. (older participant)

> Body image was different back then, social media now gives fake perceptions of what a woman and man's body should be like. (student)

Although a majority of older participants had agreed that things were easier for when they were young, over half (51.2%) still felt they had personally faced difficulties as a younger person. A higher percentage of younger participants (73%) felt that they personally face difficulties as a young person and this difference is statistically significant (Figure 2.4).

For the older participants these difficulties included the lack of educational opportunities, particularly for girls and those from low-income families, the high level of competition for university places; and the end of formal education at age 15 for many people. In contrast, younger participants referred to the pressure to go to university and the high costs and debts incurred through higher education. In relation to economic disadvantages both groups referred to low wages, unemployment and difficulties of finding work, and being treated differently in the workplace on account of age. But

Figure 2.4: Agreement or disagreement with the question 'do you think you faced difficulties as a younger person'; answers by age group

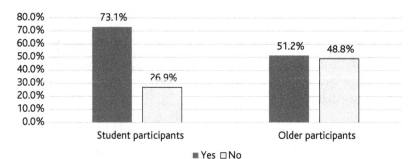

Source: Online survey 'Understanding fairness between different generations' carried out by authors July 2020

younger participants also referred to job insecurity characterised by zero-hours contracts and high competition for jobs.

Older participants reflected on the cultural norms which were often experienced as restrictive and limiting when they were young. Possibly, younger participants experience more freedom, but they also reflected on the social pressures that impact them, such as educational achievement, pressure to be financially independent and pressures around body image and sex and the negative impacts of social media.

For some older participants cultural norms and expectations were highly gendered as the traditional male breadwinner model of welfare and family norms were prevalent at the time. This meant that there were fewer work and career opportunities for women, who were expected to give up work once they got married and had children:

> There was huge discrimination against young women in the workplace – again because of the fear that they would go off and have children just when they had the skills to be really useful. I successfully concealed my first pregnancy until the week the baby was born. (older participant)

> As a girl, parents viewed a career as temporary only prior to marriage. Education would have been made a priority for a son. (older participant)

For younger participants, their experiences reflected different aspects of discrimination related racism, gender identity and disability:

> As a transgender young person I am often characterised as less deserving of equal treatment, or treated like my lived experience is not valid. (student)

> What I wear, my headscarf is my identity but most people look at me weird for wearing one. (student)

The older age group referred to wider social and historical contexts that shaped their experiences, such as growing up during World War Two. Whilst younger participants reflected on climate change and political uncertainty:

> Yes we faced different difficulties. Shortage of food during the war and when the war was over. We were rationed for years. (older participant)

I was a WW2 child and my education was disrupted by evacuation 3 times and a lack of sleep due to Air-raids at night. (older participant)

Having to live in a society with an underfunded welfare state and inadequate climate protection causing us to face mass extinction or having to spend billions of our taxes to reverse it as the previous generations have put us in an awful position. (student)

When we asked if participants agreed that generally 'younger people (18–25s) are often seen as worse off than previous generations' a higher proportion of older participants (75%) than younger participants (14.9%) agreed (Figure 2.5). This was a statistically significant difference.

The examples given by both groups mirrored responses about assumptions that older people had it easier when they were young, such as financial security and affordable housing. Again, it was older participants who reflected that the circumstances facing current younger people compare less favourably to their own younger lives. Possibly, the older participants had some understanding of the younger peoples' challenges as the majority had children and grandchildren. A larger proportion of younger participants thought their own age group is not seen as worse off than previous generations. For example, they recognised more educational opportunities and careers enabled by new technologies not available to previous generations.

COVID-19 and government responses to the pandemic

We were interested in older and younger participants' perspectives on COVID-19 and how the government responded. Participants rated their

Figure 2.5: Agreement or disagreement with the statement 'younger people (18–25s) are often seen as worse off than previous generations'; answers by age group

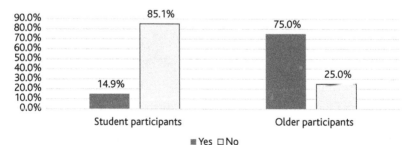

Source: Online survey 'Understanding fairness between different generations' carried out by authors July 2020

concern over a range of aspects related to the pandemic: getting the virus; their health (not COVID-19 related); the health of their family (living in different households); their wellbeing; the wellbeing of their family (living in different households); losing their job; financial worries; social isolation; childcare arrangements for children/grandchildren. Table 2.2 shows the average levels of current concern with higher scores reflecting more concern. Both age groups showed the most concern for the health and wellbeing of their families living in a different household. Younger participants had a higher level of concern for personal wellbeing, financial worries and social isolation than the older age group. Perhaps because many students had to isolate in halls of residents away from their families and support networks and this most likely also impacted on their wellbeing. The negative effects of lockdown on young people has been recognised through government funding for a recovery plan to support young people's mental health (HM Government, 2021).

Younger participants were on average more likely to disagree that 'the government has done enough to protect older people who are deemed more at health risk from the virus during the pandemic' as well as 'the government has done enough to protect younger people who are deemed more at economic risk during the pandemic'. In contrast, older participants were on average neutral, neither agreeing nor disagreeing with both statements.

Table 2.2: Average levels (medians) of current concerns related to the pandemic by age group

	Student participants	Older participants
Getting the virus	3	4
My health (not COVID-19 related)	3	3
Health of my family in different households	4	4
My wellbeing	4*	3*
Wellbeing of my family in different households	4	4
Losing job	3	1
Financial worries	4*	2*
Social isolation	4*	2*
Childcare worries	2	2

Note: *Statistically significant p<.05. Medians (the middle value in a sorted list of responses) are presented and refer to the following categories: 1 – not at all concerned, 2 – not concerned, 3 – neither not concerned nor concerned, 4 – concerned, 5 – very concerned

Source: Online survey 'Understanding fairness between different generations' carried out by authors July 2020

Figure 2.6: Main concerns arising from the pandemic; answers by age group

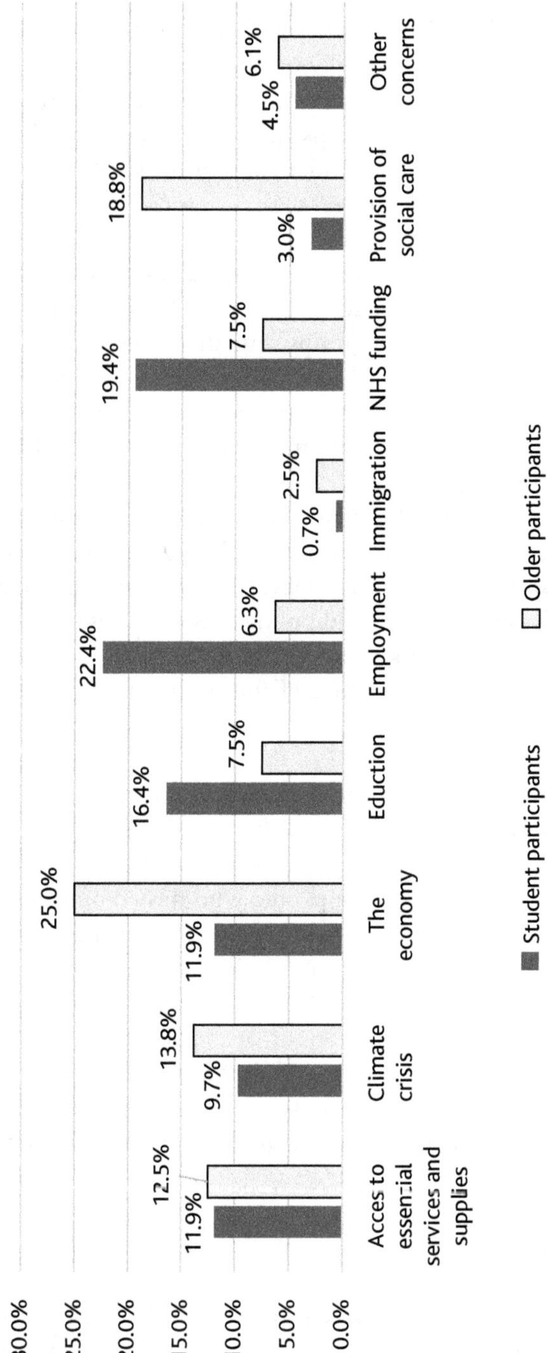

■ Student participants　　□ Older participants

Source: Online survey 'Understanding fairness between different generations' carried out by authors July 2020

When asked 'in tackling the COVID-19 pandemic which do you think the government should focus on more – the economy or people's wellbeing?', the majority of older (75.0%) and younger participants (59.7%) thought the government should focus equally on the economy and people's wellbeing during the pandemic, but over a third of younger participants (36.6%) wanted the government to focus more on peoples' wellbeing compared to 15% of older participants. Older participants (10%) were more worried about the economy than younger participants (3.7%) and these results were statistically significant.

Participants rated concerns over major issues on a scale from not at all concerned to very concerned (Figure 2.6). Most concerns were equally shared in both participant groups, but there were statistical differences for the economy and social care where older participants were more concerned than younger participants. Younger participants reported more concern for education, employment and National Health Service (NHS) funding.

Participants were asked about any other concerns related to the impacts of the pandemic and both groups indicated shared concerns about access to everyday essential services and supplies such as doctors, pharmacies and food shops as well as many social and political issues. These included increasing inequality, increases in poor mental health, impacts on children and young people, as well as political issues of future funding for the NHS and the government's handling of the pandemic:

> I am very concerned about mental health crises that are likely to have risen due to the pandemic. (student)

> The generation of young people who missed out on schooling and work experience will be affected, rising poverty and inequality. (older participant)

> The blatant carefree behaviour of the governments in front of the people's pain and grief and death. (student)

> Governmental mismanagement the deceitfulness and incompetence of the government. (older participant)

Conclusion

As we have seen, notions of a generational divide suggest that older people are enjoying benefits and privileges while younger people face difficulties and challenges, the underlying implication being that the former exist at the expense of the latter. These ideas have been circulating, particularly through media discourses for some time but in the UK increased substantially following the vote to leave the EU. Given this, we might have expected to see younger participants in our study expressing a strong sense of unfairness and little acceptance of the idea that older people experience discrimination and disadvantage. However, the survey results in fact show a consensus among the younger participants that older people do experience discrimination and disadvantage, and a clear understanding on their part that age stereotypes are prevalent in society. Although there were a few examples of responses which reflect negative stereotypes in both participant groups, there were many shared concerns over what life will be like post-pandemic and the challenging economic, social and political issues confronting all generations. There was mutual recognition of the challenges each generation is facing, and younger participants demonstrated an evident awareness about ageism and issues that older people face. Similarly, the older participants' responses indicate awareness and concern about issues that younger people experience. Although older participants tended to agree that today's younger people are worse off than previous generations, younger participants were less certain this is the case.

The responses from both groups of participants pointed to an awareness of the discourse of intergenerational conflict, the blaming of 'boomers', but these were not largely prevalent and did not feature to any large extent in either group's responses. One explanation may be that the playing out of generation wars takes place at the level of discourse rather than resonating with actual relationships that people experience in their everyday lives. The 'generational war' discourses do not appear to have deeply influenced our study participants who had a better grasp of the complexities and less inclination to simply blame the other generation.

This accords with empirical studies which have investigated solidarity and transfers of support between older and younger generations. In a qualitative study which explored whether intergenerational equity discourses resonate with peoples' everyday lives, Wildman et al (2022) make the point that conversations on these issues are taking place *about people* rather than *with people*. From their interviews with people in different generations they found that intergenerational inequity was not blamed on the older generation but rather on 'a remote state, 'socially ignorant' of the realities of the lives of people of all ages' (Wildman et al, 2022, p 14). In common with our study, the participants were aware of different generational experiences, as well as 'boomer blaming' and 'lazy younger people' tropes and discourses. However, they understood that the situations they found themselves in, such as, younger participants struggling to achieve financial independence and older participants having to support adult children, resulted from the decline in collective welfare provision rather than the individualised fault of an older generation.

Similarly, empirical studies that have investigated intergenerational transfers within families challenge the simplistic framing of intergenerational relationships as divided and in conflict. In a qualitative study of grandparents who provide childcare for grandchildren, Airey at al (2021) argue that current debates which portray older people as selfish and individualistic, depriving subsequent generations of the opportunities they themselves benefitted from, overlook the role of grandparents providing childcare for working parents. This is not only an important way that older people support younger people but demonstrates ongoing familial obligations towards adult children and intergenerational solidarity.

But, even if the generational divide exists only at the level of discourse and is not reflected in older and younger peoples' actual experiences and relationships, this does not mean discourses of generational conflict are harmless. As many have argued they provide a powerful mechanism for transmitting stigma, ageist stereotypes and even hate, all of which can have 'real' effects and implications (Walker, 1990, 2013). So, what are the dangers of the 'generational war' discourses beyond the inaccuracy of their claims and lack of resonance with lived experiences? Hurley et al (2017) argue such claims may impact public support for the universal social provision that characterises welfare states. Drawing on a study in New Zealand about superannuation proposals, Hurley et al found that when generational inequity was foregrounded in pension debates it generated antagonism and undermined widespread support for state-funded support for older people. This is similar to findings in Wildman et al's UK study where participants expressed a 'fracturing social contract, with little faith in the principles of intergenerational equity, equality and reciprocity upon which welfare states depend' (Wildman et al, 2022, p 2284).

Some have argued that the undermining of collective public support for welfare provision is not accidental, and offered this as an explanation to the intensification of intergenerational injustice claims (Bristow, 2019, 2021). From this perspective, these discourses and the claims that circulate through them, operate as a 'smokescreen' to obscure the uneven impacts of global neoliberal economics and the dramatic rise in inequalities between rich and poor (Macnicol, 2015; Phillipson, 2015). The particular ways in which young people have fared within neoliberal policy agendas provides ample ammunition here. As Wildman et al point out, the young are 'collateral damage' and disadvantaged by a system based on the private accumulation of wealth. Drawing on Resolution Foundation evidence, they argue that 'intergenerational inequalities reflect an economic system in which assets outstrip income and life chances depend heavily on inherited wealth' (Wildman et al, 2022, p. 2299).

This acknowledges the particular challenges facing younger generations, such as costs and debts associated with higher education, insecure jobs, unaffordable housing, which featured in the responses of both our participant groups, but attributes these to neoliberal economic policies rather than 'blaming' the older generation (Pickard, 2019).

Going forward: implications for policy and research

Our analysis suggests generational inequity discourses do not accurately reflect generational differences, and further that this somewhat misses the point as accurate or not they play an ideological role in policy debates on the allocation of state support for welfare provision. As we move into the post-pandemic period, how might these discourses be mobilised and resisted? Will the potential for increased solidarity through the crisis, as seen through the emergence of mutual aid at the start of the pandemic, be supported in post-pandemic recovery policy making? The dire state of the UK social care system has been highlighted since the pandemic and drawn attention to the urgent need to reform the social care system in the UK. The enduring narrative of the unaffordability of social care is one such area where pitching generations against each other to meet the costs is a real possibility. There is already some evidence within media debates that these issues are continuing to be framed in generational terms. The argument that pensioners should bear more of the costs gained some currency when the pension triple lock (which guarantees state pensions rise annually in line with either inflation or earnings whichever is higher) was suspended in September 2021 (Collinson, 2020). Others have claimed that COVID-19 affected young people disproportionately, through social restrictions and the older generation should be made to pay for the enormous sacrifices the young made to protect older people (Conway, 2022).

Such claims need critical interrogation along with the use of 'generations' as a way of explaining complex social issues. The findings from our study indicate the potential for cross-generational understandings of the challenges each is facing and more importantly that older and younger people understand the social, economic and political issues that face all generations. It is clearly important to consider the usefulness of using the concept of 'generations' as a category of analysis, given the ways in which analytical claims about generational difference are being mobilised, and even weaponised. The potential of 'generational wars' discourse to define issues, shape perceptions and take 'hold' of the public imagination suggests a more precise use of the concept of 'generation' is needed alongside the intersections of 'age' and other factors of class, race and gender.

In developing a policy framework that can address the major challenges facing post-pandemic societies, policy makers need to pay greater attention to the potential of fostering cross-generational relationships as resources, rather than reproducing the divisive politics embedded in age ideologies that set one generation against each other. We suggest that further research is needed to investigate generational relationships empirically to fully understand the nature and complexity of the challenges facing all generations. Given the significant level of common ground and mutual understanding across both generations apparent in our findings, more extensive dialogue between younger and older people would be productive in research going forward.

Acknowledgements: The authors would like to thank Dame Philippa Russell Dame Commander of the Order of the British Empire (DBE) and Peter Dale of South East England Forum on Ageing (SEEFA), Lee Towers and the participants who took part in the survey. This work was supported by the School of Applied Social Science, University of Brighton and SEEFA. Ethical approval for this study was obtained from the University of Brighton Ethics Committee, ref 2020–7093.

Note

[1] Blanket orders not to resuscitate care home residents were used at the start of the pandemic. The do not attempt cardiopulmonary resuscitation (DNACPR) orders were reportedly being put in place and recorded on patients' records without discussion or informed consent being given, against recommended best practice in this area.

References

Airey, L., Lain, D., Jandrić, J. and Loretto, W. (2021) 'A selfish generation? 'Baby boomers', values, and the provision of childcare for grandchildren', *The Sociological Review*, 69(4): 812–29.

Alexander Shaw, K. (2018) *Baby Boomers Versus Millennials: Rhetorical Conflicts and Interest-construction in the New Politics of Intergenerational Fairness*, UK: European Centre for Progressive Studies.

Blanchflower, D. and Bell, D. (2020) 'We must act now to shield young people from the economic scarring of COVID-19', *The Guardian*, [online] 22 May. Available from: www.theguardian.com/society/2020/may/22/we-must-act-now-to-shield-young-people-from-the-economic-scarring-of-covid-19 [Accessed 23 May 2020].

Bristow, J. (2019) *Stop Mugging Grandma: The 'Generation Wars' and Why Boomer Blaming won't Solve Anything*, New Haven and London: Yale University Press.

Bristow, J. (2021) 'Post-Brexit boomer blaming: the contradictions of generational grievance', *The Sociological Review*, 69(4): 759–74.

British Society of Gerontology (BSG). (2020) *COVID-19: Statement from the President and Members of the National Executive Committee of the British Society of Gerontology*, British Society of Gerontology. Available from: www.britishgerontology.org/publications/bsg-statements-on-covid-19/statement-one [Accessed 14 September 2022].

Coker, R. (2020) "'Harvesting'" is a terrible word – but it's what has happened in Britain's care homes', *The Guardian*, [online] 8 May. Available from: www.theguardian.com/commentisfree/2020/may/08/care-home-residents-harvested-left-to-die-uk-government-herd-immunity [Accessed 9 May 2020].

Collinson, P. (2020) 'Should UK pensioners be forced to pay the bill for coronavirus?', *The Guardian*, [online] 22 May. Available from: www.theguardian.com/money/2020/may/22/uk-pensioners-coronavirus-triple-lock-state-pension [Accessed 23 May 2020].

Conway, E. (2022) 'Should we reimburse the young?', *Sunday Times*, [online] 6 February. Available from: www.thetimes.co.uk/article/should-we-reimburse-the-young-lockdown-restrictions-house-prices-whnrbwczl [Accessed 9 September 2022].

Cooper, M. (2021) 'A burden on future generations? How we learned to hate deficits and blame the baby boomers', *The Sociological Review*, 69(4): 743–58.

Coren, C. (2016) 'Wrinklies have well and truly stitched us up', *The Times*, [online] 25 June. Available from: www.thetimes.co.uk/article/wrinklies-have-well-and-truly-stitched-us-up-qfz509cz8 [Accessed 3 May 2020].

Elliott, R. (2022) 'The 'Boomer remover': intergenerational discounting, the coronavirus and climate change', *The Sociological Review*, 70(1): 74–91.

European Commission. (2009) *Intergenerational Solidarity: Key to Responding to Demographic Ageing*, European Commission IP/09/651, Brussels, 28 April 2009. Available from: www.ec.europa.eu/commission/presscorner/detail/en/ip_09_651 [Accessed 29 November 2022].

Fletcher, J.R. (2021) 'Chronological quarantine and ageism: COVID-19 and gerontology's relationship with age categorisation', *Ageing & Society*, 41: 479–92.

Harris, J. (2020) 'Coronavirus has deepened prejudice against older people', *The Guardian*, [online] 26 April. Available from: www.theguardian.com/commentisfree/2020/apr/26/prejudice-older-people-coronavirus [Accessed 21 June 2020].

Hill, A. (2020) 'Favouring young over old in COVID-19 treatment justifiable, says ethicist', *The Guardian*, [online] 22 April. Available from: www.theguardian.com/world/2020/apr/22/favouring-young-over-old-in-covid-19-treatment-justifiable-says-ethicist [Accessed 28 April 2020].

HM Government. (2021) *COVID-19 Mental Health and Wellbeing Recovery Action Plan*, [online] 28 November 2022. Available from: https://assets.publishing.service.gov.uk/government/uploads/system/uploads/attachment_data/file/973936/covid-19-mental-health-and-wellbeing-recovery-action-plan.pdf [Accessed 28 November 2022].

Hurley, K., Breheny, M. and Tuffin, K. (2017) 'Intergenerational inequity arguments and the implications for state-funded financial support of older people', *Ageing and Society*, 37(3): 561–80.

Macnicol, J. (2015) *Neoliberalising Old Age*, Cambridge: Cambridge University Press.

Martin, G. and Roberts, S. (2021) 'Exploring legacies of the baby boomers in the twenty-first century', *The Sociological Review*, 69(4): 727–42.

Matthew, B. and Ross, L. (2010) *Research Methods*, Harlow: Pearson Education Limited.

Paxman, J. (2015) 'Cull the grey vote—it is an affront to democracy', *Financial Times*, [online] 27 November. Available from: www.ft.com/content/beb7f 1a2-937f-11e5-bd82-c1fb87bef7af [Accessed 3 May 2020].

Phillipson, C. (2015) 'The political economy of longevity: developing new forms of solidarity for later life', *The Sociological Quarterly*, 56: 80–100.

Pickard, S. (2019) 'Age war as the new class war? Contemporary representations of intergenerational inequity', *Journal of Social Policy*, 48(2): 369–86.

Popescu, A. (2019) 'The brief history of generation. An analysis of literature review', *Journal of Comparative Research in Anthropology and Sociology*, 10(2): 15–30.

Proctor, K. (2020) 'Longer lockdown for over-70s " 'could create sense of victimisation'", *The Guardian*, [online] 28 April. Available from: www. theguardian.com/society/2020/apr/28/longer-lockdown-for-over-70s-could-create-sense-of-victimisation [Accessed 9 May 2020].

Sodha, S. (2020) 'Coronavirus has revealed what's wrong with our approach to ageing', *The Guardian*, [online] 17 April. Available from: www.theg uardian.com/commentisfree/2020/apr/17/carers-badges-ageism-britain [Accessed 18 May 2020].

Walker, A. (1990) 'The economic "burden" of ageing and the prospect of intergenerational conflict', *Ageing and Society*, 10: 377—96.

Walker, A. (2013) 'The new ageism', *The Political Quarterly*, 83(4): 812–19.

Ward, L., Fleischer, S. and Towers, L. (2021) *Understanding Fairness Between Generations in the times of COVID-19*, Brighton: University of Brighton.

Wildman, J., Goulding, A., Moffatt, S., Scharf, T. and Stenning, Al (2022) 'Intergenerational equity, equality and reciprocity in economically and politically turbulent times: narratives from across generations', *Ageing and Society*, 42(10): 2284–303.

Williams, Z. (2020) 'Isolating the over-50s? It's an idea whose purpose is to sow discord', *The Guardian*, [online] 3 August. Available from: www. theguardian.com/commentisfree/2020/aug/03/isolating-over-50s-idea-covid-19 [Accessed 4 August 2020].

Willetts, D. (2010) *The Pinch: How the Baby Boomers took their Children's Future – and Why They Should Give it Back*, London: Atlantis Books.

3

Impacts of substance use across generations: exploring how the risk of problem substance use can be impacted by locus of control

Penelope Laycock

Introduction

Substance use has wider impacts than just to the individual, the social impacts can be seen across generations. This chapter is a consideration of childhood experiences and outcomes for adult children (aged 30–55) in Glasgow affected by a parent's problem alcohol use. Specifically, it compares the lives of 'adult children of problem drinkers' (ACoPD) and 'adult children of alcoholics' (ACoA) who undertake or undertook problem substance use (PSU) and those who have not engaged in any PSU (non-PSU). It describes and puts into context how these people's differing locus of control impacted their childhood experiences and their outcomes. This is through narrative interviews and a thematic analysis utilising locus of control as a framework. This chapter will include literature on substance use in Glasgow, the theory of locus of control, direct quotations from narrative interviews and policy implications.

Substance use in Glasgow

Substance use in Glasgow is an issue which impacts more than the individuals undertaking the act. There is a lack of research on the prevalence of 'children of alcoholics' (CoA) and their own lived experiences despite the fact that many studies have shown that ACoPD have an increased risk of negative outcomes and having PSU themselves (Templeton, Zohhadi, Galvani, and Velleman, 2006; Velleman and Orford, 1999; Velleman and Templeton, 2016). This increased risk of negative adult outcomes can be argued to occur because of their more negative childhood experiences due to their parents drinking (Velleman and Orford, 1999) and lack of beneficial influences or protective factors. Despite the lack of research, there are a few studies which take account of ACoA childhood experiences. Perhaps the most comprehensive study on adult children is that of Velleman and Orford (1999). In their book *Risk and Resilience*, they look at the outcomes of 164 ACoPD aged 16–35 in America during the 90s, and 80 individuals who did not identify as such. They found that those who identified as ACoPD had more negative outcomes, including psychological and economic (Velleman and Orford, 1999). However, Velleman and Orford (1999) also claim that they believe the risk of ACoPD having more problems than those who did not have a parent with a drinking problem has been overstated. They argue that it is disharmony in the family that predominantly influences these negative outcomes (Velleman and Orford, 1999). In their review of over 2,600 articles, book chapters, reports and books, Templeton and colleagues (2006) found that domestic violence often occurred when a parent undertook PSU and both of these combined increased the negative impact on various factors: the child's development, their experiences in adolescence, relationships and parenting abilities of adults, prediction of adolescent psychopathy, perpetrating child abuse, developing substance use problems or suffering domestic abuse in adulthood (Templeton et al, 2006). The increased risk of child abuse was not necessarily predicated by parental substance use alone. Previous research highlights the importance of context in distinguishing these differences, as children of problem drinkers often experience more adverse childhood events (Dube et al, 2003). Negative outcomes are not prescriptive, something in the ACoA lives aided them and negated their increased risk.

Things which negate increased risk of negative outcomes are called protective factors. Velleman and Templeton (2016) have an extensive list of protective factors which enhance resilience in children affected by parental substance misuse. Of these, certain protective factors have been found important by relevant reviews of literature. These are divided into individual, family and community factors. Individual factors include internal coping mechanisms and self-control, whereas family factors include factors such as a protective adult and community factors include the social norms and expectations of the community. Although the focus of more recent work is on internal protective factors, family factors appear to be central to good outcomes, especially in the early years (Velleman and Templeton, 2016). Environmental factors also impacted risk of harm, such as: poverty, social isolation and lack of family or community involvement (Velleman and Templeton, 2016). ACoA have been found to have fewer protective factors than those who did not grow up with a parent with problem alcohol use. However, these risk and protective factors could explain the differences between outcomes for individuals who are ACoA, as not all have negative outcomes in adulthood.

ACoA increased risk for negative outcomes are mirrored in other studies in the United States of America, such as Sher and colleagues' (1991) study on ACoA and alcohol and drug problems (Sher et al, 1991); Balsa and colleagues'

(2009) quantitative study on mental health problems (Balsa et al, 2009); and Balsa's (2008) paper on labour market outcomes (Balsa, 2008). In the UK, Gilvarry (2005) presents a study based on a retrospective questionnaire completed by 746 adults who grew up with a parent who either misused alcohol or suffered from mental health problems (Gilvarry, 2005). They found that the adult children had a higher likelihood of alcoholism, drug addiction, suicidal thoughts and eating disorders compared to the control group. These studies all confirm that growing up with an adult who has a drinking problem can lead to negative outcomes in later life. This is important because these individuals impact the larger society and economy. Alcohol abuse does not just impact the individual, in 2007 alcohol abuse was estimated to cost Scotland over £3.6 billion a year (Scottish Government, 2010). The Ask The Family Report (2021) found that in Scotland on average 11 people had been harmed across all family relationships for each respondent to their survey on alcohol use (Scottish Families Affected by Alcohol and Drugs, 2021). This pattern is also reflected across the country.

ACoA were found in some studies to also have an increased risk of undertaking PSU themselves (Braitman et al, 2009; Christoffersen and Soothill, 2003; Nation and Heflinger, 2006; Ross and Hill, 2001). There is evidence that individuals whose parents have an alcohol problem have an increased risk of alcohol misuse themselves (Landberg et al, 2018; Rossow et al, 2016; Yap et al, 2017). There have been many potential explanations for this such as genetic predispositions and environmental conditions (Hawkins et al, 1992). Braitman and colleagues (2009) found that college age, ACoA were more likely to be current users and initiate alcohol use earlier than non-adult children. Ross and Hill (2001) compared 20 ACoAs to non-ACoAs. They found that family history of alcoholism had a direct link to more lifetime drinks and drinking more frequently in high school. Epstein, and colleagues, (2020) found that children and teenagers of parents who had chronic alcohol and marijuana use were more likely to use these substances themselves, even if their parents had stopped use years before they were born (Epstein et al, 2020). These children were 1.8 times more likely to use alcohol compared to children whose parents who did not drink alcohol. Whereas children of individuals who had chronic usage were 2.75 times more likely to use alcohol as compared to children whose parents did not drink (Epstein et al, 2020).

Despite the transmission of potential substance abuse between parents and children, there is evidence that an adult who does not engage in this behaviour and is supportive can change the negative outcomes for their child (Dooley and Fitzgerald, 2012). The 'My World: National Study of Youth Mental Health in Ireland' study by Dooley and Fitzgerald (2012) in Ireland found that 'one good adult' is very important to the mental wellbeing of young people. With over 70% of young people reporting that they received very high or high support from an adult. They found that one good adult had a positive impact on the child's self-belief, confidence, coping skills and optimism about the future (Dooley and Fitzgerald, 2012). Werner and Johnson (2004) undertook a longitudinal study on 65 children of alcoholics spanning 32 years, the Kauai Longitudinal Study (Werner and Johnson, 2004). They found that individuals who coped more effectively with childhood trauma had more sources of support in their childhoods.

Although not all studies show this connection of intergenerational transmission of substance use, there does appear to be consistent evidence to show that if your parents undertake any form of substance use, children and adult children are much more likely to do so themselves (Werner and Johnson, 2004). ACoA are at higher risk for worse outcomes compared to those who are not ACoA, and they have an increased risk of having PSU (Gilvarry, 2005). However, as PSU and negative health impacts do not always occur, then there must be differences between the lives of individuals in this demographic.

Theory of locus of control

Childhood experiences have been shown to link to locus of control which impact adult outcomes (Galvin et al, 2018). It has been shown that differing childhood experiences can impact locus of control, particularly socioeconomic status, family dynamics and environmental factors (Galvin et al, 2018). Those individuals from more affluent areas with good family dynamics have a more internal locus of control (Ahlin and Antunes, 2015; Da Silva, 2013; García-Cadena et al, 2013). From outcomes, higher internal locus of control has been linked to outcomes such as better long-term investments in their health (Cobb–Clark et al, 2014), are better able to cope with negative life events (Buddelmeyer and Powdthavee, 2016), have higher savings (Cobb–Clark et al, 2016) and are more likely to have better mental health (Buddelmeyer and Powdthavee, 2016). A more external locus of control could in itself be a risk factor for drug use (Haynes and Ayliffe, 1991), as well as be a consequence of other risk factors (Caputo, 2019). This is due to individuals perhaps feeling helpless and threatened when they feel powerless and incapable of controlling a situation (Rabani Bavojdan et al, 2011). Some risk factors which have been linked to drug use have also been linked to external locus of control, for example lack of self-esteem (Rabani Bavojdan et al, 2011), peer drug use (Ahlin and Antunes, 2015) and parental discipline and family cohesion (García-Cadena et al, 2013). Locus of control can change and individuals with a more external locus of control who have undertaken PSU can exhibit a more internal locus of control through recovery programmes. Locus of control can be a way to show the associations between childhood experiences and potential problematic substance use in ACoA.

Locus of control can be used as a way to understand different substance use behaviours among ACoA and why some intergenerational transmission of substance use occurs. Locus of control can be used to explain the connection between childhood experiences and differing outcomes of ACoA in Glasgow. Many theories have been proposed to address the problem of differing outcomes for ACoA such as protective factors (Velleman and Templeton, 2016), resilience (Velleman and Orford, 1999), hope (Snyder, 2002) and locus of control. These all have some benefits in the way they assess outcomes for ACoA. However, it was locus of control can communicate the mechanism in which outcomes are different and can be used to examine a range of factors, which are not limited by being protective or risk factors. Children of alcoholics were more likely to have experienced more adverse childhood events (Dube et al, 2003) compared to those who did not have alcoholic parents. Their outcomes were impacted by protective and risk factors such as parental alcohol or substance use (Adamson and Templeton, 2012). Glasgow provided a unique context for these childhood experiences due to the high levels of deprivation, deindustrialisation and changes in housing, affecting children and their families socioeconomic status and access to resources (Ellaway and Macintyre, 1996; Walsh et al, 2017).

A more internal locus of control has often been linked to positive outcomes. Individuals with a more internal locus of control have been found to make better long-term investments in their health through a healthier diet and exercise (Cobb-Clark et al, 2014), are better able to cope with negative life events (Buddelmeyer and Powdthavee, 2016), have higher savings (Cobb-Clark et al, 2016) and are more likely to have better mental health (Buddelmeyer and Powdthavee, 2016). Galvin and colleagues (2018), in their theoretical review, found links between higher internal locus of control with academic success, psychological empowerment, self-efficacy, self-esteem, intrinsic task motivation, problem focused coping strategies and expectations for success (Galvin et al, 2018). Whereas, Ng, and colleagues (2006) in their meta-analysis of literature also found that in work-related locus of control, high internal locus of control was positively associated with favourable work outcomes such as being confident and determined (Ng et al, 2006). Those with a more internal locus of control were also found to be better able to cope with negative life events and be more likely to have better mental health (Buddelmeyer and Powdthavee, 2016). Use of the locus of control has been limited in substance abuse research (Hall, 2001). Connections have been found between internal locus of control and addiction onset, problem recognition, maintenance, and potential relapse and in remission (Hall, 2001). In neuroscientific works, drug addiction is also associated with brain systems which focus on self-control (Ersche et al, 2012). Locus of control may impact problematic substance use due to individuals being less able to control their dependence (Davies, 1992).

Individuals with an external locus of control were more likely to experience negative relationships with others, decreased autonomy, a lack of purpose and meaning in life, as well as decreased personal growth and development, all of which influences positive well-being (Ryff, 1989). Haynes and Ayliffe (1991) also found that high external locus of control was a good indicator of active misusing behaviour. Haynes and Ayliffe (1991), undertook a psychological test of 28 'misusers', and other groups who did not misuse substances: 25 postmen, 21 working mothers and 25 trainee social worker. They found that there was a statistically significant difference in locus of control scores between active misusers and other groups. Those who were actively using scored higher on external locus of control compared to those who were not PSUrs. Using a 17-item Likert scale to determine locus of control behaviour and an additional questionnaire to take into account a number of independent variables, Haynes and Ayliffe (1991) concluded that high external locus of control was linked to substance abuse. This is expected to be found in this study, with those who have undertaken problematic substance use having a more external locus of control.

Narrative interviews with ACoA in Glasgow

Narrative interviews can be utilised to explore the childhood experiences and outcomes of ACoA in Glasgow. The 'narrative' can be considered life story in which major events that the participants believe are important can be analysed. It can be understood as an orated or transcribed text giving an account of actions which are chronologically connected (Czarniawska, 2004). Narratives obtained from this form of method will represent the individual's interpretation of the world. This style of interviewing obtains the participants' understanding of their own childhoods and does not bias their responses (Czarniawska, 2004). This allows for their underlying motivations or locus of control to be determined. In narrative interviews, the goal is to understand the subjects, their meanings and their experiences (Kartch, 2017). The narrative interviews in this chapter highlight individuals who had parents who undertook PSU. Some individuals went on to use substances themselves and others did not, the difference between the two groups can be understood due to their locus of control. Three narratives have been chosen to highlight internal locus of control and lack of substance use, external locus of control and substance use and change in locus of control and recovery impacts. All participants have been assigned pseudonyms to maintain anonymity.

Internal locus of control

Internal locus of control was found to relate to childhood experiences. Data from the narrative interviews showed that overall there were less participants who had parents who misused substances, with an internal locus of control compared to an external locus of control. Mostly those who did not use substances had a more internal locus of control compared to individuals who undertook PSU. Sophie's locus of control could be viewed as a high internal locus of control.

Sophie had a very high internal locus of control. She believed events such as her brothers' education and drug addiction were her responsibility and events which she should be able to exhibit control over. Sophie lived with her mother and father, who she defined as an alcoholic, and two younger brothers. She was born in 1971 and her brothers were two and seven years younger than her. Sophie grew up in the city centre of Glasgow when they lived with her dad and then moved briefly to East Kilbride then to Drumchapel once her mum met her new boyfriend. Her mum's new boyfriend was 'even more of an alcoholic than my Dad was'. Therefore, Sophie felt like she had to take on more of a parental role. She mentions multiple times how she was responsible for events which she shouldn't have been:

> 'I want to look after people and if things go wrong, I blame myself and all of those things.'

Sophie mentions taking on a parental role and feeling like she needs to look after her brothers. This leads to intense feelings of having to be in control of situations as a child:

> 'You all of a sudden you have to take on this very very grown-up role which kind of makes you very responsible and you're gonna go one of two ways. You're kind of going to go off the deep end and be completely irresponsible or you become really really responsible, and my route was to become really responsible which helped at that point but as an adult it made me, it was really hard for me to like and even now to not feel responsible for other people.'

There is one instance that particularly highlights Sophie's high internal locus of control, one in which she was caring for her brother, and he cuts himself:

> 'There was a night where we were in the house on my own and my youngest brother had fallen and grazed his knee and I remember looking at this knee that was dirty and saying I have to clean it and I didn't know what I could clean it with. And I wasn't sure whether soap and water would cause a problem, whether soap would make it worse and the only thing I knew to kind of try and help him was to use the surgical spirits that

> I used for my ears, which nips and stings. I mean it's horrible, it burns, and I remember being in the bathroom [Sophie cries] and getting really upset and trying to, trying to help this little boy and he's going "it's too sore, it's too sore" and me going "but I've got to clean it", if I don't clean it and it gets an infection in it then that's my fault.'

Sophie believes that if her brother gets ill further from the cut that it will be her fault, she carries this through into other aspects of looking after her brothers, such as not telling teachers about the specifics of her home life as she did not want to be responsible for her brothers going into care, somewhere she could not protect them. As an older teenager she even changes where she wanted to go to university and continues living at home so she can keep looking after her two younger brothers. Although in the end she did not get the mathematics grades to attend university for engineering like she wanted too and believes this was entirely her own fault and that she 'failed'. Sophie has an extremely high internal locus of control which follows her into adulthood.

Internal locus of control was found in individuals who believed that they had the power to change events during their childhood. Aspects of their childhood in which locus of control were applied were socioeconomic status, family dynamics, abuse and peers. Sophie was found to have a high internal locus of control in all of these areas. Internal locus of control was found to be more positive and more prevalent in individuals who did not undertake PSU. However, as shown by examples from Sophie's narrative, sometimes a high internal locus of control can leave participants feeling that certain events are their responsibility or 'fault' when this may not in fact be the case.

External locus of control

External locus of control relating to childhood experiences was more common among participants in this study than an internal locus of control. Those who undertook PSU had higher levels of external locus of control compared to those who did not undertake PSU. Byron is used as an example of external locus of control. His narrative provides the clearest examples of external locus of control relating to childhood experiences.

Byron was an only child who lived with his grandparents from the age of four due to his parents' problematic substance use. He was born in 1987 and his mother was always a part of his life. His father he describes as 'on and off' until his father hung himself when Byron was 12. Byron describes how around this age he started experimenting with drugs. He describes himself as a 'fat kid' who was the 'class clown', always getting into trouble and suspended. He believes that his friends highly influenced his drug behaviour and that he was dealing drugs without even realising he was doing it as he was getting drugs for his friends and taking a bit of hash from that:

> 'aye I was the one that used to get everybody their bits of hash and that. I would scoop a bit aff the top for meself and put a bit less money on to make the next a bit for myself you know what I mean? I was kinda selling it before I knew that I was selling it you know what I mean? And then aye that hing that got me involved and things like that at a bigger level from a very young age.'

Byron also understands his childhood as being impacted by external forces. He went to prison at 17 for murder and references this in his interview and what he had to say at trial. A lot of how Byron discusses his life is highly influenced by his time in prison and multiple offences after his initial imprisonment at 17. He has discussed how the drugs he was taking induced psychosis which led to the offences. He reflects on how his childhood led to this:

> 'I'm not used to being, living a normal life with normal people you know what I mean. I now know that I'm an addict as well, I've got an addictive personality and that started when I was a wean you know what I mean … I'm easily led, and this is the first time that I've kinda, that I've done with that last attempt right. I thought my life was over if I'd have got done with that, convicted of it.'

Internal and external locus of control

Alfie has an internal locus of control, however there are circumstances where Alfie mentions how his perspective may have changed due to his recovery journey. Alfie was born in 1974, his father was in the navy and his mother was a housewife. Shortly after Alfie was born they all moved to Easterhouse and then his younger brother came along. His parents separated before he was a teenager. Alfie currently lives alone and works as a labourer. He actively tries to 'give back' to the neighbourhood in which he grew up in. As a child, Alfie used to try and protect his brother and mother from his father. he believed this was his responsibility as the oldest male sibling. He also felt like it was his responsibility to protect his mother from boyfriends once she had left his father. In hindsight Alfie has come to believe that he was different when he was a child, suggesting he did not believe many events were under his control and his locus of control may have been more external. Alfie also acknowledges that he didn't take responsibility when he started using drink and drugs at a young age. He used this to justify behaviours as something he was not at fault for:

'So, I found solace in the bottom of a bottle. I had my first drink when I was 8 years old. My first blackout when I was 14. That took me into gang fighting things and all that stuff and I was seeking approval, getting involved in all the gang fighting. Seeking approval, just doing things that I shouldnae have been doing. Not because, not because I didnae know the difference between right or wrong. I wanted to be accepted. Yeah. And I found that the crazier the stunts that I would do. I thought I was being accepted not realising I was getting rested as a fire in. I was being manipulated.'

Alfie makes it clear that he did know the difference between right and wrong but that he didn't think he had a positive role model to influence his behaviour. He was influenced by his older peers and being used as a 'fire in' and being made to do things for them. Alfie does talk about how his perspective has changed and has allowed a reflective hindsight:

'You're right, it's all my fault. No my upbringing, that wasnae my fault. Just life, just circumstances. My Ma, like I said my Ma done the best with what she had. My Da, I recognise that like me he suffered from an illness called alcoholism …I stopped beating myself up when I make mistakes because that's what I used to do. I used to, bury they way down shh don't tell anybody about what I done. Now to the best of my ability I get honest about them because I find that see when I'm honest about it, it doesnae hold any power on me. I don't feel any guilt, shame or remorse when I'm keeping completely honest about it. See another thing that I've realised is when I'm being honest, I don't need to have a great memory. That's just how it is for me and that's basically what it was like for me when I was growing up.'

Throughout this information given, Alfie exhibits a changed locus of control as an adult. He could be argued to have a more external locus of control when a child and applying the locus of control measures retrospectively has shown a change in his locus of control from more external to a more internal locus of control. This shows the impacts from parental alcohol use can be altered and individuals can change their locus of control and outcomes, through rehabilitation and restorative measures.

Discussion and policy implications

From the narrative interviews, it was found that locus of control varied for ACoA, however, generally a more internal locus of control led to more positive outcomes. The traumatic childhood experiences of ACoA impacted their outcomes, this could be identified due to their type of locus of control and difference between drug use behaviours. Childhood experiences have been shown to link to locus of control which impacts adult outcomes (Galvin et al, 2018). Those individuals from more affluent areas with good family dynamics have a more internal locus of control (Ahlin and Antunes, 2015; Da Silva, 2013; García-Cadena et al, 2013). For outcomes, higher internal locus of control has been linked to outcomes such as better long-term investments in their health (Cobb-Clark et al, 2014), are better able to cope with negative life events (Buddelmeyer and Powdthavee, 2016), have higher savings (Cobb-Clark et al, 2016) and are more likely to have better mental health (Buddelmeyer and Powdthavee, 2016). A more external locus of control could in itself be a risk factor for drug use (Haynes and Ayliffe, 1991), as well as be a consequence of other risk factors (Caputo, 2019). Some risk factors which have been linked to drug use have also been linked to external locus of control, for example lack of self-esteem (Rabani Bavojdan et al, 2011), peer drug use (Ahlin and Antunes, 2015) and parental discipline and family cohesion (García-Cadena et al, 2013). Locus of control can change and individuals with a more external locus of control who have undertaken PSU can exhibit a more internal locus of control through recovery programmes. Utilising locus of control as a measure in policy can enable interventions to be created based around encouraging a more beneficial locus of control for the ACoA. This then redefines the current policy focus on 'risk'. Velleman and Orford's (1999) original work provided a psychosocial analysis of qualitative and quantitative data on young adults and children affected by parental alcohol use. They argued that there was not enough of a focus on children's 'resilience' and more of a focus on the negative and 'risk' towards children (Velleman and Orford, 1999).

Using locus of control within policy would be a step towards more of a focus on 'resilience' based policy, although veering away from using the conflicting perceptions around resilience. This has implications for health and social care policy in Scotland. It would be advisable to create early interventions for children and young people, especially as drug use began in puberty in the sample used in this study and the influence of peers and schooling. Parenting programs and other models created by the local authority or alcohol and drugs partnerships could decrease intergenerational transmission. Much like similar reports such as the Drug Deaths Taskforce's final report, Changing Lives, these findings are nuanced and cannot be applied to everyone, but policy change needs to occur with more funding to drug related services and provisions and pathways through an inequalities lens (Taskforce, 2022).

Conclusion

Locus of control was discussed as a way to understand the potential associations between ACoA who had similar childhood experiences but different outcomes. The difference in outcomes affects our conceptual understanding of risk of PSU and the theory of locus of control. Overall, those individuals with an internal locus of control were more likely to not undertake PSU. Kroll's (2004) analysis of ACoA found that there were similarities in childhood including violence, abuse and fear (Kroll, 2004). Templeton and colleagues (2006) found that domestic violence often occurred when a parent was a PSUer and that both these experiences increased the likelihood of an individual developing substance use problems or suffering domestic abuse in adulthood (Templeton et al, 2006). Previous studies have found that ACoA have an increased risk of becoming PSUrs themselves (Nation and Heflinger, 2006; Ross and Hill, 2001; Braitman et al, 2009; Christoffersen and Soothill, 2003). Additionally, adolescents who had been physically assaulted, sexually assaulted, witnessed violence or had family members with alcohol or drug problems had increased risk for current substance abuse or dependence (Nation and Heflinger, 2006). The common intergenerational links in this are with parents with PSU issues themselves having histories of child abuse and neglect (Templeton et al, 2006). Having an internal locus of control has been found to be a protective factor against many differing traumatic childhood events such as parental divorce, violence and general wellbeing (Rutter, 1985; Velleman and Templeton, 2015).

Those individuals who had more traumatic childhoods and negative experiences were more likely to have more negative outcomes potentially because of their locus of control. Often negative experiences were linked to an external locus of control, but this was not always the case. In this study, locus of control is used as a way to understand different outcomes among ACoA. Locus of control was chosen because internal locus of control is a protective factor of PSU which increases resilience (Velleman and Templeton, 2016) as well as a sense of agency and ability to find a pathway out of that circumstance as in hope theory (Snyder, 2002). Locus of control can be used to explain the connection between childhood experiences and differing outcomes of ACoA in Glasgow. The impact of parental drinking is further reaching than generally acknowledged. A more internal locus of control was often associated with more positive childhood experiences and outcomes and an external locus of control with more negative experiences and outcomes. Childhood experiences can impact whether individuals believe events to be under their control (internal locus of control) or outside of their control (external locus of control). Although internal locus of control is considered beneficial and has been linked to multiple positive outcomes (García-Cadena et al, 2013), it can lead to a problematic internal belief system when individuals attribute negative external events to their own behaviour (Haynes and Ayliffe, 1991). Although in general an internal locus of control shows more positive outcomes compared to an external locus of control, this is not always the case and locus of control can change. The impacts of parental alcohol use can transmit through generations and impact many outcomes for individuals, but these negative impacts can be altered if individuals have an internal locus of control or attend programmes which can alter their locus of control.

Further research could be undertaken in this area on wider demographics, outside of Glasgow and with more diverse populations as at present the findings are hard to generalise. There could also be further research on alcohol and drug policy and a review of how this is implemented across the country due to the need for this topic to be pushed up the political agenda.

References

Adamson, J. and Templeton, L. (2012) 'Silent voices: supporting children and young people affected by parental alcohol misuse', [WWW Document]. Available from: http://dera.ioe.ac.uk/15497/1/FINAL_OCC_Report_Silent_Voices_Parental_Alcohol_Misuse_FULL_REPORT_11_Sept_2 012%5B1%5D.pdf. [Accessed 16 June 20].

Ahlin, E. and Antunes, M. (2015) 'Locus of control orientation: parents, peers, and place', *J. Youth Adolesc.*, 44 : 1803–1818.

Balsa, A.I., (2008). 'Parental problem-drinking and adult children's labor market outcomes'. *J. Hum. Resour.* 43: 454–486.

Balsa, A.I., Homer, J.F. and French, M.T. (2009) 'The health effects of parental problem drinking on adult children', *J. Ment. Health Policy Econ.*, 12: 55–66.

Braitman, A.L., Kelley, M.L., Ladage, J., Schroeder, V., Gumienny, L.A., Morrow, J.A., et al (2009) 'Alcohol and drug use among college student adult children of alcoholics', *J. Alcohol Drug Educ.*, 53: 69–88.

Buddelmeyer, H. and Powdthavee, N. (2016) 'Can having internal locus of control insure against negative shocks? Psychological evidence from panel data', *J. Econ. Behav. Organ.*, 122: 88–109.

Caputo, A. (2019) 'Addiction, locus of control and health status: a study on patients with substance use disorder in recovery settings', *J. Subst. Use*, 24: 609–13.

Christoffersen, M.N. and Soothill, K. (2003) 'The long-term consequences of parental alcohol abuse: a cohort study of children in Denmark', *J. Subst. Abuse Treat.*, 25: 107–16.

Cobb-Clark, D., Kassenboehmer, S.C. and Sinning, M. (2016) 'Locus of control and savings', *J. Bank Finance*, 73: 113–30.

Cobb-Clark, D.A., Kassenboehmer, S.C. and Schurer, S. (2014) 'Healthy habits: the connection between diet, exercise, and locus of control', *J. Econ. Behav. Organ.*, 98: 1–28.

Czarniawska, B. (2004) *Narratives in Social Science Research*. London: Sage Publications Ltd.

Da Silva, G. (2013) A therapeutic model for parents for enhancing the internal locus of control in primary school children (Doctoral Thesis). University of South Africa, Pretoria

Davies, J.B. (1992) *The Myth of Addiction: An Application of the Psychological Theory of Attribution to Illicit Drug Use*, Harwood Academic Publishers.

Dooley, B.A. and Fitzgerald, A. (2012) 'My World Survey: National Study of Youth Mental Health in Ireland (Technical Report)', Chur, Switzerland, Philadelphia: Headstrong and University College Dublin (UCD) School of Psychology.

Dube, S.R., Felitti, V.J., Dong, M., Chapman, D.P., Giles, W.H. and Anda, R.F. (2003) 'Childhood abuse, neglect, and household dysfunction and the risk of illicit drug use: the adverse childhood experiences study', *Pediatrics*, 111: 564–72.

Ellaway, A. and Macintyre, S. (1996) 'Does where you live predict health related behaviours?: a case study in Glasgow', *Health Bull. (Edinb.)*, 54: 443–6.

Epstein, M., Bailey, J.A., Furlong, M., Steeger, C.M. and Hill, K.G. (2020) 'An intergenerational investigation of the associations between parental marijuana use trajectories and child functioning', *Psychol. Addict. Behav.*, 34: 830–8.

Ersche, K.D., Turton, A.J., Croudace, T. and Štochl, J. (2012) Who do you think is in control in addiction? A pilot study on drug-related locus of control beliefs. *Addict. Disord. Their Treat*, 11: 173–223.

Galvin, B.M., Randel, A.E., Collins, B.J. and Johnson, R.E. (2018) 'Changing the focus of locus (of control): a targeted review of the locus of control literature and agenda for future research', *J. Organ. Behav.*, 39: 820–33.

García-Cadena, C.H., de la Rubia, J.M., Díaz-Díaz, H.L., Martínez-Rodríguez, J., Sánchez-Reyes, L. and López-Rosales, F. (2013) 'Effect of family strength over the psychological well-being and internal locus of control', *J. Behav. Health Soc. Issues*, 5: 33–46.

Gilvarry, C. (2005) 'Children of alcoholics: the UK's largest survey', National Association for Children of Alcoholics. [WWW Document]. Available from: https://nacoa.org.uk/wp-content/uploads/2020/11/2005-June-AT-article-CGilvarry.pdf-1.pdf [Accessed 03 April 23]

Hall, E. (2001) Feelings About Drug Use Drug-Related Locus of Control. (Doctoral Thesis). University of California, Los Angeles.

Hawkins, J.D., Catalano, R.F. and Miller, J.Y. (1992) 'Risk and protective factors for alcohol and other drug problems in adolescence and early adulthood: implications for substance abuse prevention', *Psychol. Bull.*, 112: 64–105.

Haynes, P. and Ayliffe, G. (1991) 'Locus of control of behaviour: is high externality associated with substance misuse?', *Br. J. Addict.*, 86: 1111–17.

Kartch, F. (2017) 'Narrative interviewing', in Allen, M eds *The SAGE Encyclopedia of Communication Research Methods*, Thousand Oaks California: Sage Publications, Inc.

Kroll, B. (2004) 'Living with an elephant: growing up with parental substance misuse', *Child Fam. Soc. Work* , 9: 129–40.

Landberg, J., Danielsson, A.-K., Falkstedt, D. and Hemmingsson, T. (2018) Fathers' alcohol consumption and long-term risk for mortality in offspring', *Oxford Journals Alcohol and Alcoholism.*, 53: 753–9.

Nation, M. and Heflinger, C.A. (2006) 'Risk factors for serious alcohol and drug use: the role of psychosocial variables in predicting the frequency of substance use among adolescents', *Am. J. Drug Alcohol Abuse*, 32: 415–33.

Ng, T.W.H., Sorensen, K.L. and Eby, L.T. (2006) Locus of control at work: a meta-analysis', *J. Organ. Behav.*, 27: 1057–87.

Rabani Bavojdan, M., Towhidi, A. and Rahmati, A. (2011) 'The relationship between mental health and general self-efficacy beliefs, coping strategies and locus of control in male drug abusers', *Addict. Health*, 3: 111–18.

Ross, L.T. and Hill, E.M. (2001) 'Drinking and parental unpredictability among adult children of alcoholics: a pilot study', *Subst. Use Misuse*, 36: 609–38.

Rossow, I., Keating, P., Felix, L. and McCambridge, J. (2016) 'Does parental drinking influence children's drinking? A systematic review of prospective cohort studies', *Addict. Abingdon Engl.*, 111: 204–17.

Rutter, M. (1985) 'Resilience in the face of adversity: protective factors and resistance to psychiatric disorder', *Br. J. Psychiatry*, 147: 598–611.

Ryff, C.D. (1989) 'Happiness is everything, or is it? Explorations on the meaning of psychological well-being', *J. Pers. Soc. Psychol.*, 57: 1069–81.

Scottish Families Affected by Alcohol and Drugs. (2021) 'Ask The Family Report.' [WWW Document]. Available from: https://www.sfad.org.uk/content/uploads/2021/04/Ask-The-Family-Report-March-2021.pdf [Accessed 03 April 23].

Scottish Government. (2010) 'The Societal Cost of Alcohol Misuse in Scotland for 2007', [WWW Document]. Available from: https://www.webarchive.org.uk/wayback/archive/20170701074158oe_/http://www.gov.scot/Publications/2009/12/29122804/0 [Accessed 16 June 2020].

Sher, K.J., Walitzer, K.S., Wood, P.K. and Brent, E.E. (1991) 'Characteristics of children of alcoholics: putative risk factors, substance use and abuse, and psychopathology', *J. Abnorm. Psychol.*, 100: 427–48.

Snyder, C.R. (2002) 'Hope theory: rainbows in the mind', *Psychol. Inq.*, 13: 249–75.

Taskforce, D.D. (2022) 'Final Report', [WWW Document]. Drug Deaths Taskforce. Available from: https://drugdeathstaskforce.scot/news-.info rmation/publications/reports/final-report/ [Accessed 12 January 2022].

Templeton, L. and Zohhadi, S., Galvani, S., Velleman, R. (2006) '"*Looking Beyond Risk*": *Parental Substance Misuse: Scoping Study*', Edinburgh: Scottish Executive.

Understanding Glasgow. (2016) 'Problem drug use: The Glasgow Indicators Project', [WWW Document]. Available from: https://www.understan dingglasgow.com/indicators/lifestyle/drugs/problem_drug_use [Accessed 26 March 2021].

Velleman, R. and Orford, J. (1999) *Risk and Resilience: Adults who were the Children of Problem Drinkers*. London: Routledge.

Velleman, R. and Templeton, L.J. (2016) 'Impact of parents' substance misuse on children: an update', *B. J. Psych. Adv.*, 22: 108–17.

Walsh, D., McCartney, G., Collins, C., Taulbut, M. and Batty, G.D. (2017) 'History, politics and vulnerability: explaining excess mortality in Scotland and Glasgow', *Public Health*, 151: 1–12.

Werner, E.E. and Johnson, J.L. (2004) 'The role of caring adults in the lives of children of alcoholics', *Subst. Use Misuse*, 39: 699–720.

Yap, M.B.H., Cheong, T.W.K., Zaravinos-Tsakos, F., Lubman, D.I. and Jorm, A.F. (2017) 'Modifiable parenting factors associated with adolescent alcohol misuse: a systematic review and meta-analysis of longitudinal studies', *Addict. Abingdon Engl.*, 112: 1142–62.

4

COVID-19 and intergenerational equity: can social protection initiatives transcend caste barriers in India?

Akanksha Sanil

Introduction

The COVID-19 outbreak became a field experiment to test social and economic resilience both within and between societies. However, exposure to vulnerabilities is often systemically reinforced by inequities in policies that fails to accommodate those already at the margins of multiple disadvantages and unjust differences in distribution of and access to resources. This acts as an impediment to a flourishing life for a vast population that includes not only the people today but also those of future generations. In India, the existence of caste as a form of systemic structural inequality is commonly understood as an arrangement of human hierarchy institutionalised on grounds of ritual considerations. For long, uneven and disproportionate outcomes have aggravated and deepened historic inequities among disadvantaged groups in fair access to basic services such as healthcare or education, equitable opportunity and even human dignity. This is because the nature and context of present society is embedded in its socio-cultural development through civilisations. While there exists a constant challenge to maintain equity, the failure to recognise underlying operative dimensions of social marginality, caused as an outcome of India's social structure of caste system renders multiple governance deficiencies. It is here that the idea of social protection becomes a relevant commitment for any socially responsive state apparatus. While increasing interventions points to the global expansion of social policies in general, the influence at national level reflects the dynamic interconnectedness between domestic politics and scholarly policy ideas. For India, this is marked by evolving insights on *Intergenerational Equity*, particularly in context of social protection architecture. This chapter intends to identify existing scholarship and correlate it with empirical studies by independent agencies and newspaper reports to critically examine the impact of religious-scriptural ideology of caste as a contemporary challenge that exacerbates existing disparities among the so-called '*savarna* (those with a *varna*) − *avarna*'[1] (those without a *varna*) category of continuing social divisions in India, even during the COVID-19 distress. Broadly, the chapter is divided into five sections, excluding the conclusion. The *first* and *second* sections are an introduction to the theme of social protection and equity. The *third* section further develops the theoretical context with reference to *intergenerationality* and demonstrates its renewed focus in India given the background of the recent pandemic. The *fourth* section attempts to apply the idea of caste to understand its relevance in determining the outcome of social protection measures undertaken during COVID-19. The subsequent section seeks to explore a possible framework that incorporates an intergenerational perspective within social protection architecture and caste in India, based on the world's most ambitious social protection initiative − Mahatma Gandhi National Rural Employment Guarantee Scheme (MGNREGS). Overall, the chapter is premised on the moral conviction and the argument that, if an *intergenerational* perspective to contextualise caste is ignored in social policy, future generations will continue to inherit the invisible costs and burdens of an archaic social order.

The 'Quiet Revolution' of social protection: lessons for a post-pandemic order

The existence of social protection embodies a persistent ideation to overcome diverse and multiple vulnerabilities. It is the conceptual perspective of risks, needs and rights that helps to locate alternative arrangements based on a comprehensive suitability of the specific ecosystem. In this regard, the official website of United Nations on Sustainable Development Goals (SDG) clearly recognises target 1.3 (Social Protection systems and measures for all, including floors) in order to 'implement nationally appropriate social protection systems and measures for all, including floors, and by 2030 achieve substantial coverage of the poor and the vulnerable' (see https://sdgs.un.org). It is important to note that access to basic social protection has been recognised as a human right in international conventions (Barrientos and Hulme, 2008, pp 4–5). One such significant acknowledgment has been enshrined under the 1948 Universal Declaration of Human Rights.[2] It is crucial to understand that the declaration involves a commitment to ensure a decent living for all, and hence, public interventions become necessary to secure them for each individual, household and community.[3] The most widely applicable approach is to ensure provision of guaranteed social security. It is preeminent to highlight therefore, that the term 'social protection' has a wider connotation and includes within it measures undertaken to promote 'social security', which is mainly related to financial assistance programmes (Spicker, 2014, p 215).

Social protection strategies have been integral for governments − past and present, especially for countries such as India, where the multi-dimensional nature of crisis and vulnerabilities are compounded by embedded socio-economic inequalities and exclusion. The recent pandemic has brought the discourse on social protection to the forefront. Evidently, the global crisis made pre-existing challenges more visible and far worse. While efforts are already underway to revitalise and rebuild a sustainable and fairer future, there are regions across the world where deeply entrenched everyday struggles have adversely affected some more than the others. Indeed, attempts to advance measures to protect individuals and households through compensatory fiscal stimulus plans have only had certain immediate ad-hoc outcomes. It is here, that the idea to strengthen, expand, or even introduce necessary measures for 'social protection' becomes relevant for a responsive and committed state apparatus. According to the social protection platform maintained by the International Labour Organisation (ILO), between February 2020 to April 2021, the majority of countries globally have announced some form of social protection response measures, with the highest among them being reported from Africa, Americas, Europe and Central Asia, followed by Asia and the Pacific, and the Arab states. The responses varied from access to education, food and nutrition, health, housing, pensions, income protection, unemployment, children and family. Among these, income and unemployment protection, housing and other special allowance accounted for more than 50 per cent of measures taken overall across regions. Therefore, it seems a convincing proposition that situations and challenges caused by unforeseen events similar to COVID-19 necessitate a credible and adaptable design of such a social security system that endures in its durability even beyond an emergency response plan. For emerging economies in particular, the rise of social protection has been viewed as an evolving paradigm for social policy (Barrientos and Hulme, 2009, p 3) – a 'quiet revolution' (Barrientos and Hulme, 2009, p 452) within their respective national development strategies, strongly witnessed during 1990s in such countries, including India (Spicker, 2014, p 216).

Social protection is conventionally linked to policies and programmes to advance efforts that mitigates risk of poverty and deprivation. The discourse on social protection has transformed significantly since the publication of World Development Report in 1990 by World Bank, especially in context of developing countries. Primarily, the distinguishing outcome of the World Bank's conceptualisation indicated a 'minimalist social assistance' in countries that were fiscally unsustainable to support comprehensive social welfare programmes (Devereux and Sabates-Wheeler, 2004, p 3). Invariably therefore, such initiatives began to be narrowly promoted as components necessary for what Devereux and Sabates-Wheeler argues as ' " economic protection", and not "social" protection, as it does not advocate social transformation' (Devereux and Sabates-Wheeler, 2004, p 3).

According to Devereux and Sabates-Wheeler (2004),

> Social Protection is the set of all initiatives, both formal and informal, that provides: *social assistance* to extremely poor individuals and households; *social services* to groups who need special care or would otherwise be denied access to basic services; *social insurance* to protect people against the risks and consequences of livelihood shocks, and, *social equity* to protect people against social risks such as discrimination or abuse. (p 9)

Therefore, the basic elements of social protection may be categorised as identification of:

- economic and social risks such as poverty, disability, and so on, and
- vulnerable population, including marginalised communities.

However, until September 2021, only 47 per cent of the global population are effectively covered by at least one social protection benefit, while 4.1 billion people (53 per cent) obtain no income security at all from their national social protection system (ILO, 2021). The COVID-19 pandemic also revealed wide and uneven gaps between and within countries.

Further, within the framework developed by ILO, the functions of social protection have been conceived and differentiated into Protective, Preventive, and Promotional (PPP) measures. The dominant critique against the most influential conceptualisation in policy literature recognises the need to question the 'missing integration of transformative functions' (Devereux and Sabates-Wheeler, 2004, pp 9–10) to assert the relevance of such interventions. This chapter has a substantial focus on the 'transformative' function of social protection. Nevertheless, the other three functions (as conceptualised by the ILO), have been dealt with briefly to operationalise the argument. Therefore, while each category of the 'PPP model' communicates a distinct broader purpose – *protective* to provide relief from deprivation (for example, income benefit); *preventive* to avert deprivation (for example, social insurance); and *promotional* to enhance income and capabilities, respectively – the 'transformative' element clearly advocates a vision for social equity to be defined along greater inclusion, empowerment and rights, to 'protect the vulnerable and minority groups against discrimination and abuse' (Devereux and Sabates-Wheeler, 2004, pp 9–10).

Social protection or social equity: defying the dilemma

The adoption of social protection policy requires the existence of a stable political system which indicates preferences to enhance human welfare through enlightened values over those that undermine their credibility based on patronage, clientelism and corruption (Barrientos and Hulme, 2008, p 17). Therefore, the rationale behind political choices made in order to guarantee certain entitlements determines to a great extent the aggregate implications of such policies. The occurrence of exogenous factors such as COVID-19 reflects how the desired policy counteracts under the crisis of extreme threat inflicted upon public. It is crucial to rethink about the sustainability of such ineffective social protection strategies that have caused serious disadvantages to those strongly dependent on them. For instance, Holmes and Jones (2010) conducted a multi-country research to examine the extent to which gender has been integrated into social protection approaches. The conceptual framework of the study was based on concerns of equity which held that a recognition of people's experiences of social and economic risks manifested in the underlying asymmetries of power was crucial in order to provide a sustainable strategy of extensive reform (p 4). In a way, therefore, equity is a preeminent solution to *address imbalance* in the social system.

More importantly, in an age of unforeseen socio-environmental crisis, it becomes an even greater obligation for national governments to commit themselves towards 'strengthening social equity' (American Society for Public Administration, 2013). However, 'this obligation is not only limited to administration of laws in a fair manner, but is also about the attitude to actively seek to foster its spirit through moral leadership' (Shafritz and Russell, 2005). Fundamentally, social equity implies 'fairness in the delivery of public services; it is egalitarianism in action – the principle that each citizen, regardless of economic resources or personal traits, deserves and has a right to be given equal treatment by the political system' (Shafritz and Russell, 2005). In India, inequities are most prominently, an outcome of differences in income and wealth, education, occupation, gender, religion and socioeconomic status. For instance, preference of sons over daughters is an outcome of discrimination against the girl child. This severely affects her right to educational opportunity and command decisions for any action that becomes relevant for her decent living in future. Similarly, marginalised communities such as the official category of Scheduled Castes (SCs), historically referred to as 'untouchables' remained at the bottom of the caste system, were exposed to abuse, discrimination and indignity as they are among the worst accumulator of competing advantages of social capital. For the vast majority of them, the most provocative aspect that enhances the urge to transcend their social and economic barrier and escalate upwards on the ladder of status mobility, is the desperation towards a radical transformation of the caste-based social order – an assertion of their distinct, yet an equally powerful self-identity. The 'equity lens' (World Health Organisation, 2013) therefore, is more important now than perhaps at any other point in the history of an emancipatory struggle within India. Indeed, the pertinent question to ask is: *can social policies, including those on social protection, prevent past and continuing generations of overt or prejudicial cultural customs to conquer contemporary inter-group or caste disparities, and solidify an institutional commitment to equity and social justice?*

In this context, an equity framework of social protection poses a two-front challenge (particularly, in India), even before a systematic assessment of the most unfortunate outcomes is deliberated. The *first* demands an objective identification of those more susceptible to adverse effects of natural and varied forms of crisis, and *second* to rethink on the frontiers of action that aggressively builds resilience to help minimise an intergenerational transfer of burden for the more vulnerable populations. This is because the mechanism of caste deeply penetrates the stigmatised classification of social identities. To quote,

> Caste is not a physical object like a wall of bricks or a line of barbed wire which prevents the Hindus from co-mingling and which has, therefore, to be pulled down. Caste is a notion. It is a state of the mind. The destruction of Caste does not therefore mean the destruction of a physical barrier. It means a notional change. (Ambedkar, 1936)

The idea of Intergenerational Equity in caste: a theoretical context

Intergenerational perspective offers a historical continuum of entitlements and obligations that connects generations of past, present and future. It assumes that generational transformation between younger and older members of society influences each other's lives and, therefore, particular kinds of arrangements and actions ameliorate or limit social problems across a range of contexts – social, political, economic and environmental. Significantly enough, the discourse about *intergenerationality* presents contemporary and evolving 'insights on 'intergenerational contract' underlying the provision of social welfare (Marcum and Treas, 2013), 'intergenerational justice' (Gardiner, 2006) to mitigate the impact of climate change and resource depletion, forms of 'intergenerational practice' (Moore and Statham, 2006) to improve relations between generations, intergenerational inequality as the cause of rising social and political unrest (Berry, 2011)' (Vanderbeck and Worth, 2015). The relationship between *caste and 'generational' or 'intergenerational' dimension* – a linkage that this chapter intends to establish – denotes the inheritance of the invisible privileges and burdens between members of different generations, produced by the perceived *stigmatised identity of difference* under an inherent conception of an archaic social order. This means that the process of segregation and integration embodied in citizen–state welfare interaction determines the degree of social and economic caste-specific vulnerabilities within and beyond families.

The concept of 'Intergenerational Equity' is a well-recognised core principle for environmental justice and sustainability that has its origins in the Declaration of the United Nations Conference on the Human Environment 1972, commonly referred to as the Stockholm Declaration. Principle 1 under the declaration states that, 'The natural resources of the earth, including the air, water, land, flora and fauna and especially representative samples of natural ecosystems, must be safeguarded for the benefit of present and future generations through careful planning or management, as appropriate' (United Nations Environment Programme, 1972). Interestingly, the expression does not find a clear mention in the international commitment for environmental agenda adopted by the United Nations General Assembly in 2015 under the Sustainable Development Goals (SDGs). Within the literature of climate change, Brown Weiss – a well-known scholar on international environmental law – defined

> Intergenerational Equity through three key principles of conservation of – options, quality, and access in order to protect the diversity of natural resources, quality of the environment, and the ability of future generations to equitably access the benefits are translated into obligations to prevent and mitigate climate change, together with the obligation to provide adaptation assistance. (Venn, 2019, p 718)

It must be observed that the founding pillars that underpins the conceptualisation of obligations are firmly grounded on the ethical arguments to promote social equity in order to prevent a self-perpetuating cycle of inequality, marginalisation and exclusion among particular groups and individuals. It is this contextual framework that needs wider application in decision-making on intricately complex and evolving paradigms within the domain of social policies, including issues on social protection, especially in India. The idea is to prioritise necessary processes and procedural interventions in such a way that questions of intergenerational fairness can be posed and addressed.

It is however unclear of how and to what extent the challenges can be strongly conquered so long as the dominant debates continues to surround the overlap between multiple interests and future of the legal and constitutional order, market, institutions, and the moral-human factors involved thereby. This is even more a reality for India where, there is a general absence of detailed definition, legislation, and practices for social policies to promote Intergenerational Equity within the established operational structure of the country. In fact, there exists a further challenging question about whether a recognition of caste-based deprivation in overall welfare policy is possible, especially when the larger agenda of redressal is part of an explicitly political project? Nonetheless, compelling transformation necessitates a dialogue based on extensive field research on valuable government interventions, including those related to the provision of social protection benefits, particularly during unanticipated crisis such as the COVID-19 pandemic. It is during these extremities that it becomes relevant to identify how the processes of inclusion or exclusion operate to reinforce positions of advantage or disadvantage as a result of an individual's association with a specific caste identity; or whether continuing or prior experience of identity-based disadvantage justify the case for an intergenerational focus; or can the stigma subjected to those belonging to the historically dehumanised castes reinforce the perception of 'undeserving recipients' of welfare and provoke a sense of 'welfare stigma' for future generations?

The previous analysis demonstrates that, in order to empirically redesign context-specific purpose of social protection mechanism under the prevailing social policy architecture in India, involves an opportune potential for a theoretical reinterrogation of the concept, design and practice within the ambit of welfare benefits. The framework of *intergenerationality* offers an efficient scheme of resource allocation and management, specifically during natural or human exigencies. Further, Intergenerational Equity inherently incorporates dimensions of measurement of the impact governments can have on future generations. It aims to facilitate an enabling ecosystem that helps achieve an inclusive and equitable future for historically marginalised groups, especially in context of India. Undoubtedly, decisive political action, especially radical measures such as stringent nationwide lockdowns, among other preventive strategies undertaken during the coronavirus pandemic, has communicated a dramatic absence or presence in the perceived trust by citizens on their governments and representative leaders. According to Bros (2022), 'Many leaders around the world have seen improvement in their approval ratings as the virus started its worldwide expansion' (p 51). Some studies suggest that: 'increased trust in government is not due to the epidemic itself but rather due to the measures taken and that they come more as a reward for their expertise and handling of the situation' (Bros, 2022, p 52). In this reference, the most rational interpretation from the COVID-19 pandemic unleashed a crucial point. As Bros (2022) observes, 'an exceptional event may trigger an emotional response and a surge in approval rate. As the issue loses its novelty, it becomes one of the items of the political debate and citizens eventually hold their government accountable and reward proper management and expertise' (p 62). However, extraordinary events necessitate that citizens exercise their right to seek accountability from democratic governments, as is the case in India.

COVID-19 and social protection: locating the problem of caste in India

The nature and context of any society is embedded in its socio-cultural development through civilisations. Subsequently, strong indicators of 'equality deficits' communicate not only an unequal distribution of resources and opportunities, but also represent the underlying domination that creates and mobilises such differences (Jodhka, 2018, p 2). Hence, any analysis that attempts to question structures of inequality must necessarily be located within the 'particular framework of history, culture and social configuration' (Jodhka, 2018, p 3). In India, contemporary inequalities, in particular, inequality among specific identity groups, is largely an outcome of historical exclusion and marginalisation, perpetuated through the institution of caste as a critical marker of social stratification.

The textbook view of caste presents it as an 'ancient institution based on the ideas of *varna*, *karma* and *dharma*, most explicitly elaborated in the classic Hindu text *Manusmriti*' (Jodhka 2018, p 112). While *Manusmriti* does not explicitly mention the word caste, it governed individual conduct and social interactions based on the belief that the organisation of the Hindu social order was divinely ordained through a system of hierarchy that was institutionalised on the notion of 'purity and pollution'. This was achieved by the mechanism of distinctions based on *varna*. The *varna* system established the Hindus into four mutually exclusive and hierarchically ranked categories. Beyond the four *varnas* were the *atishudra* or *achhoots* (the 'untouchables'), 'who by virtue of being classified as the *avarnas* (those without a *varna*) occupied the lowliest position in contrast to the *savarnas* (those with a *varna*)' (Deshpande, 2011, p 19). This 'intergenerational transfer of hierarchy' defining one's social standing in the overall structure was inscribed in ritual terms by a codified framework that structured almost every aspect of social and economic life of people for centuries.

The *second* related element that naturalised a caste order was the *karma* doctrine. According to it, the present life of a person is a link to the infinite chain of subsequent births and rebirths, and that, the birth of each in a specific (*varna*) position is an outcome of their own past deeds. Therefore, the only way to improve the prospects of a better future birth was to adhere to, and perform well, the role considered appropriate for the stratum in which one was born. The text *Manusmriti* clearly lays down the duties of each *varna* in its various verses. Finally, with regards to the concept of *dharma* in ancient India, it must be noted that *dharma* governed the criteria of human behaviour and social duties, as adherence to it was stated to be beneficial not only for the individual, but also for the overall welfare of society at large (Meena 2005, pp 578–9). In the text *Manusmriti*, *dharma* has been conceptualised as a creation of 'divine power' established on the idea of religion and spirituality for the execution of 'right duties' in all aspects of human life. It is important to observe here that, while conceptual conflicts between *varna* and caste is acknowledged, given the purpose, the intent is to relate both in a rather comprehensive perspective and recognise them as objects of individual or group identity that continues to determine the extent of inequality, exclusion and marginalisation in India.

Caste is not an indigenous Indian term but has its origins in the Portuguese word casta. There is no exact equivalent in Indian languages for the word caste (Galanter, 1984, p 6). Probably, theoretical ambiguities on *jati* have gradually made the term *caste* correspond directly to the former. The nature of the caste pyramid has traditionally been standardised to an imagination that is characteristic of a vast population of 'lower-castes' to assume the bottommost position. It is equally important to highlight that caste divisions between the so-called 'high' or 'low' distinction is most often indicative of the historically subjugated 'untouchable' cluster of *jatis* that were together identified as a specific social category in government schedule during the colonial period. Clearly, it is not the aim of this study to capture the micro-level complexities that intricately defines the *varna-caste-jati* relationship. Undoubtedly, the literature is vast in this regard. However, this limited discussion was a necessary prerequisite to locate the historic manifestation of the present-day complexities of caste in the everyday lives of people within a structure of caste-based social order.

As mentioned previously, a governing instrument that legitimised notions of caste can be traced to the foundation of 'untouchability', which in turn has its roots in the religious-scriptural tradition of Indian society. Dr B.R. Ambedkar, the most influential scholar in the study of *Castes In India* (also the title of his work in 1916) and architect of the Constitution of India argued that, 'untouchability was an infliction and not a choice' to ensure compulsory segregation (Ambedkar 1989 [2014], p 5). Further, in *Untouchability and Stratification in Indian Civilisation*, Shrirama (2007) noted, that 'the metaphysical doctrine of karma has provided a powerful rationalisation for inequality based on birth and made it acceptable to the wide masses' (p 49). The dynamics on the practice of untouchability have transformed and manifested differently over the years. Though there exist instances of spatial segregation and physical violence, there are also other prevalent modes that are either largely hidden or numerically low, compared to subtle, yet powerful forms of social ostracism, discrimination and humiliation. The following excerpt from *Caste and the Indian Economy* by Munshi (2019) reflects the centrality of caste society in almost all social and economic interactions. He observed that:

> Caste plays a role at every stage of an Indian's economic life. His caste will determine the type of school he has access to, the way he is treated by his teachers, and his interactions with his classmates.

> In young adulthood, his caste will determine whether or not he benefits from affirmative action in higher education and (later) access to government jobs. Over the course of his working life, his caste will determine how he is assessed by potential employers, while, in parallel, networks organized around his caste help him find new jobs. Overlapping caste- based networks will provide him with credit, help him start a business if he is endowed with entrepreneurial talent, and provide him with insurance against income shocks and major contingencies into old age. (p 781)

This suggests that traditionally asymmetrical power relations and social capital based on caste-based identities are primarily responsible for reproduction and revival of ideological faith in the hierarchical social system of caste that supports a superiority-inferiority structure in India. Nonetheless, efforts have been undertaken to evolve, despite continuous and rather regressive resistance. However, what is firmly desirable is to supplement existing struggles towards an egalitarian society by exploring the potential within policy-oriented solutions.

The mechanism of social protection initiatives introduced in India as a consequence of COVID-19 were primarily designed to mitigate concerns from the inadvertent crisis on health, income support and food distribution. In India, the social protection system encompasses a majority of legislative and policy-based approaches to overcome contemporary social policy concerns of vulnerable populations, including targeted measures to tackle sickness, unemployment, disability and old age among such groups. It would be interesting to visualise the PPP measures and transformative approach based on the functions of social protection in the context of India (Figure 4.1).

In India, the most documented fallout of the pandemic has been the challenge to minimise exclusionary tendencies in established mainstream social protection schemes. The unprecedented pressure on the country was a result of a majority of confirmed cases of COVID-19 in the region and a significant increase in the number of cases during the second half of June 2020, which was also the end of the nation-wide lockdown imposed in March 2020 (Basil and Soyer, 2020). As a result, in addition to various public health mechanism already in place, the Government of India announced socio-economic relief measures under a comprehensive package of *Pradhan Mantri Garib Kalyan Yojana* (PMGKY) to ensure continuous provision of basic needs for poor and vulnerable people. The aim was not only to 'introduce new social protection interventions but also to adapt to pre-existing benefits' (Basil and Soyer, 2020).

There have been, however, significant inequalities and massive inadequacies in providing a broad-based social protection coverage to all. Precisely, this was due to a lack of sufficient assessment of deservedness and implementation bottlenecks. Studies on uneven patterns of COVID-19 outcomes conducted

Figure 4.1: Representative programmes/schemes to communicate Devereux and Sabates-Wheeler's (2004) conception of the 'functions of social protection' in India

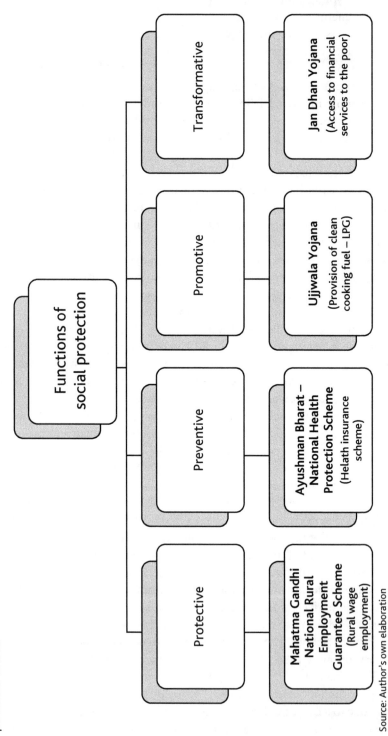

Source: Author's own elaboration

across countries worldwide have revealed disturbing evidence that suggests a systemic overlay between conditions of vulnerability and structures of marginalisation (Banerjee and Bhattacharya, 2022, p 378). While much of the discussion acknowledges the distributional asymmetries and disproportionate inequities among historically excluded identity groups, what is now needed is an increased engagement with the institutions and practices that influenced such structural deprivation.

It is noteworthy however, that among significant research that tracks India's social protection responses to COVID-19, there were a substantial number of them that clearly failed to highlight the inadequacies in relief measures as a result of caste-induced exclusion. For instance, the Discussion Paper on India's social protection response to COVID-19 released in June 2021 by World Bank Group on Social Protection and Jobs has no mention of caste-based exclusion in relief entitlements during the pandemic. However, among a few well-documented studies conducted by independent bodies such as The National Commission for Dalit Human Rights (NCDHR) in selected geographies across 14 states presented in its Report 'Delayed and Denied: Injustice in COVID-19 Relief', an inclusion assessment of India's key relief entitlements across SC/Scheduled Tribes (ST) households during April to May 2020. While the assessment is based on the first round of India's social safety net response to COVID-19, the analysis identifies how government intentions and efforts to provide relief to poor and vulnerable households have fared in implementation outcomes between April and August 2020. The findings revealed threefold trends: little or no awareness about the announced entitlements; significant scheme coverage gaps; and low benefit realisation by those enrolled under the social protection schemes (NCDHR, 2020, p 3).

At its core, social policy and the role it plays in redistributing resources is central to issues of social justice, equality and citizenship. However, as caste continues to remain a structural cause of inequality and poverty (Mosse, 2018), a purposive recognition in Indian social policy is crucial to achieve equity and promote an inclusive society. For this, it is imperative to realise that in India, the idea of power must move beyond the demands of social control, subordination and exercise of restraint on immoral conduct. Rather, and more importantly, the use of power must equally envision a commitment to introduce and nurture social change and transformation through ethical and political values in policy and practice, that are based on a larger understanding of the inherent societal structure.

Caste, intergenerational equity, and social protection in India: in search of a possible framework

Among an important role of social policy there is an underlying aim 'to serve as a cushion to reduce the worst social effects of a crisis – natural or economic – which in turn can contribute towards a direct relief and sustainability of the entire process' (Ghosh, 2015, p 285) and vulnerable people. Therefore, it is argued that to integrate social protection policies with Intergenerational Equity in India will remain impractical, unless persisting and deepening caste-based inequalities are incorporated within a social policy framework. An illustrative case of MGNREGS – has been examined here to bring greater clarity on this.

The MGNREGS Act enacted in the year 2005 by the Government of India is the world's largest work guarantee programme that provides for 100 days of guaranteed wage employment per year to rural poor households. It intends to provide social protection and livelihood security through wage employment for the most vulnerable rural population in India. Studies have documented that the initiative had tremendously empowered the socially disadvantaged segments of population, particularly, women and SCs/STs, through a rights-based legislation. Nonetheless, in practice, the positive outcomes have varied greatly across different states in India. Despite all its successes and limitations, MGNREGS has undeniably loosened the patron-client relations between low-caste agricultural labourers and their landowning caste Hindu employers (Lerche, 2010, p 64). However, a major aspect to observe in this transformation of the village economy from 'agricultural labour' to 'rural labour' is the continued over-dependence on the scheme of certain caste categories more than the others. Evidence from a series of research studies on MGNREGA, 2005 conducted in the period between 2006–12 suggests that,

> at the national level, the share of SCs (Scheduled Castes) and STs (Scheduled Tribes) in the work provided under MGNREGA has been high at 40–50 per cent across each of the years of the Scheme's implementation. In the case of both SCs and STs, the participation rate exceeds their total share in the total population. (Government of India, 2012, p 12)

Thus, as is evident here, social policies (such as MGNREGS) have an ambitious orientation to counter deeper societal challenges, while it negotiates between its financial viability and wider reform agenda. In this context, an intergenerational approach is pertinent to explore and even mitigate the influence of caste in MGNREGS. This necessitates the steps that follow:

1. *Identify the top 5 States with maximum number of 'Active Workers' under the scheme.*
   For instance, as of now, Uttar Pradesh, West Bengal, Rajasthan, Madhya Pradesh, and Bihar (NREGA State Report). Incidentally, according

to government sources the state-wise number of rural population, as on 1 April 2022 indicates that the presence of Scheduled Castes (SCs) is dominant in Uttar Pradesh, West Bengal, Bihar, Rajasthan and Madhya Pradesh.

2. *Correlate data on caste and MGNREGA uptake by rural populations in these states*, is necessary to determine the percentage of on-site caste bias – discrimination, indignity, and violence; expedite the process of irregular wage disbursements (to prevent them from severe economic hardships).

3. *Assess how far economic disabilities becomes a cause to penetrate social marginalisation of such communities*, especially in terms of generational aspirations to upscale knowledge, skills, and prospects of better work.

4. *Determine if improper healthcare practices and greater dependency on other welfare benefits such as food and nutrition is based on lack of meaningful financial inclusion* of the SCs.

The list may most commonly be understood as an over-simplification of the complexity of the issues involved. However, the purpose to curate an illustrative case such as the one mentioned above is only to promote a radical rethink on welfare and social protection in India, especially if the objective is to counter a historical continuum of an unequal social structure, and create an empathetic solidarity among diverse social groups.

Conclusion

Social policy research is not just an academic exercise; sometimes it is investigative – finding out what is happening or why something has gone wrong (Spicker, 2014, p 383). The study of social policy considers that it is necessary to place welfare policies within its related societal context to identify and reduce socio-economic inequalities, and therefore, social policies seeks to actively engage and enable wider societal transformation. This chapter intends to argue that Intergenerational Equity is not only a normative concern, but indeed a morally rational obligation for welfare democracies around the world. One of the most fundamental mechanism to promote such an *intergenerationality* can be its application in the provision of social protection. This tends to be particularly crucial for emerging economies, including India, where its growth has been among the most remarkable. However, notable benefits of social protection in these countries (this work consider India) and its effects on the reduction of social inequality, do not necessarily integrate concerns of mutually reinforcing inequalities of caste, class and gender, that not only undermines cooperative action, but also distorts the generic public policy priorities (Drèze, 2016, p 14). This is because when association to derive one's identity is based on the affiliation to region, religion or caste and is generally led by complex administrative *procedures* and the underlying bureaucratic-technocratic interplay, it is the *purpose* of social equity that will most likely achieve a collective of individuals and communities and thereby encourage greater accommodation over contestation on fundamental ideals.

In alignment with this, it is worth mentioning that the Constitution of India outlined this in its interpretation of the idea of 'fraternity' as the core of social interactions. In the area of social provision, this principle 'takes welfare as a form of collective activity and so the responsibility of the wider society rather than of individuals' (Spicker, 2014, p 217). The approach to policy, then, has centred not to abolish caste itself (the Constitution of India itself does not do so), but seeks to integrate those excluded communities who remain to be delinked from welfare outreach of governments. This is because, the lack of equity in one aspect of social life, that is on account of perceived caste identities in the determination of a fair share in public resources and opportunities, has consequences for inequity in most other aspects of life. Therefore, the 'integration strategy' (Barrientos and Hulme, 2008, p 15) employed to combine multiple interventions based on a credible assessment of the factors involved in generating persistent inequalities within countries or regions, as in the case of India, must be recognised as a feature of social protection interventions. It is the formulation and implementation of such *dynamic social policies* that can reconcile concerns of caste to produce Intergenerational Equity in the practice of social protection mechanism to transcend and gradually eradicate the cause of persistent caste barriers in India.

Over the years, the argument to challenge caste, primarily as a function of social policies in general, will not only have a diminished influence on everyday lives and struggles of such people, but equally complement to outweigh the persistence of intersecting and evolving disadvantages as a result of economic status, gender or increased technological advancements. Despite contradictions on the future envisioned so far, what remains certain of the long-term impact of an intergenerational strategy is the provocation of an ideational shift, which *recognises differences only as a mechanism to reorient the value-driven frame which is consistent with politics and policy of overall wellbeing of all.* Indeed, it is time for a rethink now more than any other time in the history of humankind.

Notes

[1] The *varna* system established the Hindus into four mutually exclusive and hierarchically ranked categories. Beyond the four *varnas* were the *atishudra* or *achhoots* (the 'untouchables'), 'who by virtue of being classified as the *avarnas* (those without a *varna*) occupied the lowliest position in contrast to the *savarnas* (those with a *varna*)' (Deshpande 2011, p. 19).

[2] The text of Article 22 under the 1948 Universal Declaration of Human Rights declares that 'Everyone, as a member of society, has the right to social security and is entitled to realization, through national effort and international co-operation and in accordance with

the organization and resources of each State, of the economic, social and cultural rights indispensable for his dignity and the free development of his personality' (un.org).

3   This is relevant from the perspective of what the World Bank termed as 'social risk management' (Barrientos and Hulme 2015, p 5). In a paper in 1999, Holzmann and Jorgensen have defined the same. However, the context implied here is not limited to prevent income risks alone.

References

Ambedkar, B.R. (1916) *Castes in India: Their Mechanism, Genesis, and Development*, Chennai: Notion Press.

Ambedkar, B.R. (1936) *Annihilation of Caste*, New Delhi: POD Only Publishing.

Ambedkar, B.R. and Moon, V. (1989 [2014]) *Dr. Babasaheb Ambedkar, Writings and Speeches: Vol. 5*, Bombay: Education Department, Government of Maharashtra. [Reprinted 2014.]

American Society for Public Administration. (2013) "Code of Ethics". https://www.aspanet.org/ASPA/ASPA/Code-of-Ethics/Code-of-Eth ics.aspx

Bacil, F. and Soyer, G. (2020) *COVID-19 and Social Protection in South Asia: India*, Brasilia-DF: International Policy Centre for Inclusive Growth (IPC-IG).

Banerjee, L. and Bhattacharya, S. (2022) 'Labour and the pandemic: a study on work, employment, and work situation', in Bhattacharyya, R., Dastidar, A.G., and Sikdar, S. (eds) *The COVID-19 Pandemic, India and the World: Economic and Social Policy Perspectives*, New York: Routledge, pp 376–90.

Barrientos, A. and Hulme, D. (2008) *Social Protection for the Poor and Poorest* (1st edn) New York: Palgrave Macmillan.

Barrientos, A., and Hulme, D. (2009) 'Social protection for the poor and poorest in developing countries: reflections on a quiet revolution' *Oxford Development Studies*, 37(4): 439–56.

Berry, C. (2011) 'How generational inequality helped set England's cities alight', Inequalities: Research and Reflections from Both sides of the Atlantic. https://inequalitiesblog.wordpress.com/2011/08/23/how–gener ational-inequality-helped-set-england%e2%80%99s-cities-alight/

Bhattacharya, S. and Roy, S.S. (2021) 'Intent to Implementation: Tracking India's Social Protection Response to COVID-19', World Bank Group, No. 2107, Washington DC: The World Bank.

Bros, C. (2022) 'Riding the wave or going under? The COVID-19 pandemic and trust in governments', in Bhattacharyya, R., Dastidar, A.G., and Sikdar, S. (eds) *The COVID-19 Pandemic, India and the World: EcoDnomic and Social Policy Perspectives*, New York: Routledge, pp 50–63.

Deshpande, A. (2011) *Grammar of Caste: Economic Discrimination in Contemporary India*, New Delhi: Oxford University Press.

Devereux, S. and Sabates-Wheeler, R. (2004) *Transformative Social Protection*, IDS Working Paper 232, Institute of Development Studies, Sussex: England.

Drèze, J. (2016) *Social Policies*, Hyderabad: Orient Blackswan.

Dukelow, F., Whelan, J. and Bolton, R. (2022) 'Interrogating welfare stigma: an introduction', *Social Policy & Society*, 21(4): 627–31.

Galanter, M. (1984) *Competing Equalities: Law and the Backward Classes in India,* Berkeley, Los Angeles: University of California Press.

Ghosh, J. (2015) 'Social policy in Indian development', in Mkandawire, T. (ed.) *Social Policy in a Development Context*, New York: Palgrave Macmillan, pp 284–307.

Government of India. (2012) *MGNREGA SAMEEKSHA: An Anthology of Research Studies on the Mahatma Gandhi National Rural Employment Guarantee Act, 2005:* 2006–2012, Ministry of Rural Development, Government of India., New Delhi: Orient Blackswan Private Limited.

Guy, M.E. and McCandless, S.A. (2012) 'Social equity: its legacy, its promise', *Public Administration Review*, 72(S1): S5–S13.

Holmes, R. and Jones, N. (2010) *Rethinking Social Protection using a Gender Len.,* Working Paper 320, London: Overseas Development Institute.

International Labour Organisation. (2021) 'World Social Protection Report 2020–22: Social Protection at the Crossroads – in Pursuit of a Better Future', International Labour Office', Geneva: ILO.

Jodhka, S.S., Rehbein, B. and Souza, J. (2018) 'The Indian story of inequality', in Jodhka, S.S., Rehbein, B., and Souza, J. (eds) *Inequality in Capitalist Societies*, New York: Routledge, pp 108–25.

Kallio, K.P. (2015) 'Intergenerational recognition as political practice', in Vanderbeck, R.M. and Worth, N. (ed.) *Intergenerational Space*, New York: Routledge.

Lerche, J. (2010) 'From 'rural labour' to 'classes of labour': class fragmentation, caste and class struggle at the bottom of the Indian labour hierarchy', in Harris-White, B. and Heyer, J. (eds) *The Contemporary Political Economy of Development: Africa and South Asia*, New York: Routledge, pp 64–85.

Marcum, C.S and Treas, J. (2013), 'The intergenerational social contract revisited' in M. Silverstein and R. Giarrusso (eds) *Kinship and Cohort in an Ageing Society: From Generation to Generation,* Baltimore, MD: The Johns Hopkins University Press, pp 293–313.

Meena, S.L. (2005) 'Relationship between state and Dharma in Manusmriti', *The Indian Journal of Political Science*, 66(3): 575–88.

Mosse, D. (2018) 'Caste and development: contemporary perspectives on a structure of discrimination and advantage', *World Development*, 110: 422–36.

Munshi, K. (2019) 'Caste and the Indian economy', *Journal of Economic Literature*, 57(4): 781–834.

National Campaign on Dalit Human Rights. (2020) *Delayed and Denied: Injustice in COVID-19 Relief National Factsheet*, New Delhi: National Campaign on Dalit Human Rights (NCDHR). Available from: http://www.ncdhr.org.in/wp-content/uploads/2020/09/10-NCDHR-natio nal-factsheet_weclaim_April-May-2020.pdf

Shafritz J., and Russell E.W. (2005) *Introducing Public Administration*, New York: Pearson/Longman.

Shafritz J., Russell E.W., Borick, C. and Hyde, A. (2017) 'Social equity', in Shafritz, J., Russell E.W., Borick, C., and Hyde, A. *Introducing Public Administration* (9th edn), New York: Routledge.

Shrirama,. (2007) 'Untouchability and stratification in Indian civilisation', in Michael, S.M. *Dalits in Modern India: Vision and Values*, New Delhi: Sage Publications India, pp 45–75.

Spicker, P. (2014) *Social Policy: Theory and Practice*, Bristol: Policy Press.

United Nations Environment Programme. (1972). *Environmental Law Guidelines and Principles 1 Stockholm Declaration*, United Nations Environment Programme (UNEP), Stockholm: UNEP, 1972.

Vanderbeck, R.M. and Worth, N. (2015) 'Introduction', in Vanderbeck, R,M. and Worth, N. (eds) *International Space*, New York: Routledge.

Venn, A. (2019) 'Social justice and climate change', in Letcher, T.M. (ed.) *Managing Global Warming: An Interface of Technology and Human Issues*, Amsterdam: Elsevier.

World Health Organisation. (2013). Demonstrating A Health In All Policies Analytic Framework For Learning From Experiences: Based on literature reviews from Africa, South-East Asia and the Western Pacific, Geneva: WHO, 2013.

5

Two levels of agency: the negotiation of intergenerational support in Chinese families

Jiaxin Liu

Introduction

Intergenerational family support has been playing a vital role in China's welfare provisions, especially regarding the old-age support arrangements. Filial piety, intergenerational contract, and intergenerational solidarity are among the most discussed theoretical frameworks that explain the nature of these support arrangements. However, given the rapid changes in demographic and family structure, the shifts in social and cultural norms, and the extended coverage of public pension schemes, little is known about how older Chinese and their families arrange and negotiate intergenerational support under the new circumstances. It also remains to be examined how far these theoretical frameworks may offer renewed insights in understanding intergenerational support relationships in a changing context. This chapter aims to provide new empirical evidence on the negotiation of intergenerational support in Chinese families. Moreover, it proposes a two-level analytical framework to understand both individual agency and familial agency in the arrangement and negotiation of intergenerational support.

By the end of 2020, more than 264 million Chinese had reached the age of 60 years and above, accounting for 18.7% of the total population in China; meanwhile, the working-age population (15 to 59 years old) had decreased to 63.4% (National Bureau of Statistics of China, 2021). Such demographic change not only poses an enduring challenge to the society and its welfare provisions, but also has a significant impact on older individuals and their families. For instance, one of the implications of the ageing population in China, reflected at the family level, is the changes in family structure (Peng, 2011; Su, Hu and Peng, 2017). With the 'baby-boomer generation' entering their old age, and the one-child generation having now reached the age of marriage and childrearing, the '4–2–1/+' multi-generational family structure becomes more common in China – where a working-age couple needs to take care of four older parents and one or more young children (for example, see Abrahamson, 2016; Zang and Zhao, 2017).

The changes in demographic and family structure and their impact on intergenerational families also need to be contextualised in China's recent socio-economic developments. For instance, the regional disparities in economic growth and imbalanced labour market have been contributing to the massive domestic migration from less developed areas to more developed ones (for example, see Cheng et al, 2019). One of the major impacts of domestic migration, at the family level, is an increasing geographic distance among family members, which further challenges the informal old-age support arrangements in both urban and rural China. In the meantime, the Chinese cultural and social norms are also undergoing a series of changes. The traditional Chinese filial piety, which requires one to unconditionally provide for and show obedience to their older parents (Yeh et al, 2013), is being contested particularly by the younger generations and re-interpreted by both generations during the process of modernisation (Mehta and Ko, 2004; Croll, 2006; Guo et al, 2020).

In 2009, after a successful pilot public pension programme in Baoji, Shaanxi Province, the Chinese government initiated the nationwide New Rural Social Pension scheme (NRSP). This new public pension scheme aims to extend the formal public pension coverage to the long-excluded rural residents. In 2011, a parallel programme in urban areas, the Urban Resident Social Pension scheme (URSP) was introduced to include urban residents who were not eligible for the existing employees' pension schemes. The new public pension system aims to provide a fully covered income protection to older Chinese. However, given the primary role of the Chinese (intergenerational) family in protecting and providing for its members, there is little research exploring in depth the arrangement and negotiation of intergenerational support in the context of the changing family structure and the new public pension arrangements.

Based on 14 in-depth semi-structured interviews with older Chinese in Baoji, Shaanxi Province, where the New Rural Social Pension scheme was first initiated, this study aims to explore how older Chinese and their families arrange and negotiate for intergenerational support. The remainder of the chapter will first explore the existing intergenerational and family theories (for example, Bengtson and Schrader, 1982; Connidis and McMullin, 2002; Papadopoulos and Roumpakis, 2019) and propose a theoretical framework of two levels of agency – individual agency and familial agency – for the analysis of intergenerational support. It then moves on to describe the interviewing and thematic analysis approaches used in this study. After that, the chapter draws together the findings on the main themes, including gendered support arrangement, ambivalent attitudes and suppressed need, negotiation strategies, and the cross-generational consensus that family is a primary socio-economic actor. The chapter concludes with a discussion on the two levels of agency in the arrangement and negotiation of intergenerational support in Chinese families.

Family, intergenerational relationships and two levels of agency

As one of the most influential theoretical models for studies of intergenerational relationships, Bengtson and his colleagues' intergenerational solidarity model (Bengtson and Schrader, 1982; Bengtson and Roberts, 1991; Parrott and Bengtson, 1999; Bengtson et al, 2002) provides a framework for understanding the 'building blocks' of relationships and interactions between generations within the family sphere. The six inter-related constructs, including family structure, associational solidarity, affectional solidarity, consensual solidarity, functional solidarity, and normative solidarity, highlight the multidimensionality of intergenerational interactions and have been applied in studies on intergenerational relationships both in China and beyond (for example, see Izuhara, 2010; Guo, Chi and Silverstein, 2012; Brandt and Deindl, 2013; Lin and Yi, 2013).

Admitting the significant contribution of the solidarity model to the understanding of the multidimensionality of intergenerational relations, however, one may argue that solidarity alone is hardly enough to capture the whole picture of the relationships between generations, especially in the changing time when different values and norms collide. Prior to the intergenerational ambivalence approach, studies on intergenerational relations tended to interpret consensus and shared values as solidarity and the negative aspects of family life as 'an absence of solidarity' (Lüscher and Pillemer, 1998, p 414). This approach simplified the complex and dynamic relationship between generations within the family sphere and reduce it to an 'either-or' situation. Instead, conflicts arise from daily interactions, and sometimes conflicts may even result from solidarity itself (Lüscher and Pillemer, 1998). For instance, intergenerational conflicts are more likely to be generated among inter-dependent generations (Braiker and Kelley, 1979).

Many scholars have been trying to define intergenerational ambivalence and explore its implications for studies on intergenerational relationships. For instance, Lüscher and Pillemer (1998, p 416) define intergenerational ambivalence as 'contradictions in relationships between parents and adult offspring that cannot be reconciled'. The contradictions in this context are discussed at two levels, that is, contradictions at the social structure level such as roles, norms, and expectations, and contradictions at the subjective level such as cognitions, emotions and motivations (Lüscher and Pillemer, 1998). Connidis and McMullin (2002, p 558) further develop the concept of intergenerational ambivalence as 'structurally created contradictions that are made manifest in interaction'. They agree with Lüscher and Pillemer's (1998) definition of the two-level of contradictions, but they underline individuals' agencies in the negotiation of relationships within the constraints of structured social relations (Connidis and McMullin, 2002).

The previous discussion paves the way for using intergenerational ambivalence as a bridging concept to link the analyses of contradictions at the micro, meso, and macro levels (Lüscher, 2002; Connidis, 2015). For instance, the concept links psychological ambivalence experienced by the individuals, the contradictions in social institutional resources and requirements, and the macro-level systemic inequalities caused by the structured social relations such as gender and age. Moreover, it also links individuals' attempt to exercise agencies to negotiate in the intergenerational relationships to 'the opportunities and constraints embedded in social institutions, social structure, culture, and economic and political processes' (Connidis, 2015, p 79). The latter, especially social policies, are also crucial to understand 'sources of ambivalence, their implications for negotiating relationships, and solutions to socially created ambivalence that go beyond individual adaptation' (Connidis, 2015, p 83). For instance, the way in which the relationship is negotiated is not only determined by the resources owned by the individuals and the cultural values and beliefs held by them, but might also be shaped by (the lack of) social policies which can either contribute to avoiding intergenerational conflicts via eliminating and/or reducing social structural contradictions (Bengtson et al, 2002; Connidis and McMullin, 2002).

The intergenerational ambivalence theory highlights the individual agency in the negotiation process; however, it fails to take familial agency into account. To understand family and the role of familial agency in the arrangement and negotiation of intergenerational support under the wider social structure, one should consider the economical, sociological, ideological, and political implications of family. For instance, family plays an important role in income redistribution, labour supply and consumption; family provides for care needs and arranges relations across generations; family has an impact on the continuity and change in values; family can be viewed as a site of social control (Daly, 2010). Family can also be seen as an economic actor in terms of stocking 'moral capital', a concept coined by Silverstein et al to refer to 'the internalised social norms that obligate children to support their older parents' (2012, p 1246).

The concept of family as a socio-economic actor is further developed by Papadopoulos and Roumpakis (2017, 2019), where the roles of family in generating relational goods and organising different types of economic practices are highlighted. Their work has also drawn attention to the familial agency in mobilising and redistributing resources to absorb social risks and maximise the collective wellbeing (Papadopoulos and Roumpakis, 2017, 2019). Empirical studies on China's intergenerational relationships have, to a greater or lesser extent, touched the dual roles of family in organising and facilitating social production and reproduction (see Roumpakis, 2020 for informality in social production and social reproduction) and highlighted the familial agency in coping with structural constraints such as geographic distance caused by China's massive domestic migration (Lee, Parish and Willis, 1994; Cong and Silverstein, 2012; Gruijters, 2018; Qi, 2018; Gu, 2021; Zhou, Kan and He, 2021). The familial agency is realised by, among others, the flexibility and resilience of China's intergenerational support network and the renegotiation and reinterpretation of filial piety (Huang and Chang, 2020; Wang, 2021). The new patterns of intergenerational relationships in Chinese families indicate that the Chinese family acts as a corporate group (Lee, Parish and Willis, 1994; Cong and Silverstein, 2012; Gruijters, 2018) which actively adjusts to new challenges and situations, makes familial rational choices (Huang, 2011) and long-term arrangements to protect its members.

Bringing intergenerational theories and family theories together, this chapter proposes an analytical framework of two-level agency to understand the arrangement and negotiation of intergenerational support in Chinese families. It examines both individual agency – how older individuals make sense, manage, or adapt to the intergenerational ambivalence at different levels – and familial agency – how family as a socio-economic actor protect its members by mobilising, allocating, and redistributing resources via intergenerational support network.

Research design

Research data were collected via one-to-one, semi-structured, telephone interviews with older Chinese people. Ideally face-to-face interviewing approach would have been used to better collect non-verbal information (for example, the body language, the facial expressions, and the atmosphere) and build rapport relationship (Brinkmann, 2013). However, given the COVID-19 pandemic restrictions at the time of the study being carried out and followed the instructions of the Ethics Committee, the interviews were conducted via telephone calls.

As a special form of conversation (for example, 'conversation with a purpose' as mentioned in Burgess, 1984, p 102), qualitative interview allows the researcher to use interactional dialogues (Brinkmann, 2013) to explore in-depth the lived experience of older individuals about their arrangement and negotiation of intergenerational support. By talking interactively with older people, the researcher can obtain everyday knowledge of the arrangement and the process of negotiation via older people's account and interpretation. A topic guide was developed based on the research aims and refined after a pilot interview, which aims to serve as a tool to facilitate the interviews with both consistency as well as flexibility.

Participants were recruited from Baoji, a prefecture-level city in western Shaanxi province (as shown in Figure 5.1), and one of the first pilot cities of NRSP. Baoji is the second largest city in Shaanxi province with more than three million residents by the end of 2020. Among them, 57% of the population are urban residents and 43% are rural residents, and residents aged 60 or older account for 23% of the total population (Shaanxi Statistics Office, 2021). At the time the interviews were conducted, the flat-rate NRSP/URSP benefits were ¥148 (ca £16) per month, plus a monthly ¥50-yuan (ca £5.5) cash transfers to residents aged 70 and above. Although there were no official statistics of the average pensions for employees in Baoji, for example, the Enterprise Employee Basic Pension (EEBP) or the Government and Institution Pension (GIP) benefits. To provide a general picture at the national level, according to Zhu and Walker's (2018) analysis, the average pension benefits for EEBP or GIP recipients can be as great as 14–20 times as the average pension benefits for NRSP or URSP recipients. The inclusion criteria for participation in this study were that participants need to be aged 60 or older, in physical and mental condition that allows for verbal communication, and receiving or used to be receiving any kind of support from adult children. Purposive sampling strategy was applied to establish 'a good correspondence' between research questions and participants (Bryman, 2016, p 458), and to achieve representativeness regarding the experience, knowledge, and practice of the phenomenon (Flick, 2007). Specifically, participants included both urban and rural residents, as well as people with different public pension status. Fourteen participants took part in the interviews with informed consent. Among them, there are 11 women and three men; ten rural residents and four urban residents; one recipient of GIP, one recipient of EEBP, nine recipients of NRSP, two recipients of URSP, and one participant who did not enrol into any public pension scheme; five participants aged between 60 and 69, seven participants aged between 70 and 79, and two participants aged above 80 (more information about the participants can be found in Table 5.1).

The interviews were audio-recorded (informed consent obtained) and transcribed anonymously into text materials for analysis. The thematic analysis approach, as informed by Braun and Clarke's (2006, 2022) and Attride-Stirling's (2001) work, was applied to identify, analyse, report, and interpret themes that are related to the arrangement and negotiation of intergenerational support in Chinese families.

Gendered support arrangement

The interviews show that intergenerational family support in China can be in different forms (such as financial, practical, emotional, care, and housing support) and flows upward and downward across three generations. But such

Figure 5.1: Location of Baoji within Shaanxi province

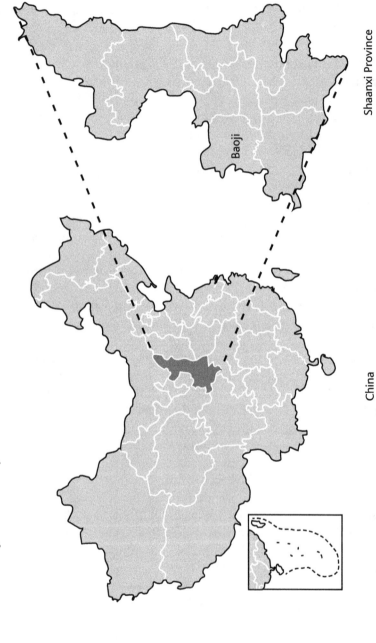

Baoji

Shaanxi Province

China

Source: This map was obtained from Ding et al (2021) under an open access licence (Creative Commons Attribution 4.0 International License). Text was added to indicate the location of Baoji within Shaanxi Province.

Table 5.1: Profiles of the 14 participants

Interviewee code	Gender	Age	Urban/ rural	Public pension	Co-residence with adult children	Marital status	No. of adult children
Interviewee 1	Male	81	Urban	Government and Institution Pension (GIP)	No, living alone	Widowed	2 sons & 1 daughter
Interviewee 2	Female	69	Rural	New Rural Social Pension (NRSP)	Yes, living with daughter	Widowed	2 sons & 2 daughters
Interviewee 3	Female	70	Rural	Not participated into any public pension schemes	Yes, living with son	Widowed	1 son & 1 daughter
Interviewee 4	Female	70	Rural	New Rural Social Pension (NRSP)	Yes, living with son	Married	3 sons
Interviewee 5	Male	72	Urban	Enterprise Employee Basic Pension (EEBP)	No, living with partner	Married	1 son & 1 daughter
Interviewee 6	Female	63	Rural	New Rural Social Pension (NRSP)	No, living alone	Widowed	2 sons & 1 daughter
Interviewee 7	Male	65	Rural	New Rural Social Pension (NRSP)	No, living with grandchildren	Married	2 sons & 1 daughter
Interviewee 8	Female	66	Rural	New Rural Social Pension (NRSP)	Yes, living with son	Married	1 son & 3 daughters
Interviewee 9	Female	79	Rural	New Rural Social Pension (NRSP)	No, living alone	Widowed	2 sons & 2 daughters
Interviewee 10	Female	67	Urban	Urban Resident Social Pension (URSP)	No, living with partner	Married	1 son & 1 daughter
Interviewee 11	Female	80	Urban	Urban Resident Social Pension (URSP)	No, living with partner	Married	2 sons & 1 daughter
Interviewee 12	Female	74	Rural	New Rural Social Pension (NRSP)	No, living with grandchildren	Married	1 son & 2 daughters
Interviewee 13	Female	76	Rural	New Rural Social Pension (NRSP)	Yes, living with son	Widowed	2 sons & 2 daughters
Interviewee 14	Female	74	Rural	New Rural Social Pension (NRSP)	Yes, living with son	Widowed	2 sons & 1 daughter

support arrangements tend to be highly gendered. Taking a rural multi-generational family as an example, Figure 5.2 illustrates how intergenerational support is arranged asymmetrically between a son and a daughter, and how older people's expectations of support differs between a son and a daughter. Before adult children get married, both the daughter and the son received financial support from their parents (denoted by the 'F' in the downward arrow at the very left of Figure 5.2). However, such support was highly skewed to the son (denoted by the solid shaded figure in the upper stream of Figure 5.2) to increase the son's prospect of getting married and having children, or the son's 'marriageability' as described by Eklund (2018). This is due to the social expectation that being a homeowner is the precondition for a man to marry a wife and that the husband's parents need to provide such housing-related financial support (denoted by the 'H' in the downward arrow in the upper stream of Figure 5.2).

After the son's marriage, older people might continue to provide financial support to the son and his new nuclear family. Furthermore, once the son has a child, older people would also provide grandparental childcare support (denoted by the 'CC' in the downward arrow in the upper stream of Figure 5.2). But such support, along with practical support on household chores, is often deemed by older people as to daughter-in-law specifically (denoted by the dotted light figure in the upper stream of Figure 5.2). This, in a sense, is also a reflection of the gendered view of older people on the division of caring and housework task. As a return, the son's family is expected to provide financial support and co-residence living arrangement to older parents (denoted by the 'F' and 'R' in the upward arrow in the upper stream of Figure 5.2). Such expectation grows with age, especially when older people are no longer capable of taking care of themselves. Similarly, implicitly or explicitly, daughters-in-law are then expected to perform the duties of daily care (denoted by the 'DC' in the upward arrow in the upper stream of Figure 5.2).

On the other side, the daughter (as shown in the lower stream of Figure 5.2) is treated by her natal family as a part-outsider once getting married: compared to her brother, the daughter (denoted by the dotted light figure in the lower stream of Figure 5.2) will only receive negligible financial and/or childcare support from older parents. Accordingly, daughters are not assumed or expected to take the responsibility of taking care of their parents.

Following is an example where the daughter was excluded from receiving extensive support from her parents, meanwhile, she was also exempted from the obligations of supporting her own parents.

> 'I didn't help my daughter with childcare. Her parents-in-law were responsible for that. It is just the tradition. When my daughter got married, she became one of their [her partner's]

Figure 5.2: Intergenerational support arrangement from a gendered perspective

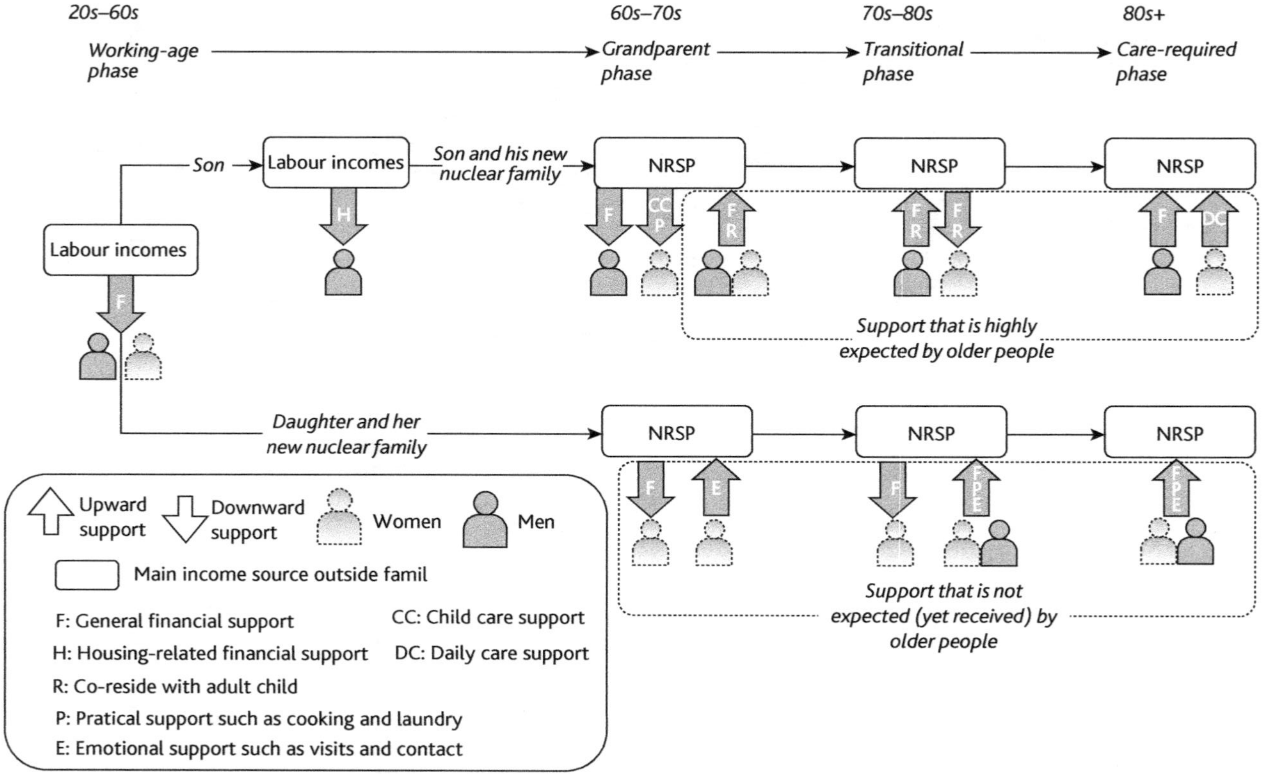

20s–60s	60s–70s	70s–80s	80s+
Working-age phase	*Grandparent phase*	*Transitional phase*	*Care-required phase*

Son

Son and his new nuclear family

Daughter and her new nuclear family

Labour incomes

NRSP

H:

F:

CC:

R:

P:

DC:

E:

Support that is highly expected by older people

Support that is not expected (yet received) by older people

Upward support

Downward support

Main income source outside famil[y]

Women

Men

F: General financial support

H: Housing-related financial support

R: Co-reside with adult child

P: Pratical support such as cooking and laundry

E: Emotional support such as visits and contact

CC: Child care support

DC: Daily care support

Source: Researcher's own work, based on the interviews

family members. Her responsibility lies in her parents-in-law. I don't count on my daughters, either.' (Interviewee 9, female, 79 years old, rural hukou, recipient of NRSP)

Nevertheless, the interviews show that daughters not only provided more emotional and practical support such as frequent visits and help with housework but would also, sometimes together with their partners (denoted by the solid shaded figure in the lower stream of Figure 5.2), provided financial support to older parents. For instance, the following participant had two sons and a daughter. He offered more than ¥300,000 housing-related financial support to his sons. He had also been providing childcare support to both sons, but he had never helped his daughter with childcare or purchasing a home. When he talked about his daughter, he said:

> 'The meat and vegetables I eat, clothes and shoes I wear, they are all bought by my daughter. When my wife went into the hospital, when I went to see a doctor, it was my daughter and son-in-law who paid for it. When I was busy with reaping wheat, my son-in-law came to see me and gave me a few hundred yuan before he left. He said I might need money for reaping wheat. I didn't want the money, but he just left it on the cupboard and walked away. [long sigh] Sometime I think I am relying too much on my daughter. My daughter and son-in-law are taking care of everything. If I need something, I don't need to do anything but just open my mouth (say it), and they would always bring it to me. They would come back every two or three weeks, always get me some daily necessities. Even my sons couldn't treat me better.' (Interviewee 7, male, 65 years old, rural hukou, recipient of NRSP)

Ambivalent attitudes and suppressed need

It is found in the interviews that older people experience ambivalent attitudes towards the negotiation of intergenerational support. On one hand, negotiation is often stigmatised, and such stigmatisation has been internalised by older people themselves – it is interpreted by older people as a sign of being dependent/needy, disharmony, or the failure of filial parenting. For instance, interviewees would feel "being a burden/trouble" (Interviewee 2, 69 years old, recipient of NRSP; Interviewee14, 74 years old, recipient of NRSP) if they need to ask for support from adult children. Some interviewees might also claim that there is no need for negotiation because "they (adult children) are filial children" (Interviewee 4, 70 years old, recipient of NRSP), or that they are "not at that point (to discuss about intergenerational support arrangement) yet" (Interviewee 6, 63 years old, recipient of NRSP). The ideal arrangement, in the narratives of almost all interviewees, is that adult children take the initiatives to offer support, regardless older parents need/accept it or not, as such initiatives demonstrate good relationships and filial behaviours.

At the same time, participants have shown a strong apprehension of the financial pressures on the younger generation, for example:

> 'I don't want to ask (adult children) for help. They have family to support and mortgages to repay. My eldest grandson is going to get married this year. It will cost (his father, the eldest son of the interviewee) a fortune. My youngest son and daughter-in-law are street vendors, and their children are going to college this year. They are all exhausted.' (Interviewee 13, 76 years old, rural hukou, recipient of NRSP)

Although family is institutionalised in old-age support arrangements in China, in practice, these feelings make it difficult for older people to seek support from adult children. Moreover, the ambivalent attitudes towards the negotiation of support suggest that the long-trenched family-oriented support arrangement might become less tangible. However, without adequate public pensions, older people must either suppress their needs and make adaptions to their living standard, or to adopt a series strategies to justify or negotiate for intergenerational support.

For instance, it was shown in the interviews that intergenerational support is often only sought for the purpose of meeting very essential needs such as food and medicines. In the lack of material resources, social needs such as participation in social interactions were considered by older people as less important and therefore often be suppressed.

> 'My children give me money, even then I won't go to weddings or funerals or rituals like that. I can't afford to buy a gift or to prepare a red envelope. I don't have extra money for that. I need to live.' (Interviewee 9, 79 years old, rural hukou, recipient of NRSP)

Negotiation strategies

In other cases where intergenerational support is required, for instance to meet the financial, care, or emotional needs that cannot be met elsewhere, older people will apply a range of strategies to negotiate for such support.

The longest-term strategy that both sides often apply unconsciously is the cultural and social norms and expectations. Adult children are expected to behave in accordance with filial piety, which is not only acting as a 'golden standard' of being a good child but also mentioned across interviewees as a determinant of a good life in retirement. The content and scope of filial piety, in this context, includes frequent interactions such as visits or phone calls, evident respects for and affections to the older, excessive initiatives to offer support and strong commitments to caring obligations.

An example of the application of this strategy in practice is through parenting education:

> 'We have a good family education in traditional values. My parents had taught me to respect and love the older since my childhood. I continued this tradition. We have strict (filial) education for children ... Because my parents educated me in this way, I treat them very well. I was a filial son myself, taking good care of my mom. They (adult children) have seen it for themselves. They saw how I treated their grandma, so they wouldn't treat me badly. I was educating them by words and deeds, wasn't I?' (Interviewee 1, 81 years old, urban hukou, recipient of GIP)

On the other side, social norms also require older people to continue to provide housing-related support and childcare support for adult children, particularly for sons (as discussed earlier), for example:

> 'If they (her son and daughter-in-law) need you to be there [to take care of the grandchild], as a parent you have to. Surely you can't say no ... For us older people, it is our role and duty to take good care of them, even it means suffering a little. It is okay.' (Interviewee 6, 63 years old, rural Hukou, recipient of NRSP)

> 'It is a matter of course for us to help with childcare ... It is a parental obligation to spend on son's marriage and housing. I didn't think much about it.' (Interviewee 9, 79 years old, rural hukou, recipient of NRSP)

Such continuous downward support was sometimes interpreted by older people as a long-term exchange for, or a way to secure future support. Parents provide support throughout their lifetime for their children, with an expectation that adult children would take care of them in future when they are in need. For example,

> 'You have to help [with childcare]. Otherwise, when you get older, they won't take care of you. They would say you didn't take care of their children either. It's just how it is.' (Interviewee 6, 63 years old, rural hukou, recipient of NRSP)

> 'If I don't count on my children, who else can I count on? I take good care of them and bring them up so that I can count on them one day.' (Interviewee 10, 67 years old, urban hukou, recipient of URSP)

Family as a socio-economic actor

At the centre of the negotiation of intergenerational support, either within or outside the family sphere, is the cross-generational consensus that family is a primary socio-economic actor.

It is shown in the interviews that participants believe that the responsibility of care and support lies in family, and that family should play the primary role in protecting its members. For example,

> 'Everyone has their family, right? Everyone should be cared for by their family members. That's how the society works.' (Interviewee 9, 79 years old, rural hukou, recipient of NRSP)

Within the family sphere, resources were mobilised and redistributed via the intergenerational support network so that the needs of both generations can be met and the risks from outside family can be absorbed or mitigated. The following quotes provide examples for the mobilisation and redistribution of resources within the family sphere.

> 'Her (the eldest daughter of the interviewee) children need to go to school. Sometimes she couldn't even scratch together the tuition fees. So I need to save as much as possible. The money that my sons give me, I always spend carefully, so that I can save, say, two or three hundred yuan and give it to my eldest daughter. So that her children can go to school. As a parent, of course, I want all my children to do well. If one of them is better off, I can ask for a little more money; and if anyone is experiencing hardships, then I can give them a bit of help.' (Interviewee 9, 79 years old, rural hukou, recipient of NRSP)

'[My youngest daughter has] children to support, medicines to take, she often found herself in difficult situations. If I happen to have 50 or 100 yuan, I would give it to her. I don't have money myself. When her elder sister and brother give me some money, and if I can save a hundred or two, I might be able to help her out.' (Interviewee 12, 74 years old, rural hukou, recipient of NRSP)

It shows that family resources are mobilised and reallocated through upward and downward support networks across generations, where older people are playing a vital role in the redistribution process within the family.

Outside the family sphere, intergenerational support, especially the grandparental childcare arrangement, is arranged so that the collective wellbeing can be maximised. For instance, the grandparental childcare arrangement, sometimes along with the relocation of older people, is an example of the agency and resilience of intergenerational families in addressing the conflicts between the dual roles of the Chinese family in social production and social reproduction. This is especially evident in the intergenerational families with migrant workers.

'My daughter-in-law isn't working for the time being, but she plans to find a job after the Chinese New Year. If she successfully finds a job and needs me to take care of my grandson at some point after the Chinese New Year, then I will go back to Beijing and live together with them.' (Interviewee 6, 63 years old, rural hukou, recipient of NRSP)

'They (the eldest son and his wife) asked one of us (the interviewee and his partner) to go there and help with looking after the youngest one (granddaughter), who just turned one year old at that time. My daughter-in-law couldn't manage it while she was working as a full-time schoolteacher. My wife went there and helped with childcare for a few months. ... she (daughter-in-law) couldn't leave her job, could she?' (Interviewee 7, 65 years old, rural hukou, recipient of NRSP)

'I told them that I can take care of the child so that both my son and daughter-in-law could do their work.' (Interviewee 10, 67 years old, urban hukou, recipient of URSP)

Conclusion

Findings from the interviews have highlighted the role of Chinese families in both social production and social reproduction. It also demonstrates how such a role is achieved via the negotiation of intergenerational support arrangements in this process. In families where the members are geographically dispersed (for instance, families of migrant workers), intergenerational support arrangements can also be negotiated and tailored over spatial distance so that the young couples can participate in the paid labour market. The interviews have confirmed the malleable role of grandparents, as described in Gu (2021, p 17) as 'the reserve workforce in the domestic sphere'. In this way, the responsibilities and costs of social reproduction are in fact transferred to older members in the extended family (Papadopoulos and Roumpakis, 2019) via the intergenerational support network.

The interviews also demonstrated the ways in which resources, either in financial, care, co-residence, or practical form, are mobilised at the family level and redistributed intergenerationally so that the collective welfare can be enhanced. For instance, the financial transfers from adult children to their older parents might be partly channelled back to support other adult children when the latter were in need. Those arrangements and the negotiation process corroborate the idea that family, as a socioeconomic actor, copes with structural constraints and maximises the interests and wellbeing of its members via exercising its agency (Huang, 2011, 2018; Cong and Silverstein, 2012; Daly and Kelly, 2015; Papadopoulos and Roumpakis, 2019; Gu, 2021). In this view, family is seen as a 'corporate group' (Cong and Silverstein, 2012, p 427) or a 'strategic coordinator' (Papadopoulos and Roumpakis, 2019, p 245) that makes 'familial rational choice' (Huang, 2011, p 485) and strategical decisions (Laslett and Brenner, 1989) through long-term arrangements and ongoing negotiations within and outside the family sphere.

One of the examples of family exercising its agency to cope with constraints and protect its members is the (re)negotiation and (re)interpretation of intergenerational contract. For a long time, at the core of the Chinese intergenerational contract has been the filial piety and related obligations and expectations such as the unconditional provision for and obedience to older parents (for example, Shi, 2009). The interviews, in line with the findings from previous literature (for example, Teo et al., 2003; Croll, 2006; Izuhara, 2010; Chen, Liu and Mair, 2011; Izuhara and Forrest, 2013; Abrahamson, 2017; Zhong and Li, 2017; Huang, 2018; Gu, 2021), suggest that new filial practices and patterns have emerged, negotiated, and accepted by both generations. For instance, instead of older parents being dependent on adult children, the findings reveal a mutual interdependence where housing-related financial support and childcare support provided by older people has become an essential element of a reciprocal intergenerational support arrangement. It on one hand reflects the influences of social structural factors such as changing family structure and booming housing market. On the other hand, it demonstrates the efforts of Chinese families to adjust for those changes and seek for the improvement of familial wellbeing by pooling together resources.

The (re)negotiation and (re)interpretation of intergenerational contract is also reflected in the gender aspect, in particular, in the changing relationship between (married) daughters and their older parents in natal families. The traditional patrilineality and patrilocality embedded in the Chinese filial piety indicates that daughters become outsiders of their natal families upon marriage (Croll, 2001; Shi, 2009; Eklund, 2018). The manifestations include, among many others, that married daughters are excluded from the extensive intergenerational support arrangements from their natal families and simultaneously exempted from the obligations and duties of caring and providing for their natal parents. The interviews, however, identified a changing pattern where older people in fact received both tangible and intangible support from their married daughters. It is found that daughters are more likely to provide emotional support and practical support, more caring, and visiting and contacting more frequently than sons. If conditions permit, daughters also voluntarily share the financial responsibility of providing for their older parents. Meanwhile, older people provide occasional support to their married daughters as well.

Findings from the interviews have illustrated the potential of intergenerational ambivalence as a bridging concept that links micro, meso, and macro level of analysis (as suggested in Connidis, 2015). For example, one of the reoccurring sources of ambivalence among rural families comes from the dependence vs. autonomy of older people. Although support from adult children demonstrates successful parenting and good behaviours in accordance with filial piety as well as care and love between generations, the fact that rural people 'have no choice but to' rely on their adult children due to lack of resources in old age often leads to negative feelings. This presents the psychological ambivalence that is experienced by older people (at the individual level), the expected, but not always realised, role of Chinese families in protecting its older members (at the familial level), and the potential risks caused by the lack of adequate public pensions after retirement (at the structural level). In fact, the interviews revealed the inadequacy of the new pensions and a lack of formal childcare support, which contribute to the continuous role of intergenerational family but also a potential source of conflict. Social policies that address these issues will help intergenerational families to better manage their relationships.

The negotiation of intergenerational support reflects older people's experience, sense-making, and adaptation/reaction to the individual, institutional, and structural levels of intergenerational ambivalence. The findings not only demonstrate the individual agency of older Chinese but also highlight the familial agency by viewing the Chinese family as a socio-economic actor in the negotiation of intergenerational support.

The study is subjected to certain limitations. For instance, although the purpose of the study is to offer in-depth understanding of the process, strategies, and experience of intergenerational support arrangement and negotiation rather than the discovering generalisable patterns, the external validity from a quantitative perspective (generalisability beyond the specific research context) can be an inherent weakness of the study, as the sample size is relatively small and not representative in terms of demographic structure. Another limitation regarding the sample is that some analytical categories (by public pension status and *hukou* types) are overrepresented while other are underrepresented (as shown in Table 5.1). The main reason is the difficulties and challenges in recruiting participants during the COVID-19 pandemic. Future research engaging with URSP recipients or rural residents who didn't participate into any public pension schemes can be helpful to understand the arrangement and negotiation of intergenerational support in China.

References

Abrahamson, P. (2016) 'End of an era? China's one-child policy and its unintended consequences', *Asian Social Work and Policy Review*, 10(3): 326–38. Available from: Doi: 10.1111/ASWP.12101

Abrahamson, P. (2017) 'East Asian welfare regime: obsolete ideal-type or diversified reality', *Journal of Asian Public Policy*, 10(1): 90–103. Available from: Doi: 10.1080/17516234.2016.1258524

Attride-Stirling, J. (2001) 'Thematic networks: an analytic tool for qualitative research', *Qualitative Research.*, 1(3): 385–405.

Bengtson, V., Giarrusso, R., Mabry, B., Merril. (2002) 'Solidarity, conflict, and ambivalence: complementary or competing perspectives on inter-generational relationships?', *Marriage and Family*, 64 (3): 568–76. Available from: Doi: 10.1111/j.1741-3737.2002.00568.x

Bengtson, V.L. and Roberts, R.E.L. (1991) 'Intergenerational solidarity in aging families: an example of formal theory construction', *Journal of Marriage and the Family*, 53(4): 856–70. Available from: Doi: 10.2307/352993

Bengtson, V.L. and Schrader, S.S. (1982) 'Parent-child relations', in Mangen, D.J. and Peterson, W.A. (eds) *Social Roles and Social Participation*, NED-New. University of Minnesota Press (Research Instruments in Social Gerontology, Vol. 2), pp 115–86. Available from: http://www.jstor.org/stable/10.5749/j.cttttsv1.9 [Accessed: 2 December 2018].

Braiker, H.B. and Kelley, H.H. (1979) 'Conflict in the development of close relationships', *Social Exchange in Developing Relationships*, 135 : 168.

Brandt, M. and Deindl, C. (2013) 'Intergenerational transfers to adult children in Europe: do social policies matter?', *Journal of Marriage and Family*, 75(1): 235–51. Available from: Doi: 10.1111/j.1741-3737.2012.01028.x

Braun, V. and Clarke, V. (2006) 'Using thematic analysis in psychology', *Qualitative Research in Psychology*, 3(2): 77–101.

Braun, V. and Clarke, V. (2022) *Thematic Analysis: A Practical Guide*, London: Sage.

Brinkmann, S. (2013) *Qualitative Interviewing*, Oxford: Oxford University Press.

Bryman, A. (2016) *Social Research Methods*, Oxford: Oxford University Press.

Burgess, R.G. (1984) *In the Field: An Introduction to Field Research*, London: Allen and Unwin.

Chen, F., Liu, G., and Mair, C.A. (2011) 'Intergenerational ties in context: grandparents caring for grandchildren in China', *Social Forces*, 90(2): 571–94. Available from: Doi: 10.1093/sf/sor012.

Cheng, Y., Gao, S., Li, S., Zhang, Y., Rosenberg, M. (2019) 'Understanding the spatial disparities and vulnerability of population aging in China', *Asia and the Pacific Policy Studies*, 6(1): 73–89. Available from: Doi: 10.1002/app5.267.

Cong, Z. and Silverstein, M. (2012) 'Caring for grandchildren and intergenerational support in rural China: a gendered extended family perspective', *Ageing & Society*, 32(3): 425–50.

Connidis, I.A. (2015) 'Exploring ambivalence in family ties: progress and prospects', *Journal of Marriage and Family*, 77(1): 77–95.

Connidis, I.A. and McMullin, J.A. (2002) 'Sociological ambivalence and family ties: a critical perspective', *Marriage and Family*, 64(3): 558–67. Available from: Doi: 10.1111/j.1741-3737.2002.00558.x

Croll, E. (2001) 'The generations: expectations and entitlements', in *Endangered Daughters: Discrimination and Development in Asia*, Taylor & Francis Group, pp 106–31.

Croll, E.J. (2006) 'The intergenerational contract in the changing Asian family', *Oxford Development Studies*, 34(4): 473–91. Available from: Doi: 10.1080/13600810601045833

Daly, M. (2010) 'Families versus state and market', *The Oxford Handbook of the Welfare State*.

Daly, M. and Kelly, G. (2015) *Families and Poverty: Everyday Life on a Low Income*, Policy Press.

Ding, L., Zhang, N., Zhu, B., Liu, J., Wang, X., Liu, F. et al (2021) 'Spatiotemporal characteristics and meteorological determinants of hand, foot and mouth disease in Shaanxi province, China: a county-level analysis', *BMC Public Health*, 21(1): 374. Available from: Doi: 10.1186/s12889-021-10385-9

Eklund, L. (2018) 'Filial daughter? Filial son? How China's young urban elite negotiate intergenerational obligations', *NORA-Nordic Journal of Feminist and Gender Research*, 26(4): 295–312.

Flick, U. (2007) *Designing Qualitative Research*, Sage Publications Ltd.

Gruijters, R.J. (2018) 'Daughters' and sons' remittances in rural China: findings from a national survey', *Journal of Family Issues*, 39(11): 2911–34.

Gu, X. (2021) 'Sacrifice and indebtedness: the intergenerational contract in Chinese rural migrant families', *Journal of Family Issues*, 43(2): 509–33.

Guo, M., Chi, I., and Silverstein, M. (2012) 'The structure of intergenerational relations in rural China: a latent class analysis', *Journal of Marriage and Family*, 74(5): 1114–28. Available from: http://www.jstor.org/stable/41678779 [Accessed: 5 December 2018].

Guo, Q., Gao, X., Fei, S., Feng, N. (2020) 'Filial piety and intergenerational ambivalence among mother–adult child dyads in rural China', *Ageing & Society*, 40(12): 2695–710.

Huang, J. and Chang, Y. (2020) 'Is the role of the family in elderly care weakened? an analysis based on "financial support" and "caring service"', *Chinese Social Security Review*, 4(2): 131–45.

Huang, P.C.C. (2011) 'The modern Chinese family: in light of economic and legal history', *Modern China*, 37(5): 459–97.

Huang, Y. (2018) 'Changing intergenerational contracts: gender, cohorts and elder care in central rural China, 2005-2013', *Asian Population Studies*, 14(1): 5–21. Available from: Doi: 10.1080/17441730.2017.1341090

Izuhara, M. (2010) *Ageing and Intergenerational Relations: Family Reciprocity from a Global Perspective*, Bristol: Policy Press.

Izuhara, M. and Forrest, R. (2013) '"Active families": familization, housing and welfare across generations in East Asia', *Social Policy and Administration*, 47(5): 520–41. Available from: Doi: 10.1111/spol.12002

Laslett, B. and Brenner, J. (1989) 'Gender and social reproduction: historical perspectives', *Annual Review of Sociology*, 15(1): 381–404.

Lee, Y.-J., Parish, W.L. and Willis, R.J. (1994) 'Sons, daughters, and intergenerational support in Taiwan', *American Journal of Sociology*, 99(4): 1010–41.

Lin, J.P. and Yi, C.C. (2013) 'A comparative analysis of intergenerational relations in East Asia', *International Sociology*, 28(3): 297–315. Available from: Doi: 10.1177/0268580913485261

Lüscher, K. (2002) 'Intergenerational ambivalence: further steps in theory and research', *Marriage and Family*, 64(3): 585–93. Available from: Doi: 10.1111/j.1741-3737.2002.00585.x.

Lüscher, K. and Pillemer, K. (1998) 'Intergenerational ambivalence: a new approach to the study of parent child relations in later life', *Journal of Marriage and Family*, 60(2): 413–25. Available from: Doi: 10.2307/353858

Mehta, K.K. and Ko, H. (2004) 'Filial piety revisited in the context of modernizing Asian societies', *Geriatrics & Gerontology International*, 4(s1): S77–S8. Doi: 10.1111/J.1447-0594.2004.00157.X

National Bureau of Statistics of China. (2021) 'Main Data of the Seventh National Population Census'. Available from: http://www.stats.gov.cn/english/PressRelease/202105/t20210510_1817185.html [Accessed: 29 June 2021].

Papadopoulos, T. and Roumpakis, A. (2017) 'Family as a socio-economic actor in the political economies of East and South East Asian welfare capitalisms', *Social Policy and Administration*, 51(6): 857–75. Available from: Doi: 10.1111/spol.12336

Papadopoulos, T. and Roumpakis, A. (2019) 'Family as a socio-economic actor in the political economy of welfare', in Heins, E., Rees, J. and Needham, C. (eds) *Social Policy Review 31: Analysis and Debate in Social Policy*, Bristol: The Policy Press, pp 243–66.

Parrott, T.M. and Bengtson, V.L. (1999) 'The effects of earlier intergenerational affection, normative expectations, and family conflict on contemporary exchanges of help and support', *Research on Aging*, 21(1): 73–105. Available from: Doi: 10.1177/0164027599211004

Peng, X. (2011) 'China's demographic history and future challenges', *Science*, 333(6042): 581–7. Available from: Doi: 10.1126/science.1209396

Qi, X. (2018) 'Floating grandparents: rethinking family obligation and intergenerational support', *International Sociology*, 33(6): 761–77.

Roumpakis, A. (2020) 'Revisiting global welfare regimes: gender,(in) formal employment and care', *Social Policy and Society*, 19(4): 677–89.

Shaanxi Statistics Office. (2021) *Seventh National Population Census Main Results: Shaanxi*. Available from: http://tjj.shaanxi.gov.cn/tjsj/ndsj/tjgb/qs_444/202105/t20210528_2177393.html

Shi, L. (2009) '"Little quilted vests to warm parents' hearts": redefining the gendered practice of filial piety in rural North-eastern China', *The China Quarterly*, 198: 348–63.

Silverstein, M., Conroy, S.J. and Gans, D. (2012) 'Beyond solidarity, reciprocity and altruism: moral capital as a unifying concept in intergenerational support for older people', *Ageing & Society*, 32(7): 1246–62.

Su, Z., Hu, Z. and Peng, X. (2017) 'The impact of changes in China's family patterns on family pension functions', *International Journal of Health Planning and Management*, 32(3): 351–62. Available from: Doi: 10.1002/hpm.2436

Teo, P. Graham, E., Yeoh, B., Levy, S. (2003) 'Values, change and inter-generational ties between two generations of women in Singapore', *Ageing & society*, 23(3): 327–47.

Wang, H. (2021) 'Caregivers being cared: care for grandchildren and support from grown-up children interact', *Population Journal (Chinese)*, 43(4): 74–88.

Yeh, K.-H., Yeh, K., Yi, C., Tsao, W., Wan, P. (2013) 'Filial piety in contem-porary Chinese societies: a comparative study of Taiwan, Hong Kong, and China', *International Sociology*, 28(3): 277–96. Available from: Doi: 10.1177/0268580913484345

Zang, X. and Zhao, L.X. (2017) 'State of the field: the family and marriage in China', *Handbook on the Family and Marriage in China*, Cheltenham: Edward Elgar Publishing Ltd., pp 1–19. Available from: Doi: 10.4337/9781785368196.00006

Zhong, X. and Li, B. (2017) 'New intergenerational contracts in the making? – The experience of urban China', *Journal of Asian Public Policy*, 10(2): 167–82. Available from: Doi: 10.1080/17516234.2017.1290864

Zhou, M., Kan, M.-Y. and He, G. (2021) 'Intergenerational co-residence and young couple's time use in China', *Chinese Sociological Review*, 54(4): 401–31.

Zhu, H. and Walker, A. (2018) 'Pension system reform in China: who gets what pensions?', *Social Policy and Administration*, 52(7): 1410–24. Available from: Doi: 10.1111/spol.12368

Part II

Research developments in social policy analysis

6

The impact of COVID-19 on the residential care sector for the elderly: employment and care regimes in the European comparative perspective

Marco Arlotti and Stefano Neri

Introduction

The COVID-19 crisis had a tremendous impact on social services.[1] Among these, residential care for the elderly was particularly hit (Declercq et al, 2020; de Girolamo et al, 2020; OECD, 2021; Aalto et al, 2022; Eurofound, 2022). Several studies have highlighted the higher incidence of infections and mortality which occurred in this sector compared to the general population, with elderly residents representing one of the most severely affected group (Mirales et al, 2021). Care workers employed in residential care facilities have also been disproportionately exposed and affected by the pandemic crisis (OECD, 2020; Rocard et al, 2021).

A crucial factor that potentially explains such a crude impact concerns the specific profile of elderly people living in residential long-term care facilities (OECD, 2021; Rocard et al, 2021). In fact, high levels of frailty coupled with increasingly complex and compromised individual profiles (for example, the presence of multiple chronic conditions, comorbidities, and so on) have entailed greater risks of infections and adverse effects, as well as difficulties for elderly residents particularly affected by cognitive impairments, in complying with quarantine rules and specific measures (like isolation) to contrast the spread of the infection (OECD, 2021; Rocard et al, 2021).

Specific organisational features characterising most residential care facilities may have also played a crucial role. The large size of many residential care facilities often combined with high occupancies, presence of shared rooms and the need for proximity and contacts between care workers and elderly residents (Declercq et al, 2020; OECD, 2020, 2021) may explain the higher risk of infection and the strong impact of COVID-19 in this sector.

Nevertheless, according to some scholars, the critical impact of the pandemic in the residential care sector may also be interpreted by considering specific pre-existing structural and institutional conditions that already characterised this sector in various European countries even before the emergence of the COVID-19 crisis (OECD, 2020; Ellison et al, 2022; Daly and Leon, 2022). These conditions include poor employment conditions, and the weak embeddedness of residential care services within the broader dynamics of the labour market and the regulation of social protection systems.

In fact, like the elderly care sector in general (Simonazzi, 2009), the residential care system is mainly recognised as a low-status sector (with a high presence of female and migrant care workers), characterised by difficult and poor employment and working conditions due to intensive staff turnovers, low wages, the predominance of non-standard employment and high job insecurity (OECD, 2020; Rocard et al, 2021; Daly and Leon, 2022). These critical conditions have been coupled in many cases with low professionalisation standards and the absence of appropriate training of care workers in the management of geriatric conditions and of protocols concerning prevention and control of infections (OECD, 2020; Declercq et al, 2020; Pitkälä, 2020), in spite of growing care needs of the elderly resident population (Meagher et al, 2016; Eurofund, 2020; OECD, 2020). The relationship between job quality and service quality is evident and has been largely recognised by literature.

Furthermore, public funding in this sector has been undermined over the years, due to chronic underinvestment, marketisation and privatisation processes, and ageing in-place strategies (Declercq et al, 2020; Rocard et al, 2021) aimed at keeping elderly people as long as possible at home, to avoid institutionalisation and recourse to residential facilities.

These combined features have made the residential care sector particularly vulnerable and unprepared to deal with the COVID-19 crisis (OECD, 2020; Pitkälä, 2020). However, it is important to note that this critical impact seems to have not been uniform from a comparative perspective, and important variations have also emerged across countries (Frisina Doetter et al, 2021; Rocard et al, 2021; Aalto et al, 2022; Ellison et al, 2022).

Against this background, this chapter investigates the effects of the COVID-19 crisis in the residential care sector for the elderly from a European comparative perspective, by focusing on the pre-existing structural and institutional conditions characterising this sector when the pandemic crisis emerged.

While several contributions in literature have already provided important insights in this regard (OECD, 2020; Frisina Doetter et al, 2021; Aalto et al, 2022; Ellison et al, 2022; Daly and Leon, 2022), this chapter aims to further contribute to such debate by providing a combined analysis of two dimensions, which are the characteristics of employment in the residential care sector and the embeddedness of this sector within the general structure of national care regimes, which have already been considered relevant in literature, but mostly analysed separately so far.

Given the strong impact that the COVID-19 crisis had on the residential care sector, particularly during the first months of the pandemic (from March to June 2020), the focus of analysis will consider this phase.

We will adopt a comparative perspective by analysing quantitative indicators based on secondary data drawn from Eurostat and OECD online databases (https://ec.europa.eu/eurostat/data/database; https://stats.oecd.org/#). We selected these indicators so as to operationalise the key analytical dimensions under investigation and according to data availability.

In order to consider the variations across countries, the European countries selected were: Denmark, Sweden, Germany, France, the United Kingdom, Italy and Spain.

After this introductory section, the chapter is organised in four main parts. Firstly, we will analyse the effects of the pandemic crisis in the residential care sector in a comparative perspective. Secondly, we will focus on pre-existing structural and institutional conditions of the residential care sector before the emergence of the COVID-19 crisis by identifying the main similarities and differences across countries. Thirdly, we will analyse the effects of the pandemic in the light of pre-existing structural and institutional conditions in search of common patterns in terms of configuration of factors. Finally, the chapter concludes with a discussion about the potential limitations of this study, as well as the implications arising from a scientific and policy perspective.

Effects of the pandemic crisis in the residential care sector

The first step in our analysis will focus on the impact of the COVID-19 crisis on the residential sector in comparative terms. Despite the strong resonance in public debate on the issue of the mortality of the elderly in residential structures, especially during the first wave of the pandemic crisis, information and data about this phenomenon are still limited. Data comparability also represents a critical aspect in the analysis of this phenomenon due to the adoption of differentiated testing strategies, registration and coding practices of COVID-19 deaths across countries (Declercq et al, 2020; Rocard et al, 2021).

Despite such limitations, Comas-Herrera and colleagues have importantly contributed to the research on this field by collecting and analysing various national data concerning mortality in care homes during the first wave of the pandemic (Comas-Herrera et al, 2020). Although this study also highlights the need for caution in the comparative analysis, the scenario emerging from this type of data clearly illustrates the existence of important similarities as well as differences across countries (see Table 6.1).

Table 6.1: COVID-19 deaths and older people in residential care facilities, first wave

Countries	Number of resident deaths in residential care facilities as % of all COVID-19 deaths		Older people 65+ in residential care facilities as % total population, 2019	Ratio of deaths in residential care facilities as % of all COVID-19 deaths to older people in residential care facilities as % of total population	
	Values	Intensity		Values	Intensity
DK	35.0	-	0.68	51.4	-
SE	47.0	+/-	0.84	56.0	+/-
DE	39.0	+/-	0.89	43.7	-
FR	49.0	+	0.82	60.1	+/-
IT[a]	32.0	-	0.49	65.3	+/-
ES	68.0	+	0.43	158.0	+
UK[b]	41.0	+/-	0.62	66.6	+

Notes: [a]Estimated data drawn from Pesaresi (2020).

      [b]Data refer to England and Wales.

Note about degree of intensity:

(-) Low degree of intensity: ≤ First quartile (Q1);

(+/-) Medium degree of intensity: > First quartile (Q1) ≤ 3rd Quartile (Q3);

(+) High degree of intensity: > 3rd Quartile (Q3).

Source: authors' elaborations on data retrieved from Comas-Herrera et al (2020) and Eurostat online database.

For instance, by considering a specific indicator aimed at describing the impact of COVID-19 in terms of mortality in the residential care sector, that is, the number of COVID-19 deaths in residential care facilities as a percentage of total COVID-19 deaths in the general population, the data confirm the strong impact that the pandemic crisis had in this sector. Indeed, the number of COVID-19 deaths among the elderly living in residential care facilities have accounted for more than one third of all COVID-19 deaths during the first wave of the pandemic.

In addition, significant variations across countries also emerged (see Table 6.1). For instance, in terms of intensity, France and particularly Spain, seem to present the most problematic conditions, with percentage values of 49% and 68% respectively. Sweden, the United Kingdom and Germany are in an intermediate position, (with percentage values ranging between 39–47%), while Denmark and Italy show the lowest values (35% and 32% respectively).

However, the recording of COVID-19 deaths in residential care facilities has also been heavily influenced by testing strategies adopted in each national context. For instance, in Italy testing was very limited in the residential care sector, particularly during the first wave of the pandemic

(Iss, 2020), and this may have entailed a sort of under-estimation of the phenomenon. Furthermore, the indicator considered should also be carefully analysed by considering in parallel, the 'weight' that the residential care sector had in each country when the pandemic crisis emerged. In this case, the number of older people living in residential care facilities expressed in percentage of the total population (see second main column in Table 6.1) may represent an important dimension to take into account in the analysis.

By considering the ratio between the percentage of COVID-19 deaths in residential care facilities within the total COVID-19 deaths and the incidence of elderly people in residential care facilities (as a percentage of total population, see last main column in Table 6.1), the comparative scenario confirms the existence of important similarities across countries. However, the differentiations previously identified assumed a different articulation.

In fact, the critical impact that the pandemic crisis had on the residential care sector is clearly confirmed. In every country, the share of deaths in residential care facilities out of the total COVID-19 deaths of the entire population greatly exceeded the share of elderly people in residential facilities out of the total population. At the same time, the differentiations across countries only partly reflect what we saw earlier.

Also, in this case, Spain confirmed the most critical condition as the country with the highest level of COVID-19 deaths in residential care facilities despite the lowest incidence of older people living in residential care facilities. At the same time, in terms of critical intensity, important changes emerge when we look at the case of the United Kingdom and, particularly, of Italy, which had earlier represented the country with the lowest impact and now stands in an intermediate position with a higher value (due to the residuality of the residential care sector in this country) as compared to countries like France and Sweden. Instead, Denmark and Germany (the latter previously in intermediate position in terms of intensity) represent countries with the lowest impact in relative terms.

To sum up, although potential data limitations were discussed previously, these first comparative data indicate how the COVID-19 crisis significantly affected the residential care sector during the first phase, without exceptions among the European countries considered in our analysis. However, also important differences across countries emerged.

Starting from what the literature has highlighted about the crucial role played by pre-existing structural and institutional conditions in shaping the effects of the pandemic (see previous 'Introduction'), in the next paragraphs we will explore these two dimensions in parallel.

In other words, our research question is: can we explain the differentiated impact of the pandemic in the light of the variations across countries affecting employment and its characteristics in the residential care sector and also by denoting how this sector was peculiarly embedded within each national care regime?

Employment conditions and care regimes in the European comparative perspective

Since Esping-Andersen's seminal work on comparative welfare regimes and the related critiques concerning the gender blindness of his approach (O'Connor, 1993; Saraceno, 2016), a vast literature has investigated the care issue.

From this perspective, the concept of 'care regime' has been developed in order to analyse how care needs, including those of elderly people, are shaped in each country by a complex intersection and interrelation between the three main spheres of the regulation of social life, such as the family, the market and the state (Bettio and Plantenga, 2004; Leon and Daly, 2022).

Initially, literature (Antoneen and Sipila, 1996; Alber, 1995) identified the emergence across Europe of important differentiations, particularly, on the one hand, between countries characterised by the presence of universal entitlements and strong provisions of public care services (mostly Nordic countries, the Netherlands and to some extent also the United Kingdom) and on the other hand, national contexts characterised instead by informal care and the marginal role of public policies (particularly Southern European countries and to some extent also the Continental ones).

Over the years, additional variations have also been detected. For instance, in the case of Continental countries, important national reforms were introduced during the 1990s to expand the care coverage through public interventions, including cash-for-care schemes (Da Roit and Le Bihan, 2010; Theobald, 2011). In the case of the United Kingdom, severe austerity and retrenchment have deeply reduced and undermined the supply of public care services (Glendinning, 2017; Daly, 2020).

However, a point missed in this literature concerns how employment characteristics and working conditions of care workers are also potentially differentiated across countries. For instance, Simonazzi (2009) pointed out the existence of an important variation in the main features of the care labour market, in terms of 'quantity' and 'quality', strongly interrelated with the main characteristics of care regimes and national employment models.

Nordic countries, for instance, have been traditionally characterised by a significant expansion of a formal care market coupled with high standards of employment and working conditions. Also in the case of the United Kingdom, the expansion of a formal care labour market has been relevant but affected more by critical and poor working conditions. In Continental and Southern European countries, the development of the care labour market has been more limited. However, also important differentiations have emerged over the years (particularly France with a higher level of extension and regulation, in contrast to Italy and Spain) in the light of specific trajectories of institutional change and the types of policy strategy adopted (Simonazzi, 2009).

Against this background, in the following two parts we will analyse the characteristics of the European countries considered in this study just before the emergence of the pandemic crisis, in terms of pre-existing structural and institutional conditions of their residential care sectors. We will refer to the level of employment and characteristics of employment and workers on the one hand, and on the other, to the institutional embeddedness of the residential care sector within the broader structure of national care regimes.

We will start by analysing the dimension of employment and the type of clustering emerging. Subsequently, we will focus on care regimes in a comparative perspective, and assess whether and how this dimension is overlapped with the previous one in terms of clustering.

Employment in the residential care sector: a comparative analysis

As a first step in this section, the main characteristics of the employment in the residential care sector will be studied from a comparative perspective.

Unfortunately, data availability does not allow a 'fine' disaggregation of this dimension at the level of the elderly care sector. In this sense, the data that will be analysed here refers to the residential care sector as a whole. However, it is important to note that elderly care represents the largest part of this sector. So, even when considering overall data, we assume that this information represents a useful proxy to obtain specific indications regarding what is also happening in the sector of residential care for the elderly, in the strict sense.

The following Figure 6.1 shows the relative weight of the residential care sector in terms of employment. We have already seen how the incidence of older people living in residential care facilities differ greatly across countries (see Table 6.1). This aspect is also reflected in the variation of the employment base.

Data analysis identifies three main clusters which are partly coherent with the clustering already identified in literature (see previous discussion). In particular, Italy and Spain show the lowest incidence of the employment rate in the residential care sector, whereas Sweden and Denmark reach the highest values. In an intermediate position, the Continental countries (France and Germany), and also the United Kingdom (with an employment rate equal to that of Germany).

The following Figure 6.2 considers the employment rate in the residential care sector in parallel with another piece of crucial information, such as the incidence of workers with low education.

Figure 6.1: Employment rate in the residential care sector, 15–64, 2019

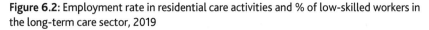

Source: Authors' elaborations on data retrieved from Eurostat online database

Figure 6.2: Employment rate in residential care activities and % of low-skilled workers in the long-term care sector, 2019

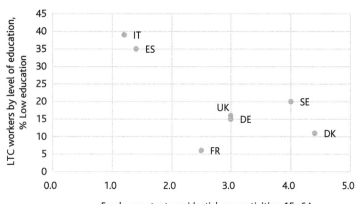

Source: Authors' elaborations on data retrieved from Eurostat and OECD online databases

This information provides direct evidence about the profile of workers involved in this sector, their professionalisation standards and, in indirect terms, also the type of quality-of-care standards guaranteed within residential facilities. For this last indicator, unfortunately, the information refers to the long-term care sector in general, but we can assume it is a good proxy in the light of our research focus.

Three main clusters also emerge in this case, albeit with some internal differentiations in relation to what we have seen previously.

In fact, Scandinavian countries (Sweden and Denmark) show the highest level of employment in residential care facilities associated with a lower share (between 11–20%) of low-skilled workers. In an intermediate position are the Continental countries (and the United Kingdom) where the share of low-skilled care workers is substantially similar to that in Scandinavian countries (or even lower, as in the case of France), however in conjunction with a limited expansion of the employment basis.

Finally, Southern European countries (like Italy and Spain) show an extreme residuality of the residential care sector, which goes hand in hand with the highest incidence of low-skilled workers (in Italy, the share of these workers reaches 40%). The high share of low-skilled workers reflects the elderly care sector's lack of professionalisation and attractiveness for workers. These are critical issues in many European countries (Eurofound, 2020), but are particularly evident in Mediterranean countries, despite recent attempts to tackle these issues (Aguilar-Hendrickson, 2020). Moreover, although the low pay and poor working conditions are suffered by many occupational groups in the long-term care sector, low-skilled workers are those who are mostly hit by these problems and were mostly affected by the deterioration of pay and working conditions connected to the processes of outsourcing and privatisation in service provision, which characterised long-term care and residential care services during the last decades (Eurofund, 2020). Therefore, a higher presence of low-skilled workers in the employment system of residential care services in a country, with its consequences in terms of poor working conditions, may negatively affect service quality and health safety in residential care homes.

The residential care sector within national care regimes: a comparative analysis

We have just seen how pre-Covid pandemic levels and features of employment and working conditions in the residential care sector were characterised by the existence of different paths, with distinctive clusters of countries emerging from the comparative analysis.

Another crucial dimension to be explored in the complexity of factors behind the acute impact of the pandemic crisis and variations across countries is the pre-existing institutional conditions concerning the residential care sector. From this perspective, as already said, we will refer to the concept of 'care regime' (Bettio and Plantenga, 2004; Simonazzi, 2009).

Also, in this case, we first selected specific indicators operationalising the dimensions under investigation, which we then analysed in comparative

Figure 6.3: Employment rate in residential care facilities and for activities of households as employers of domestic personnel, 15–64, 2019

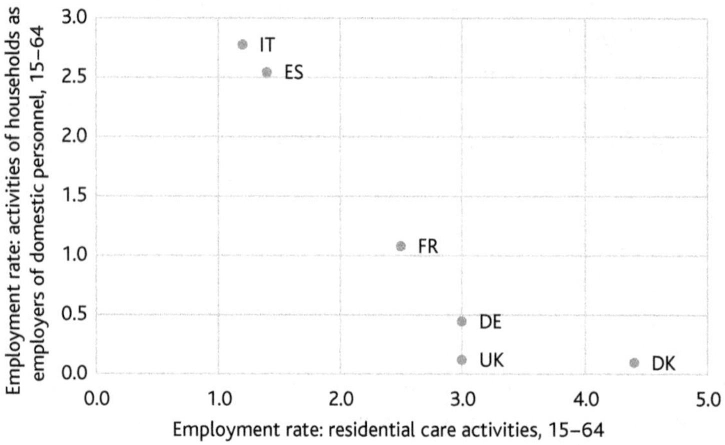

Note: Data for Sweden about employment for activities of households unavailable

Source: Authors' elaborations on data retrieved from Eurostat online database

terms by examining the specific clustering of countries emerging from this analysis against the backdrop of literature.

The first dimension concerns the embeddedness of the residential care sector within more general dynamics of the functioning of the labour market in each national context. Given limited data availability, we opted for a combined analysis of two indicators, which are the employment rate in the residential care sector (already considered previously) compared with the employment rate in a potentially 'competing' sector, such as domestic care, provided by care workers directly recruited by households (see Figure 6.3).

By analysing these two indicators, the emerging comparative map seems to reproduce the clustering previously discussed (see Figure 6.2) and already advanced in literature.

In Italy and Spain, in fact, the residuality of the residential care sector within the labour market seems to be largely explained by a strong presence of home care supports, provided not by professional care workers but mostly by domestic care workers recruited directly (and often also irregularly, without labour contracts) by families (Da Roit and Sabatinelli, 2013). The consolidation of such a feature has also been largely supported by the extensive use in these two countries of unconditional cash-for-care schemes, instead of the direct provision of formal in-kind services (including residential care) (Simonazzi, 2009; Da Roit and le Bihan, 2010). The extended recourse to domestic care workers directly employed by families, and who are not usually provided with specific training, have contributed to further exacerbate the persisting lack of professionalisation of work in the long-term care sector seen in these two countries, as earlier said.

In Denmark, the exact opposite happened. The share of care workers directly recruited by families is extremely low, while there is a very relevant share of formal employment in the residential care sector. Also for this dimension, between these two extremes, we have the cases of the United Kingdom and the Continental countries in an intermediate position. However, the case of France is slightly differentiated in the light of a higher share of care workers directly recruited by families. In France, this feature is related to the central role played by public policies (for example, tax reductions, cash benefits and so on) that aim to subsidise the household's demand for domestic workers and the promotion of the domestic services sector as a way to respond to increasing social care needs in a context of budgetary constraints (Morel, 2015).

The second dimension considered here refers to the embeddedness of the residential care sector within national care regimes gauged through the analysis of the role of welfare policies, particularly in terms of financial investments and resources implemented to support the activities of the residential care sector.

Given the scarcity of available data, and in the light of literature (see Pavolini, 2021), this dimension was operationalised by considering two macro indicators related to the expenditure in the residential care sector: the public (health) expenditure implemented for funding the residential care sector and the weight of this expenditure as a share of the current expenditure for healthcare. The last indicator also represents a good proxy for considering potential dynamics of resource inequality within the health care system, that is, between the residential sector and the other components (for example, primary and community care, hospital care, and so on).

As Figure 6.4 shows, the clustering reproduces important overlaps with literature on 'care regimes' and the comparative scenario emerging from the analysis of the previous dimensions. In particular, Italy and Spain show the most critical condition, due to the lowest level of expenditure coupled with the strongest levels of resource inequality (health expenditure for residential facilities represent less than 7% of current health expenditure).

The Continental countries and the United Kingdom are in an intermediate position. At the same time, an important and more articulated than expected differentiation concerns the clustering of the Nordic countries, and seems to indicate a different strategic approach concerning the role of welfare policies in supporting the residential care sector.

In fact, while Sweden confirms the peculiarity of the Nordic countries in terms of the strongest development of the residential care sector also

Figure 6.4: Long-term (health) expenditure in residential care facilities, per capita and as a share of current expenditure on health, 2019

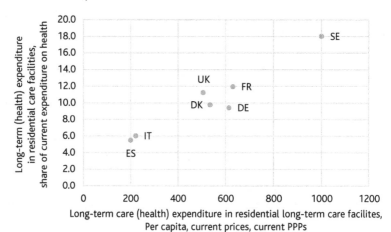

Source: Authors' elaborations on data retrieved from OECD online database

in the light of highest level of investments provided by welfare policies, Denmark is instead closer to the Continental countries and, in particular, to the United Kingdom in terms of a more limited investment in residential care facilities. This goes in parallel with an intermediate degree of resource inequality. This aspect, however, should be interpreted not in relation to a scarce consideration in general of the care issue in Denmark, but more in the light of this country's greater orientation of welfare policies, towards the deinstitutionalisation of elderly care and the promotion of ageing in place strategies (Kvist, 2018; European Commission, 2019). This orientation has presumably penalised the residential care sector in terms of a strategic allocation of public funding.

Discussion

In this chapter, we have investigated the critical effects of the COVID-19 crisis in the sector of residential care for the elderly, focusing on the first wave of the pandemic. We analysed these effects in the light of the pre-existing structural and institutional conditions characterising the residential care sector just before the emergence of the pandemic crisis. Specific analytical dimensions were considered through a review of the employment features in the residential care sector and its embeddedness within the more general structure of national care regimes.

Literature has already highlighted the importance of considering these dimensions in analysing the differentiated impacts of the pandemic in the residential care sector from a comparative perspective (OECD, 2020; Frisina Doetter et al, 2021; Aalto et al, 2022; Ellison et al, 2022; Daly and Leon, 2022), which have mostly been considered separately so far.

By developing a combined analysis of these dimensions (see the following summary Table 6.2), the empirical findings illustrated in this chapter have confirmed important aspects already evidenced in literature.

In particular, we refer to the fact that the effects of the COVID-19 crisis in the residential care sector have been more problematic especially in countries affected by the most critical situation in terms of pre-existing structural and institutional conditions of residential care.

In this regard, Spain and Italy represent two paradigmatic countries where the critical impact of the pandemic took place in a sector strongly affected by limited employment and problematic working conditions and an extreme residuality of the residential care system, due to low public investments and the centrality of a care market based on the direct recruitment of care workers by families for homecare assistance.

Nonetheless, our analysis also shows a more nuanced picture concerning the intersection between the impact of the COVID-19 crisis and the characteristics of each country in terms of pre-existing structural and institutional conditions.

For example, just before the COVID-19 crisis the United Kingdom and Germany shared important similarities from a comparative perspective, considering the level and characteristics of employment in the residential care sector and the support provided to this sector by welfare policies. Despite that, these two countries have been affected by a different impact of COVID-19 mortality in residential care facilities, which are higher in the United Kingdom, while decisively lower in Germany (see Table 6.2).

An important differentiation emerged from the comparative analysis also in the case of Nordic countries, where, according to literature, a greater development of care policies has been coupled with better employment and working conditions.

In the case of Denmark, the more limited effects of the COVID-19 health crisis in the residential care sector took place in a national context where employment and working conditions, as well as the insertion of the residential care sector in the more general dynamics of the labour market, were characterised by an unproblematic configuration, according to the indicators considered in this analysis. However, the picture is quite different when looking at the degree of investment of public policies in the residential sector. Though significant in comparative terms, the level of long-term (health) expenditure in residential care facilities was in Denmark far from those of other Nordic countries, like Sweden, at the onset of the pandemic crisis.

Indeed, according to the indicators selected in our analysis, Sweden was the country with the highest level of investment in residential care services

Table 6.2: Summary table: degree of intensity of the phenomena investigated, main findings

Countries	Ratio deaths in residential care facilities (as % of all COVID-19 deaths) to older people in residential care facilities (as % of total population), first wave	Employment characteristics		National care regimes		
		Employment rate residential care activities, 15–64, 2019	LTC workers by level of education % low education 2019	Employment rate activities of households as employers of domestic personnel, 15–64, 2019	Long-term care (health) expenditure in residential long-term care facilities, per capita, current prices, current PPPs, 2019	Long-term care (health) expenditure in residential long-term care facilities, share of current health expenditure, 2019
DK	-	+	-	-	+/-	+/-
SE	+/-	+	+/-	n.a.	+	+
DE	-	+/-	+/-	+/-	+/-	+/-
FR	+/-	+/-	-	+/-	+	+
IT	+/-	-	+	+	-	-
ES	+	-	+	+	-	-
UK	+	+/-	+/-	-	+/-	+/-

Notes: n.a. data not available.

Note about degree of intensity:

(-) Low degree of intensity: ≤ First quartile (Q1);

(+/-) Medium degree of intensity: > First quartile (Q1) ≤ 3rd Quartile (Q3);

(+) High degree of intensity: > 3rd Quartile (Q3).

Source: Authors' elaborations

and, hence, with greater embeddedness of these services in institutional terms within the general structure of the national care regime. However, this dimension does not seem to be the only sufficient condition to limit the impact of COVID-19 in the residential sector.

In Sweden, in fact, although the issue of COVID-19 deaths did not reach the most critical levels recorded in Southern European countries and the United Kingdom, the impact was nonetheless higher than, for instance, in Denmark. This aspect could presumably be read in relation to specific criticalities affecting in this country the employment composition in the residential care sector, given an intermediate level (but still higher than that of Denmark) of low-skilled workforce (see the previous Figure 6.2). This could indicate the existence of low professionalisation standards and the lack of appropriate training and specialisation of care workers in this sector.[2]

Finally, the case of France seems to illustrate how great investments of welfare policies in the residential care sector combined with highly qualified care workers in the sector are two crucial conditions. Such factors, however, are presumably insufficient to guarantee a robust protection of residential care facilities against the COVID-19 crisis, as shown by the intermediate intensity level recorded in terms of COVID-19 deaths in this country.

In this regard, the comparative analysis shows how the development of the residential care sector in France has been constrained by the presence of alternative options for covering the care needs of the elderly, like home care assistance recruited directly by families. The incidence of this type of employment is higher than that of other Continental countries such as Germany (see Figure 6.3).

This could indicate the presence of potential selection effects concerning the composition of the elderly in the residential care sector with a stronger predisposition to the most critical consequences of the pandemic, such as the presence of higher levels of frailty among the elderly in residential settings in contrast to those living at home, supported by home care assistants directly recruited by households.

Conclusion

The analysis we have previously discussed has illustrated how difficult it is to identify a unique configuration of factors common to all the countries considered, regarding the effects of the COVID-19 crisis in their residential care sectors, and pre-existing structural and institutional conditions.

This result, of course, could be conditioned by potential limitations in our study. Though the analysis was based on a careful selection of indicators aimed to operationalise the dimensions under investigation, the methodological selection has also been shaped by data availability, representing a critical issue for any comparative analysis in the field of long-term care policies (Pavolini, 2021). This aspect could have undermined the robustness of our analysis.

In addition, in the overall scope of this article, we have not expanded the analytical focus to also consider other dimensions that might be likewise explored, to disentangle the complexity of the phenomena in question.

For instance, several studies identified a significant correlation between the impact of the pandemic in the residential care sector and that of the general population (Aalto et al, 2022). In this sense, variations across countries might also reflect different infection rates in the general population (Frisina Doetter et al, 2021; Rocard et al, 2021; Ellison et al, 2022) related to national strategies adopted to contrast the COVID-19 pandemic.

In view of our empirical findings, this dimension could be an important factor to consider in the light of the variations between countries and also within the main clusters identified. For instance, as far as the Nordic cluster is concerned, we have seen how the impact of the pandemic crisis in the residential care sector during the first wave differed in each country, with a higher intensity in Sweden than in Denmark. At the same time, it is also important to point out that these two countries suffered a different pandemic pressure which was more intense in the Swedish case (Ellison et al, 2022).

Despite the limitations caused by the aforesaid limited data availability and comparability, the analysis of employment characteristics in the residential care sector could be enriched and deepened by focusing on additional dimensions directly related to employment and working conditions, such as the share of workers with atypical or flexible contracts, wage levels, working hours and work shifts among the main groups of the care workforce. This could help us to better understand the relationship between quality of work and quality of service in residential care, with possible relevant effects on the way the pandemic was tackled in residential care settings.

Another crucial dimension may concern the role played by national policies adopted in coping with the pandemic crisis in the residential care sector. Even though in many European countries, the degree of preparedness of this sector to address the health crisis was, to a large extent, already very critical in advance (Rocard et al, 2021), this aspect was further exacerbated by the primary focus attributed to the hospital systems in terms of emergency strategies, which entailed negative implications for the residential care sector during the crisis (Declercq et al, 2020; OECD, 2021).

However, this came about across countries in a different manner. In countries like Spain, the United Kingdom and also Italy where, according to our analysis, the impact of the pandemic crisis was very critical, for instance, the discharge of hospital patients to residential care facilities represented a crucial measure adopted to alleviate the pressure on the hospital system during the first wave of the pandemic (Daly, 2020; Mirales et al, 2021).

However, this determined negative effects in the residential care sector, in terms of the spread of the virus (OECD, 2020).

In addition, the specific trajectory of change in the residential care sector over the years should also be carefully considered, namely, through the consideration of a longitudinal dimension in the analysis of both pre-existing structural and institutional conditions.

As an example, upon examining the situation of Germany and the United Kingdom just before the advent of the pandemic crisis, we saw how these two countries shared, according to our analysis, strong similarities in terms of employment and institutional conditions. However, the impact of the pandemic on their residential care sectors differed. Such differentiation could be interpreted in the light of the transformations which occurred in the residential care sector of the two countries over the last decade.

In the case of the United Kingdom, it is important to remark how marketisation, austerity and welfare retrenchment have been largely predominant over the years, with a significant impact also on the residential care sector in terms of resource cutting and reduction in bed capacity (Daly, 2020; Béland et al, 2022, Elisson et al, 2022). Germany, instead, in the years before the pandemic experienced quite a distinctive trajectory, based on higher levels of public investment and expansion of the residential care sector (Elisson et al, 2022). In other words, this type of differentiation in the trajectory of change may represent a crucial dimension to better contextualise how similar pre-existing structural and institutional conditions may determine dissimilar effects, due to different trends that have influenced the capacity of the residential care sector to respond to the crisis.

To conclude, this comparative study across seven European countries was achieved through an in-depth analysis of the initial effects of the COVID-19 crisis in the residential care sectors of these countries, combined with the analysis of their pre-existing structural and institutional conditions. The results brought to light a remarkable overlapping of the pandemic effects, with differentiations across the countries, as identified in the literature about the main characteristics of the employment and care regimes in Europe.

At the same time, the empirical results have also shown how the intersections between the impact of the COVID-19 crisis and the pre-existing structural and institutional conditions are more complex and seem to go beyond the expected. This highlights the complexity of factors shaping the effects of the COVID 19 health crisis and, for analytical purposes, the importance of developing multidimensional analytical frames in order to identify the multifaceted patterns of configurational dimensions behind the crisis.

Furthermore, this research result also has policy implications because it stresses the importance of adopting multi-dimensional policy strategies aimed to support the residential care sector by considering multiple lines of intervention.

Firstly, specific recruitment and retention policies need to be designed and implemented to improve pay and working conditions, to make the residential and care services more attractive to workers; these policies should be matched with employment policies addressed to increase the share of medium and high-skilled workers employed in these services.

Secondly, policy makers should be aware of the interrelations of the residential care policies with other social policy sectors (for example, the health care system), both in terms of employment policies and of service planning. Thirdly, policy design in residential care and in social services as a whole should be carried out by considering not only the relationships with single policy sectors, but also its embeddedness in the overall political economy of each country.

The adoption of such a multi-dimensional approach in policy making may be fundamental for improving the conditions of those who receive and provide care in residential care facilities, as well as the preparedness and resilience of the residential care sector in tackling COVID-19 and other potential health threats in the future

Notes

[1] The paper was written in the context of the project 'Sowell-Social Dialogue in Welfare Services'. The project has been funded by by the EU Commission – DG XII Employment, Social Affairs and Inclusion (VS/ 2020/ 0242).

[2] Regarding this aspect, in a Eurobarometer (2007) survey conducted in 2007, which also studied the perception of insufficient standards of care in nursing homes, the existence of a big difference between Sweden and Denmark was identified. Sweden recorded a higher value in terms of negative perception (53%), whereas in Denmark, the percentage of those who agreed about the insufficiency of care standards was instead much lower (36%).

References

Aalto, U., Pitkälä, K.H., Andersen-Ranberg, K., Bonin-Guillaume, S., Cruz-Jentoft, A.J., Eriksdotter, et al (2022) 'COVID-19 pandemic and mortality in nursing homes across USA and Europe up to October 2021', *European Geriatric Medicine*, 13: 705–9.

Aguilar-Hendrickson, M. (2020) 'Long-term care in Spain: a reform failure or the regulation of a development path?', *International Journal of Sociology and Social Policy*, 40(11/12): 1301–17.

Alber, J. (1995) 'A framework for the comparative study of social services', *Journal of European Social Policy*, 5(2): 131–49.

Anttonen, A. and Sipila, J. (1996) 'European social care services: is it possible to identify models?', *Journal of European Social Policy*, 6(2): 87–100.

Béland, D., Jingwei He, A. and Ramesh, M. (2022) 'COVID-19, crisis responses, and public policies: from the persistence of inequalities to the importance of policy design', *Policy and Society*, 41(2): 187–98.

Bettio, F. and Platenga, J. (2004) 'Comparing care regimes in Europe', *Feminist Economics*, 10(1): 85–113.

Comas-Herrera, A., Zalakaín, J., Litwin, C., Hsu, A. T., Lemmon, E., Henderson, D., et al (2020) 'Mortality associated with COVID-19 outbreaks in care homes: early international evidence', *International Long Term Care Policy Network*, [online] 26 June 2020, Available from: https://ltccovid.org/wp-content/uploads/2020/10/Mortality-associated-with-COVID-among-people-who-use-long-term-care-26-June.pdf. [Accessed 6 December 2022].

Daly, M. and Lewis, J. (1998) 'Introduction: conceptualizing social care in the context of welfare state restructuring', in J. Lewis (ed.) *Gender, Social Care and Welfare State Restructuring in Europe*, Aldershot: Ashgate, pp 1–24.

Da Roit, B. and Le Bihan, B. (2010) 'Similar and yet so different: cash-for care in six European countries' long-term care policies', *The Milbank Quarterly*, 88(3): 286–309.

Da Roit, B. and Sabatinelli, S. (2013) 'Nothing on the move or just going private? Understanding the freeze on child- and eldercare policies and the development of care markets in Italy', *Social Politics: International Studies in Gender, State & Society*, 20(3): 430–53.

Daly, M. (2020) 'COVID-19 and care homes in England: what happened and why?', *Social Policy Administration*, 54: 985–98.

Daly, M. and Leon, M. (2022) 'Care and the analysis of welfare states', in K. Nelson, R. Nieuwenhuis and M. Yerkes (eds) *Social Policy in Changing European Societies*, Cheltenham: Edward Elgar Publishing, pp 20–33.

de Girolamo, G., Bellelli, G., Bianchetti, A., Starace, F. Zanetti, O., Zarbo, C., et al (2020) 'Older people living in long-term care facilities and mortality rates during the COVID-19 pandemic in Italy: preliminary epidemiological data and lessons to learn', *Aging Psychiatry*, 11: 1–7.

Declercq, A., de Stampa, M., Geffen, L., Heckman, G., Hirdes, J., Finne-Soveri, H., et al (2020) 'Why, in Almost All Countries, was Residential Care for Older People so Badly Affected by COVID-19?', OSE Working Paper Series, Opinion Paper No. 23, Brussels: European Social Observatory.

Ellison, N., Blomqvist, P. and Fleckenstein, T. (2022) 'Covid (In) equalities: labor market protection, health, and residential care in Germany, Sweden, and the UK', *Policy and Society*, 41(2): 247–59.

Eurobarometer. (2007) 'Health and long-term care in the European Union', Special Eurobarometer 283/ Wave 67.3 – TNS Opinion & Social, Brussels: European Commission.

Eurofound. (2020) *Long-term Care Workforce: Employment and Working Conditions*, Luxembourg: Publications Office of the European Union. Available from: https://www.eurofound.europa.eu/publications/customi sed-report/2020/long-term-care-workforce-employment-and-working-conditions.

Eurofound. (2022) *COVID-19 and Older People: Impact on their Lives, Support and Care*, Luxembourg: Publications Office of the European Union.

European Commission. (2019) *Joint Report on Health Care and Long-Term Care Systems & Fiscal Sustainability*, Luxembourg: Publications Office of the European Union.

Frisina Doetter, L., Preuß, B. and Rothgang, H. (2021) 'Taking stock of COVID-19 policy measures to protect Europe's elderly living in long-term care facilities', *Global Social Policy*, 21(3): 529–49.

Glendinning, C. (2017) 'Long-term care and austerity in the UK—a growing crisis', in B. Greve (ed.) *Long-term Care for the Elderly in Europe Development and Prospects*, New York: Taylor and Francis, pp 107–25.

Iss. (2020) 'Survey nazionale sul contagio COVID-19 nelle strutture residenziali e sociosanitarie', *Istituto Superiore di Sanità*, [online] 5 May. Available from: https://www.epicentro.iss.it/coronavirus/pdf/sars-cov-2-survey-rsa-rapporto-finale.pdf. [Accessed 6 December 2022].

Kvist, J. (2018) *ESPN Thematic Report on Challenges in Long-term Care. Denmark*, Directorate-General for Employment, Social Affairs and Inclusion, Brussels: European Commission.

Meagher, G., Szebehely, M. and Mearset, J. (2016) 'How institutions matter for job characteristics, quality and experiences', *Work, Employment & Society*, 30(5): 731–49.

Mirales, O., Sanchez-Rodriguez, D., Marco, E., Annweiler, C., Baztan, A., Betancor, É, et al (2021) 'Unmet needs, health policies, and actions during the COVID-19 pandemic: a report from six European countries', *European Geriatric Medicine*, 12(1): 193–204.

Morel, N. (2015) 'Servants for the knowledge-based economy? The political economy of domestic services in Europe', *Social Politics: International Studies in Gender, State & Society*, 22(2): 170–92.

OECD. (2020) *Who Cares? Attracting and Retaining Care Workers for the Elderly*, OECD Health Policy Studies, Paris: OECD Publishing.

OECD. (2021) *Rising from the COVID-19 Crisis: Policy Responses in the Long-term Care Sector*, Paris: OECD Publishing.

O'Connor, J.S. (1993) 'Gender, class and citizenship in the comparative analysis of welfare state regimes: theoretical and methodological issues', *The British Journal of Sociology*, 43(4): 501–18.

Pavolini, E. (2021) *Long-term Care Social Protection Models in the EU*, European Social Policy Network (ESPN), Luxembourg: Publications Office of the European Union.

Pesaresi, F. (2020) 'COVID-19. La mortalità nelle strutture residenziali per anziani', Welforum, [online] 7 July. Available from: https://welforum.it/covid-19-la-mortalita-nelle-strutture-residenziali-per-anziani/ [Accessed 6 December 2022].

Pitkälä, K. (2020) 'COVID-19 has hit nursing homes hard', *European Geriatric Medicine*, 11: 889–91.

Rocard, E., Sillitti, P. and Llena-Nozal, A. (2021) *COVID-19 in Long-Term Care: Impact, Policy Responses and Challenges*, Paris: OECD Health Working Paper, No 131.

Saraceno, C. (2016) 'Varieties of familialism: comparing four southern European and East Asian welfare regimes', *Journal of European Social Policy*, 26(4): 314–26.

Simonazzi, A. (2009) 'Care regimes and national employment models', *The Cambridge Journal of Economics*, 33(2): 211–32.

Theobald, H. (2011) *Long-term Care Insurance in Germany. Assessments, Benefits, Care Arrangements and Funding*, Stockholm: Institut för Framtidsstudier.

7

Curating Spaces of Hope: exploring the potential for Faith Based Organisations in uncertain times

Matthew Barber-Rowell

Introduction

In this paper, I will explore the potential a new paradigm of Faith Based Organisations (FBOs) can offer social policy in practice, for uncertain times. I will explore this potential by introducing a new paradigm of FBOs, namely, 'Curating Spaces of Hope' (Barber-Rowell, 2021a), set out in terms of its capacity to coproduce local leadership, assets and alliances pertinent to diverse areas within social policy and practice.

As a prelude to my argument, I will define FBOs, contextualising them internationally using Esping-Andersen's (1990) typology for welfare regimes, the Faith Based Organisations and Exclusion in European Cities (FACIT) project exploring FBOs in Europe (Beaumont and Cloke, 2012a) and then in a UK policy context using Johnsen (2014). The case I make is that FBOs are ill-defined and so require a new definition. This section will set out the understanding for FBOs and offer a basis in social policy for the argument that I make throughout the rest of the paper regards the potential for FBOs in uncertain times. I will develop my argument through three sections.

In section one, I will consider contexts of uncertainty. I will argue that there are multiple contexts of uncertainty shaping the environment within which (ill-defined) FBOs are working. These contexts of uncertainty are understood in terms of trajectories of the postsecular (Habermas, 2005) and geographies of postsecularity (Cloke et al, 2019), the diversifying of the belief landscape (Woodhead, 2017 and Clarke and Woodhead, 2018) and liminality as the new norm in social policy (Baker and Dinham, 2018).

In section two, I draw through the conclusions from the contexts of uncertainty section and explains how mapping uncertainties enables redefine and develop responses by FBOs. In this section, I use data from ethnographic research across three sites in the north west of England characterised by Christian and non-religious worldviews, to show how Curating Spaces of Hope can map uncertainties by opening up the 'socio-material nuances of space' framework (Barber-Rowell, 2021a). I will evidence how this mapping facilitates the coproduction of shared values and practices and the potential implications for contributions by FBOs in social policy and practice.

In section three, I will set out responses to uncertainty, where I discuss applications for Curating Spaces of Hope. I will bring the discussion of FBOs up to date with reference to FBO responses during COVID-19 in the UK. I use mixed-methods research conducted across the UK between June 2020 and November 2020, reflecting on the first lockdown of the pandemic, which sets out the role of FBOs in partnership with local authorities in responding to COVID-19 (Keeping the Faith, 2020). I will show that the pandemic accelerated the conditions for a new definition of FBOs, and that there is a desire to consolidate pandemic partnerships, policy and practice for the future. I will then use pilot research from workshops in 2022 to illustrate the potential Curating Spaces of Hope offers. This data will set out applications in non-religious and Muslim contexts associated with international networks, namely, Fellows of the Royal Society of Arts, and volunteers and activists from the Dialogue Society. This data will be used to locate the Curating Spaces of Hope approach relative to different areas of social policy and practice.

Faith Based Organisations

To begin, a prelude, setting up understanding of FBOs. The premise for this paper and the new paradigm of FBOs that I set out in later sections, is that FBOs are ill-defined. This is not the same as ill-considered. To develop my argument, I will consider FBOs in terms of international welfare regimes, in terms of European-wide research in to the work of FBOs, and in terms of UK contexts. I will conclude the paper by asking whether a new definition of FBOs offered from the UK can be shared back out into the rest of the world.

In terms of international welfare regimes, Esping-Andersen (1990) offers a typology for three different types of welfare regime: the Nordic, social Democratic regime; the continental conservative (or corporatist or Christian democratic); and the liberal regime. Additional regimes were added later, including analysis of Mediterranean and Eastern Bloc countries and their welfare contexts. The third of these regimes characterises liberal Anglo-Saxon approaches that advocate market-based solutions and means-tested social assistance. While the term 'welfare state' originated in the UK,[1] the UK model is now one of many welfare regimes within which FBOs are found working within policy and practice.

In terms of FBOs themselves, they are defined as an 'organisation [embodying] some form of religious belief in the mission statements of staff and volunteers' (Cloke and Beaumont, 2012b). FBOs are providers, protesters and everything in-between, making a contribution to voluntary activity and public service. This is well documented in the US (Beaumont, 2004, 2008a, 2008b and Beaumont and Dias, 2008) and in European contexts (Beaumont and Cloke, 2012a). There are different typologies of FBO that satisfy this definition. Cnaan et al (1999) defines FBOs by scale (local to global). Smith (2002) defines FBOs in terms of belief saturation (secular to overtly evangelical). Herman et al (2012) offers suggested types of engagement (community, sanctuary, faith, care, learning, market interaction and so on). However, Cloke and Beaumont (2012b) note that there are as many typologies as there are studies on FBOs. As a result, FBOs have become difficult to define in social policy and practice to the extent that they are indistinguishable from non-FBOs in practice (Johnson, 2014). This is the basis from which I have developed a new definition of FBOs through offering a new paradigm and methodology of Faith Based Organisation called Curating Spaces of Hope. I will use the rest of the paper to set a context for and applications of Curating Spaces of Hope.

Contexts of uncertainty

I will begin by setting out contexts of uncertainty in the UK. These contexts will underline numerous rationales for seeing uncertainty as a constant in the social policy landscape and a defining characteristic of any new understanding of FBOs. These contexts raise questions, which I argue, a paradigm of FBOs must be able to address. The first question, how might we frame the philosophical and cultural engagement with faith in public life in the UK? For this framing I will turn to 'geographies of postsecularity' (Cloke et al, 2019). The second question, if we are acknowledging the place of faith in public life, how diverse is the faith and belief landscape in the UK? Here I reference the 'rise of the nones' and the work of Woodhead (2016, 2017) which is then clarified with reference to 2021 Census data. Third, regards FBOs contributing to social policy and practice, what are the prevailing conditions? Here I will utilise Baker and Dinham's (2018) Arts and Humanities Research Council (AHRC) funded study which includes discussion of 'liminality as the new norm' in social policy.

Geographies of postsecularity

The role of faith in public life is contested. Juergen Habermas offers a postsecular understanding, which is articulated not as the decline of either the importance of religion or the secular in twenty-first century Britain, but the coexistence of both in often unexpected, open and creative ways within an increasingly pluralistic society (see Habermas (2005),). Parmaksiz (2018) offers a dispassionate assessment of this noting, 'the concept [of the postsecular] cannot be much more than an eloquent way to disguise a sophisticated religious revivalism' (p 111). Beckford (2012) argues the postsecular, while talked about widely, does not possess any meaningful definition or application at all, noting six separate definitions (pp 2–13). Others argue it simply describes swaths of history, which are recognised in other areas of the literature, or simply ignores existing literatures regarding the role of religion in the public sphere (see, Kong (2010); Ley (2011); Wilford (2010) Calhoun et al (2011)). With these critiques in mind, I want to be more specific in terms of the development of my argument, utilising a contextual reading of the postsecular offered by geographies of postsecularity (Cloke et al, 2019). What I mean by this is, are there spaces that are postsecular in nature, the content and expressions of which can be looked at specifically, and then set in relationship with other spaces? These spaces exhibit different values and practices which shape and define new forms of engagement and partnership between people of different worldviews. These spaces can be generated by and could also generate for themselves, social movements and networks, hopeful expressions of care and community action by FBOs and pedagogical spaces opening up interdisciplinary dialogues with FBOs.[2]

The diversifying belief landscape

Clarke and Woodhead (2018) note that we are in the midst of 'the single biggest change in the [faith and belief] landscape of Britain for centuries, even millennia' (p 4). This is most clearly expressed by the 'rise of the nones' (people of no religious affiliation), who represent 37.2% of the population (Census, 2021).[3] Lee (2016) notes it is not possible to take for granted the belief base and worldview that people of no-religion hold. Lee notes, they are 'not a vague or marginal population, but a large, often committed and heterogeneous one that should certainly be accounted for alongside religious ones'. On the one hand, this casts uncertainty in terms of the understanding of the diversity of views shaping geographies of postsecularity. On the other, it points to the need for a far more nuanced engagement with this shifting landscape within policy and practice. This is not only in terms of the different worldviews contributing, but it is also in terms of the synthesis of these different worldviews and the values and practices they create.

Liminality as the new norm (?)

Liminality gets to the conceptual heart of what is meant by uncertainty in this paper, and touches on the basis for the Curating Spaces of Hope paradigm I will turn to next. Liminality is a 'disorienting and non-binary' experience or rite of passage explore by Turner (1967, 1969) which causes confusion and inherent uncertainty. This phenomenon is normally found in anthropological and ethnographic research in community contexts. Expert interviews conducted through AHRC funded research with global experts in interdisciplinary fields (Baker and Dinham, 2018) suggest that the experience of liminality is becoming more common than not, characterised by the increase in globalised, fluid and frictionless environments, punctuated by market efficiency and new technology, along with 'intense flows of migration, ideology, innovation, investment and knowledge that show little respect for existing forms of local identity and community' (pp5-6). What is produced are increased expressions of social and economic inequality, fear and anxiety, populist politics and challenges to identity and democracy.

The emergence of liminality as the new norm is indicative of the bubbling up of crises and the need for revolutionary new approaches to long-standing problems (Kuhn, 2012 [1962]). Cottam (2018) highlights this shift in social policy in her work *Radical Help*. Cottam asks how the state might relate to and support people and communities in the twenty-first century, citing the power of personal relationships as a basis for living a good life. In 2021 Cottam called for '[A] fundamental rethink ... a new Beveridge ... a moment for revolution, not for patching and mending'. What is meant here is a new social settlement akin to the post-1945 welfare state, which was rooted in the Beveridge report. Alongside such a call, we must also understand its context. Underpinning the welfare state, was a partnership that included the then Archbishop of Canterbury William Temple, who's work *Christianity and Social Order* (Temple, 1976 [1942]) sets a basis for the role of citizens and the influence of different worldviews on civic life as a coupling for the welfare state settlement. The question must be asked then, where might the contributions akin to that of Temple, which responds to the postsecular context of today, the diversifying belief landscape and the liminal policy landscape in the UK, come from?

Mapping uncertainties

I begin answering this question by introducing a new paradigm and consultative methodology for FBOs, namely Curating Spaces of Hope (Barber-Rowell, 2021a). This paradigm is defined in terms of embodying liminality (Turner 1967, 1969), opening up differences and creative potential (Deleuze 1968), modelling rhizomatic or non-linear forms (Deleuze and Guattari, 1988), and productive of shared values and practices. I will open these terms of reference up through a process of mapping uncertainties across: 1) social movement and networking, 2) hopeful expressions of care and community action by FBOs and 3) pedagogical engagement with *terra incognita*, to show how Curating Spaces of Hope addresses the contexts of uncertainty I have set out previously and enable responses to uncertainty in the following.

Social movement and networking

From 2010 to 2020, I encountered unemployment, poor mental health, social isolation, coercive and controlling behaviour, blackmail, abuse and discrimination (Barber-Rowell, 2021a, pp 26–44).

From 2016, and in response to these social ills and those of others, I encountered along the way, a social movement emerged that drew in close to 1,000 people across 14 communities and 70+ organisations, engaging one another in dialogue around social ills, hopelessness and finding solutions to help make life better. This movement was called Spaces of Hope (Barber-Rowell, 2021a, pp 44–47).

In 2017, as the movement grew, I was commissioned by a local authority in northwest England to develop networked dialogues to support the faith, community and voluntary sector to respond to the impacts of austerity, divisions exposed by Brexit, unprecedented changes to public services and a growing epidemic in mental health (Marmot, 2020). The issues faced struck at the heart of civil society, impacting personal resilience and the community resources public services relied on. These dialogues took place at different community hubs across the area ranging from a weekly Wellbeing Drop In, to a church hall, to a doctor's or General Practitioner's (GP) surgery, to social enterprise cafe (Barber-Rowell, 2021a, pp 47–52).[4] A case study for the Inquiry into the Future of Civil Society in England summarised these dialogues as 'bringing together innovative mixes of civil society actors – from professional community practitioners through to individual community activists – to "meaning-make" as a response to experiences of pointlessness and emptiness in personal, community and professional life' (Civil Society Futures, 2018, p 22). The gatherings raised interesting questions for the inquiry.

> In a public sphere which has struggled to talk about religion and belief, how might faith-based actors be held to account? Should public spaces attempt to preserve the idea of secular neutrality? Or does that stifle the fullest explanations of why certain actors act … In an increasingly religiously diverse landscape these questions have traction … Spaces of Hope appears to open [these] questions up and this in turn is opening up an innovative space in public policy making and practice. (Barber-Rowell, 2021a, pp 53–5)

In terms of the gatherings, 65% of respondents (n = 282) associated Spaces of Hope with values of personal vulnerability, personal freedom and social connection and 40% (n = 281) understood people's suspicions and perceptions around different cultures and world-views to be barriers to Spaces of Hope (Barber-Rowell, 2021a, pp 47–8). This intervention opened up scope for values-based dialogues within this locality. In terms of impact, a senior advisor within public health in Greater Manchester noted that Spaces of Hope 'delivers both added value in existing work and produces new projects and networks across neighbourhoods and localities' (Spaces of Hope, 2019).

One in three respondents said that the Spaces of Hope dialogues had catalysed something new within their own work. Further, 90% of respondents (n = 168) said that they valued the Spaces of Hope dialogues and would participate in them in the future. Spaces of Hope gatherings continued. All told, 35 dialogues took place in 36 months from October 2016–2019 (Barber-Rowell, 2021a, pp 48–52). This movement and network approach had suggested a broad albeit shallow understanding of how sense making might emerge from different spaces, characterised by the different and creative potential responses to personal experiences to uncertainty. The movement and network approach had suggested something, which i investigated through ethnographic research.

Hopeful expressions of care and community action by FBOs

I engaged in ethnographic research across three sites in northwest England: a town centre church, a faith-based café and an estate church in an area of significant multiple deprivation. The purpose of this research was to test the terms of reference for the new paradigm of FBOs namely: 1) embodying liminality, 2) difference and creative potential, 3) rhizomatic or non-linear forms, and 4) producing shared values and practices. I adopted a transformative methodology that utilised assemblage theory (Deleuze and Guattari, 2016 [1988]) which was finessed with Actor Network Theory (ANT) (Latour, 2007). This methodology took nothing for granted in term of its potential to affect anything else. Instead, everything was held as a 'matter of concern' (Latour, 2007, pp 114) in relationship with one another and the affective or affected nature of those relationships was not presumed based on prior knowledge, but rather was mapped as things changed. Latour summarises thus, 'Matters of Concern, whilst highly uncertain and loudly disputed, these real, objective, atypical, and above all, interesting agencies are taken ... as gatherings [which precludes us from] deciding in advance what the furniture of the world should look like' (Latour, 2007, pp 114–15).

This approach opened up the relational, affective and territorial character of the ethnographic sites through the different data gathering methods adopted. I conducted 27 interviews, 114 surveys and 90 hours of participant observations including document analysis (Barber-Rowell, 2021a, pp 145–154). The research was produced with reference to Christian, and non-religious ethnographic sites. Following Thematic Network Analysis

Table 7.1: Modalities and characteristics produced by thematic network analysis, which comprises the socio-material nuances of space framework

Modalities	Characteristics
1) Types of Relationships	1.1 Relationship with Place 1.2 Relational Service 1.3 Transformative Potential
2) Leadership, Roles and Responsibilities	2.1 Incarnational and Negotiated 2.2 Roles and Responsibilities
3) Sources of Motivation	3.1 Emergent Beliefs, Values and Worldviews 3.2 The Significance of Context 3.3 Foundations 3.4 Formation
4) The Interface between FBOs and the Public Space	4.1 Communication: Prayer and Dialogue 4.2 Welcome and Caring for Others 4.3 Professionalising
5) Stories: Prophecy and Authenticity	5.1 Stories 5.2 Prophecy 5.3 Authenticity
6) Administrative and Relational Flows	6.1 Changing Expressions of FBO: Finding the Flow 6.2 Alliances; Partnerships, Networks and Movements 6.3 Counting the Cost and Embracing Change

(Attride-Stirling, 2001), a set of six global themes and 18 organising themes, or modalities and supplementary characteristics, emerged as common across these ethnographic sites. The six global themes are: 1) Types of Relationships, 2) Leadership Roles and Responsibilities, 3) Sources of Motivation, 4) the Interface with the public space, 5) Stories, Prophecy and Authenticity, 6) Relational and Administrative Flows (see Table 7.1). Each of the six modalities provided a distinct vantage point on the complex gatherings of overlapping contents and expressions of each of the FBOs. I set out these modalities and characteristics as the 'socio-material nuances of space'. The socio-material nuances of space are the heart of the Spaces of Hope paradigm. Each are distinct and simultaneously interdependent characteristics that map the different and creative potential affects expressed within geographies of postsecularity. The emergence of these themes was indicative of the potential for one conceptual framework, to map the relationships between different content and expressions across multiple spaces and put these spaces in dialogue with one another with respect to shared matters of concern pertinent to FBOs (Barber-Rowell, 2021a, pp 173–262). The socio-material nuances of space also offer the means by which mapping uncertainties can take place as prelude to responding to uncertainties in ways pertinent to policy and practice. The rhizomatic or non-linear structure of the paradigm means that any of the six modalities can emerge as a guiding influence on the others. This means that as the different and creative potential affective flows of socio-material nuance of space are opened up, so is the capacity to map liminal or uncertain contexts.

Pedagogical engagement with terra incognita

Through the mapping of hopeful expressions of care and community action by FBOs and as a result, the opening up of the socio-material nuances of space, the Curating Spaces of Hope paradigm can contribute to knowledge by redefining FBOs for twenty-first century social policy and practice, and offering a new consultative methodology comprising: mapping tools for geographies of postsecularity; a new basis for defining assets in terms of their normative, resource, governance and prophetic characteristics; and a new means of discerning different beliefs values and worldviews, as part of the diversifying faith and belief landscape derived from the affective flows of the socio-material nuances of space (Barber-Rowell, 2021a, pp 323–39).

This offers Curating Spaces of Hope as a means of mapping values and practices that emerge from uncertain times and offer means of coproducing leadership, assets and alliances for policy and practice. In terms of opening up the socio-material nuances of these spaces of uncertainty and redefining what is meant by 'F' that is faith from FBOs, this would be understood primarily by looking at modality 3, Sources of Motivation, which opens up emergent beliefs, values and worldviews, the contextual nature of these, the foundations upon which lived values are built and the normative assets they form[5]. It is important to emphasise that modality 3 is defined in relationship with the other five modalities. This grounds and relates the motivations that drive action in the affective flows of relationships, leadership, action at the interface with others, the wider stories that articulate experience and the administrative flows of organisational change. This offers a polyphonic and productive means of mapping operant motivations, which opens up the understanding of different worldviews as not just dogmatic and abstract truth claims, but as the contextual and productive driving force behind the assets expressed by people of faith acting in uncertain times. This paradigm shift enables responses to 'liminality as the new norm' in social policy by mapping and testing the driving force behind hopeful expressions of care and community action by FBOs.

Responding to uncertainties

In this final section I will show how Curating Spaces of Hope can be used to respond to uncertainties. I will first consider the response by FBOs to the COVID-19 pandemic in lockdown one in the UK. This will look at how faith groups mobilised and how this was received in policy contexts and what recommendations for future action might look like.[6] I will build on this new context of responding to uncertainty, by applying the Curating Spaces of Hope approach to the coproduction of new learning networks drawing on new forms of dialogue with Spaces of Hope set out in Barber-Rowell (2021b) and pilot research funded by the William Temple Foundation.

Keeping the faith: responses by faith groups during the COVID-19 pandemic

In March 2020, the UK entered a lockdown, mandated by the government, in an effort to respond to the threat of the COVID-19 pandemic. Each one of us were subject to changes in day-to-day life, which created inherent uncertainty characterised by experiences of disorientation, loss, illness, grief and hopelessness. Faith groups responded. Rt Hon Sir Stephen Timms, Member of Parliament for East Ham noted, 'collaboration between local authorities and faith groups has dramatically increased during the pandemic. The imperative of providing support to vulnerable families has overcome decades of wariness' (Keeping the Faith, 2020, p 2).

The Keeping the Faith Report (2020), commissioned by the All-Party Parliamentary Group (APPG) for Faith and Society and conducted by the Faith and Civil Society Unit at Goldsmiths, University of London, sets out the response by faith groups to the pandemic in relationship with local authorities. The report analysed how local authorities and FBOs across the UK worked together during the first lockdown of the pandemic. Headlines from the report include:

- 60% of local authorities who participated in this research involved food banks operated by a faith group or faith-based organisation as part of their response to the pandemic;
- 67% of local authorities report that there has been an increase in partnership working with faith groups since the start of the pandemic;
- Partnership has grown most since the start of the pandemic in relation to food poverty (up from 66% of local authorities before COVID-19 to 78% now) and mental health and wellbeing (up from 43% to 48% now);
- 91% of local authorities describe their experience of partnership with faith groups as 'Very Positive' or 'Positive';
- 93% of local authorities in our survey consider wider sharing of best practice in co-production between faith groups and local authorities to be 'Very Important' or 'Important' (Keeping the Faith, 2020, p 4).

A key finding was that following the experience by Local Authorities of Faith Groups during the pandemic, there is a wide spread commitment 'to build on their pandemic partnerships, supporting long-term policy interventions in ways that are different to the current practice and norms'. (Keeping the Faith, 2020, p 3).

As I have set out through my argument to this point, sustaining and developing these partnership needs a clear understanding of FBOs for policy and practice. As such, more resources are needed to realise the aspiration and commitment to sustaining and developing relationships between religious and secular partners in a post-COVID society, which is characterised by liminal policy contexts. The question is, how will the contexts of uncertainty set out earlier be overcome and learned from in conjunction with these responses to uncertainty experienced during the pandemic?

Curating Spaces of Hope

Since February 2022 I have been exploring this question in terms of the potential for FBOs in uncertain times. This project is in its pilot phase and deploys the movement and network, organising and pedagogical development typology I have set out. This new research engages in dialogues within spaces of uncertainty, in the following terms, 'mapping and listening to shared matters of concern and socio-material practices that emerge from secular and religious actants who share and shape the same postsecular public spaces' (Barber-Rowell, 2021b, p 1). This research goes beyond the production of the Curating Spaces of Hope paradigm, and deploys and test elements of it, to produce networks that can guide hopeful expressions of care and action by faith groups and continue the exploration of terra incognita between urban studies, religion and social policy and practice (see Barber-Rowell, 2022a, 2022b, and 2022c). Thus far, different partners have been engaged, namely, the Royal Society of Arts and the Dialogue Society, based in the city of Liverpool. Dialogues have taken place with each, with a view to developing networked responses to matters of concern in the city that contribute to the common good. I will set out each case study and projected outcomes in turn.

The Royal Society of Arts (RSA)

The RSA has a gathering and dialogue approach at its core. William Shipley convened the Society of Arts as it was in the late 1800s using a dialogue model in coffee houses in London (Howes, 2020, p 15). The RSA is seeking to explore similar approaches to renew its fellowship post-pandemic. There are a plethora of threads that run through the work of the RSA with the one common concern being the production of public goods (Howes, 2020, p 20). The Curating Spaces of Hope dialogue was designed to explore these different concerns, based on pandemic experience, and to seek what might emerge. The group was representative of fellows from freelance consultant, system leader and artist collective backgrounds, with interests relating to housing, mental health, heritage and civic space, ecology, sustainable development and community activism. Through the storied approach we took to the dialogue, explaining to one another what had happened to us, we acknowledged a vulnerability would be present at least at first, but there was an aspiration to bring the joy back to gathering together and to the experience of authentically shaping the city through festival-like encounters in spaces such as the bombed-out church – one of many cultural spaces in Liverpool.

Authenticity was expressed with respect to the hybrid experiences of the pandemic and named in contrast to anonymity, shyness and anxiety. Could we be authentic and anonymous akin to cameras off in a zoom room, authentic and shy as a symptom of being starved of social ties for a long time? Yes the pandemic lockdowns have ceased, but something changed. How might we become authentically ourselves as we return from two dimensional (2D) digital spaces to meeting 'IRL' (in real life)? This hybridity and disorientation was characterised by reference to the Philip K. Dick book *Blade Runner* with the questions asked, how do physical and virtual space become so tough to separate? And if our mental model or norm becomes virtual, how do we see IRL, therefore, which one comes first? Virtual/actual or actual/virtual? What role do our virtual lives play in shaping our values? One suggestion to explore this sense was to curate spaces that mimicked the conditions of a Zoom room by hanging a curtain for people to sit behind allowing them to recreate 'camera off' conditions, while talking to others who were there behind the curtain. This would facilitate reconnection while soothing the anxiety of the attendee and opening up opportunity for us to identify ourselves; our story, our hopes for the future. The outcomes from this dialogue have been developed with RSA Fellows in the following ways: 1) development of a learning network hosted by Liverpool Hope University considering the conceptual implications for Curating Spaces of Hope in the city of Liverpool. 2) Convening of a network of third sector organisations who are seeking a new vision for their work in the city combatting social inequalities such as worsening mental health in the city. 3) A further dialogue with the Gramsci Society, UK, which has catalysed exploration of Curating Spaces of Hope as a means of Democratic Party building. 4) The launch of an international network supported by an RSA Fellow who is an associate at the European Innovation Council, which opens up digital spaces to explore global collaborative leadership.

Dialogue Society

The Dialogue Society uses a network and Branch model to establish associations in cities in the UK and to gather interested parties together to share. This is often done using food as the basis for a gathering. In Liverpool there is not a Branch and so we are exploring whether Curating Spaces of Hope can offer the basis for a Dialogue Society Branch in the city. The Dialogue Society has drawn on the inspiration of the Gulen Movement, a Turkish Muslim inspired approach to dialogue (Weller, 2022). As a result, the first gathering that was convened using Zoom was attended by Turkish Muslim asylum seekers who had moved to Liverpool during the pandemic.

Themes from narratives of those gathered included the safety and education of their children, loss of loved ones, the limitations created by a language barrier, limitations to body language due to use of digital spaces and the stress and insecurity of being in an unknown city in an unknown country due to their experience of migration. For some, this was the first time they had been offered space to reflect on their journeys and the difficulties they faced. One attendee noted that they would want to say a great deal more than their English could allow them to. They asked for the opportunity to write down their feelings and their experiences and to share these with those gathered with the hope that it could develop an opportunity for further reflection. Those gathered expressed a deep resilience to overcome barriers and to connect with people in the new communities they were part of. The small actions of others, a phone call from a friend in Turkey, a cup of tea from a fellow community member in Liverpool, these were significant. What had become clear is that through the transition into the UK the group gathered had found a new appreciation for the role social connection plays in their lives. They noted that they had lost work (in business and science and education sectors) but gained a sense of togetherness and common humanity. This offered the basis for gatherings to continue, exploring a common humanity with others in the city to which they have just moved, not shaped by their own preconceptions and worldviews per se, but finding common and shared ground with those communities that had welcomed them in to contribute to the place they now live.

Conclusion

Curating Spaces of Hope offers a basis upon which FBOs can be reimagined, opening up new ways of responding to uncertain times through social policy and practice. I will conclude by setting out some of the prospects for development, pointing also to areas that have not been addressed in this paper.

Throughout this paper I have explored contexts of uncertainty. I did this initially by engaging with literatures to set out geographies of postsecularity, the diversifying belief landscape in the UK, and liminality as the new norm in social policy. These contexts offered the basis for exploration of the Curating Spaces of Hope approach in terms of mapping uncertainties and then responding to uncertainties through dialogue based and networked leadership. This thread running through the paper, punctuated by data and recommendations from the Keeping the Faith Report (2020) and data from pilot networks in Liverpool, UK, points to the opportunities for interdisciplinary scholarship that can deepen understandings of FBOs.

Curating Spaces of Hope emerged from lived experiences of uncertainty and a social movement, which flowed into hopeful expressions of care by FBOs. This transition could be explored further in terms of the implications for Curating Spaces of Hope and the different types of capital that are on offer from FBOs, for example the significance of the socio-material nuances of space for spiritual capital (see Baker and Skinner, 2006) and social capital (see Putnam, 2000 and Putnam and Campbell, 2010). This question is given emphasis by fact that the paradigm shift exhibited by Spaces of Hope is away from the paradigm of FBOs offered by through the work of Robert Putnam.

The pilot data explored herein touched on policy agendas of localism, immigration, leadership and health inequalities as responses to the COVID-19 pandemic. These are areas that will received continued attention during 2023, in the UK context in which Curating Spaces of Hope is being developed. However, the introduction of Curating Spaces of Hope to European and international contexts prompts questions as to which other areas of social policy and practice can Curating Spaces of Hope be applied, and which other catalysts of uncertainty could be addressed? Responses to climate change and a just transition to net zero, through resilient and inclusive social policy, is one brief example.

Finally, one area this paper touched on but did not explore in detail is understandings of FBOs as brokers of resources and trusted partners in social policy and practice. Elsewhere this conversation is taken up through the question of whether FBOs are an asset to be harnessed or a problem to be solved in social policy and practice (see Levin, (2020), Levin et al (2021) and Levin (2022) for US and International contexts and Baker and Dinham, (2018) for UK and international contexts)? Through this paper I have set out that Curating Spaces of Hope offers scope for mapping and responding to uncertainties, such that it can provide new answers to this perennial question.

Notes

[1] The term welfare state was first coined by Archbishop William Temple in 1928 and went on to define the post-World War Two welfare regime in the UK (Temple, 1928).

[2] I will explore this third framing later in the paper, where I will suggest how a new paradigm of FBO might integrate the dialogue between urban studies and religion, with social policy and practice.

[3] The 2019 British Social Attitudes Survey noted 52% of the population in the UK identified as 'nones'. Both this stat and the 2021 Census data show that Christianity is a minority worldview in the UK for the first time (46.2%).

[4] These dialogues took place in majority white British environments. The Inquiry into the Future of Civil Society in England considered this data alongside findings from other studies from non-majority white contexts.

⁵ Whilst I have opened up the Sources of Motivation Modality here in a way that allows general application, it is important to note that the research took place within Christian and non-religious settings. This indicates a limitation of the research. Christian and non-religious worldviews clearly do not represent the diversity of worldviews within the belief landscape in the UK. As a result, further research is needed to test the Curating Spaces of Hope Paradigm in environments characterised by other religious and secular beliefs, values and worldviews. This being said, I do not feel that this limitation delegitimises the claims made regards the opportunities for understanding Sources of Motivation provided by modality three.

⁶ The pandemic brought about a global experience of uncertainty unlike anything in modern history. It can be argued that that the contexts of uncertainty set out in terms of postsecular spaces and liminality as the new norm, which were observed in scholarship that predates the pandemic, have intensified as a result.

References

Attride-Stirling, J. (2001) 'Thematic networks: an analytic tool for qualitative research', *Qualitative Research*, 1(3): 385–405.

All Party Parliamentary Group for Faith and Society (APPG). (2020) 'Keeping the Faith: Partnerships between Faith Groups and Local Authorities during and beyond the Pandemic', All Party Parliamentary Group for Faith and Society. Westminster. Available from: https://static1.squarespace.com/sta tic/5aa7ae58266c07fe6b48eb76/t/5fabc1475ae8b92bcf64f30c/160509 1658307/APPG_CovidReport_Full_V4.pdf. [Accessed 27 July 2022].

Baker, C. and Dinham, A. (2018) 'renegotiating religion and belief in the public square: definitions, debates, controversies', in Baker, C., Crisp, B. and Dinham, A. (eds) *Re-imagining Religion and Belief: 21st Century Policy and Practice*, Bristol: Policy Press, pp 15–32.

Baker, C., & Skinner, H., (2006). Faith in Action: The Dynamic connection between religious and spiritual capital, Manchester: William Temple Foundation.

Barber-Rowell. (2021a) *Curating Spaces of Hope: Towards a Liminal, Rhizomatic and Productive Paradigm of Faith Based Organisations (FBOs)*, London: Goldsmiths, University of London.

Barber-Rowell, M. (2021b) 'Curating Spaces of Hope: exploring the potential for Intra-Communities' Dialogue (ICD) and Faith-Based Organisations, in a post-COVID society'. *Journal of Dialogue Studies*, 9: 11–33.

Barber-Rowell, M. (2022a) 'Curating Spaces of Hope: Intra-Communities Dialogue and Local Leadership in Post-pandemic Society', London: William Temple Foundation Blog. Available from: https://williamtemplefoundat ion.org.uk/curating-spaces-of-hope/ [Accessed 31st July 2022].

Barber-Rowell, M. (2022b) 'Curating Spaces of Hope: Intra-Communities Dialogue and Post-Pandemic Society' London: William Temple Foundation. Available from https://williamtemplefoundation.org.uk/curating-spaces-of-hope-2/ [Accessed 14th March, 2023]

Barber-Rowell, M. (2022c) 'Curating Spaces of Hope: Local Leadership for Post-pandemic Society', William Temple Foundation Blog. Available from: https://williamtemplefoundation.org.uk/curating-spaces-of-hope-3/ [Accessed 31st July, 2022].

Beaumont, J., (2004). 'Workfare, associationism and the 'underclass' in the United States: contrasting faith-based action on urban poverty in a liberal welfare regime'. In: *European churches confronting poverty: Social Action against exclusion*. Bochum: SWI Verlag, pp. 249–278.

Beaumont, J., (2008a). Dossier: 'Faith-based organisations and human geography'. *Tijdschrift voor Economishe en Sociale Geografie*, 99(4), pp. 377–381.

Beaumont, J., (2008b). 'Faith Action in urban social issues.' *Urban Studies*, 45(10), pp. 2019–2034.

Beaumont, J., & Dias, C., (2008). 'Faith Based Organisations and Urban Social Justice in the Netherlands.' *Tijdschrift voor Economishe en Sociale Geografie*, Volume 99, pp. 382–392.

Beaumont, P. and Cloke, P. (2012a) *Faith Based Organisations and Exclusion in European Cities*, Bristol: Policy Press, University of Bristol.

Beaumont, J. and Cloke, P. (2012b) 'Introduction', in Beaumont, J. And Cloke, P., (eds) *Faith Based Organisations and Exclusion in European Cities*, Bristol: Policy Press, University of Bristol, pp 1–36.

Beckford, J. (2012) SSSR Presidential Address Public Religions and the Postsecular: Critical Reflections. Journal for the Scientific Study of Religion. Wiley. 51(1) pp1–19.

British Social Attitudes Survey. (2019). 'British Social Attitudes Survey. Religion, identity, behaviour and belief over two decades', [Online]. Available from: https://bsa.natcen.ac.uk/media/39293/1_bsa36_religion.pdf [Accessed 30 March 2020].

Calhoun, C., Juergensmeyer, M. and Van Antwerpen, J. (2011) *Rethinking Secularism*, Oxford: Oxford University Press.

Census. (2021) 'Religion in England and Wales: Census in 2021', [Online]. Available from: https://www.ons.gov.uk/peoplepopulationandcommun ity/culturalidentity/religion/bulletins/religionenglandandwales/census2 021 [Accessed 10th December 2022].

Civil Society Futures. (2018) 'Inquiry into the Future of Civil Society in England', [Online]. Available from: https://civilsocietyfutures.org/wp-cont ent/uploads/sites/6/2018/11/Civil-Society-Futures__Civil-Society-in-England__small-1.pdf [Accessed 27 July 2022].

Clarke, C. and Woodhead, L. (2018) 'Westminster faith debates: a new settlement revised – religion and belief in schools', [Online]. Available from: http://faithdebates.org.uk/wp-content/uploads/2018/07/Clarke-Woodhead-A- New-Settlement-Revised.pdf [Accessed 30 March 2020].

Cloke, P., Baker, C., Sutherland, C. and Williams, A. (2019). *Geographies of Postsecularity: Re-envisioning Politics, Subjectivity and Ethics*, London: Routledge.

Cottam, H. (2018) *Radical Help: How we can Remake the Relationships between us and Revolutionise the Welfare State*, London: Virago.

Cnaan, R.A., Wineburg, R.J. and Boddie, S.C. (1999) *A Newer Deal: Social Work and Religion in Partnership*, New York: Columbia University Press.

Deleuze, G. (2014 [1968]). *Difference and Repetition*, London: Bloomsbury.

Deleuze, G. and Guattari, F. (2016 [1988]). *A Thousand Plateaus*, London: Bloomsbury.

Esping-Andersen, G. (1990) *The Three Worlds of Welfare Capitalism*, Cambridge: Polity Press.

Habermas, J. (2005) 'Equal treatment of cultures and the limits of post-modern liberalism,. *Journal of Political Philosophy*, 13(1): 1–28.

Habermas, J. (2008a) 'Notes on post-secular society, *New Perspectives Quarterly*, 25(4): 17–29.

Habermas, J. (2008b) 'Religion in the public sphere: cognitive presuppositions for the 'public use of reason' by religious and secular citizens', in *Between Naturalism and Religion: Philosophical Essays*, London: Routledge, pp 114–47.

Herman, A., Beaumont, J., Cloke, P. and Walliser, A. (2012) 'Spaces of postsecular engagement in cities', in *Faith Based Organisations and Exclusion in European Cities*, Bristol: Policy Press, University of Bristol, pp 59–80.

Howes, A. (2020) *Arts and Minds: How the Royal Society of Arts Changed a Nation*, Oxford: Princeton University Press.

Johnsen, S. (2014) 'Where is the 'F' in FBO? The evolution and practice of faith based homelessness services in the UK', *Journal of Social Policy*, 43(2): 413–30.

Kong, L. (2010) 'Global shifts, theoretical shifts: changing geographies of religion', *Progress in Human Geography*, 34(6): 755–76.

Kuhn, T. (2012 [1962]) *The Structure of Scientific Revolutions: 50th Anniversary Edition*, Chicago: University of Chicago Press.

Latour, B. (2007) *Reassembling the Social: An Introduction to Actor Network Theory*, Oxford: Oxford University Press.

Ley, D. (2011) 'Preface: towards a postsecular city?', in Beaumont, J. and Baker, C. (eds) *Postsecular Cities: Space, Theory and Practice*, London: Continuum, pp xii–xiv.

Levin, J. (2020) 'The faith community and the SARS-CoV-2 outbreak: part of the problem or part of the solution?', *Journal of Religious Health*, 59: 2215–28. Available from: https://doi.org/10.1007/s10943-020-01048-x

Levin, J., Idler, E. and VanderWeele, T. (2021) 'Faith-Based Organizations and SARS-CoV-2 vaccination: challenges and recommendations'. Available from: https://journals.sagepub.com/doi/full/10.1177/003335 49211054079]

Levin, J. (2022) 'Human flourishing in the era of COVID-19: how spirituality and the faith sector help and hinder our collective response', *Challenges*, 13(1): 12. Available from: https://doi.org/10.3390/challe13010012

Parmaksiz, U. (2018) 'Making sense of the postsecular', *European Journal of Social Theory*, 21(1): 98–116.

Putnam, R., (2000). *Bowling Alone*. 1st ed. New York: Simon and Schuster.

Putnam, R. and Campbell, D. (2010) *American Grace: How Religion Divides Us and Unites Us* (1st edn), New York: Simon and Schuster.

Smith, G. (2002) *Faith in the Voluntary Sector: A Common or Distinctive Experience of Religious Organisations*, London: Centre for Institutional Studies, University of East London.

Spaces of Hope. (2019) 'Curating Spaces of Hope: The Hubs Network Stockport Metropolitan Borough Council', [Online]. Available from: https://www.spacesofhope.co.uk/our-latest-work.html [Accessed 31st July 2022].

Temple, W. (1928) *Christianity and the State*, London: MacMillan.

Temple, W. (1976 [1942]) *Christianity and Social Order*, London: Penguin.

Turner, V. (1967) 'Betwixt and Between; The Liminal Period in Rites of Passage', La Salle. Illinois: Open Court, [Online]. Available from: https://books.google.co.uk/books?id=Y0h0OEe19pcC&lpg=PA3&dq=victor%20turn er%20liminality&lr&pg=PA18#v=onepage&q&f=false [Accessed 31st July 2022].

Turner, V. (1969) *Liminality and Communitas, in the Ritual Process: Structure and Anti-Structure*, Chicago: Aldine Publishing.

Weller, P. (2022) *Hizmet in Transitions: European Developments of a Turkish Muslim Inspired Movement*, Cham: Palgrave MacMillan. Available from: https://doi.org/10.1007/978-3-030-93798-0

Wilford, J. (2010) 'Sacred archipelagos: geographies of secularisation', *Progress in Human Geography*, 34: 328–348.

Woodhead, L. (2016). 'The rise of "no religion" in Britain: the emergence of a new cultural majority', *Journal of the British Academy*, 4: 245–61.

Woodhead, L. (2017) 'The rise of "no religion": towards an explanation', *Sociology of Religion: A Quarterly Review*, 78(3): 247–62.

8

The 'Innovative Job Agency': an experiment in renewing local social services in Pisa (Italy)

Elena Vivaldi, Andrea Blasini and Federico Bruno

Introduction

This chapter analyses and evaluates, from the perspective of social innovation, the *Agenzia per il Lavoro Innovativo* (ALI – 'Agency for Innovative Work') project, an experimental social policy project promoted and co-designed by Pisa (Italy) Società della Salute (SdS),[1] together with the social cooperatives Arnera, Aforisma, and Il Simbolo, and with the Scuola Superiore Sant'Anna – the latter involved in the assessment of social impact.[2] The project aimed to foster the autonomy of socially vulnerable people by promoting their job placement. To this end, ALI involved participants in highly personalised individual projects that included access to a series of services aimed at providing new skills to participants (for example, training courses) and bringing them closer to the labour market, both directly (through internships), and indirectly – that is by providing services that can alleviate the family, relational and personal conditions that hinder individual autonomy (for example, childcare services, basic home care and psychological support). The experiment consisted of two rounds: the first from October 2020 to December 2021, and the second from January 2022 to June 2022. Overall, ALI involved 207 participants, selected from citizens assisted by Pisa social services.

Despite the limited number of participants involved (207 people overall), and its experimental nature, ALI presents two interesting social innovation aspects concerning the approach to social exclusion and the governance of service provision. The first aspect concerns the kind of intervention proposed by ALI. ALI offers a range of services to tackle the different dimensions that determine social vulnerability and to empower the participants. This is particularly evident in some personalised projects (some of which are reported in this chapter) where ALI addressed the various vulnerabilities of the participants and of their families (for example, parenting problems, psychological distress and unemployment) to create the conditions for their empowerment. The second aspect concerns its governance, which sees the public actor – the SdS – taking a central role in coordinating and managing the work of the third sector organisations – the cooperatives – that carry out the interventions. ALI is therefore an attempt by the public social services to modernise their methods of intervention and offer a service capable of tackling the various risk factors that determine social vulnerability.

This chapter aims to verify whether, and to what extent, ALI has realised its potential for social innovation. Based on observations and interviews made from October 2020 to June 2022, throughout the project's duration, the chapter reconstructs ALI's individual projects and their outcomes, identifies the factors that hindered or favoured the implementation of the measures and examines the balance of ALI's experiences. The chapter is structured as follows. The next section defines the theoretical framework, focusing on the social innovation aspects that best characterise the ALI project. The methodology and data of the research are then described, followed by the functioning of ALI, and the characteristics of the participants and the activated services. Then, the results of the focus groups and interviews will be presented, which reconstruct the outcome of the individual paths, and identify ALI's strengths and criticalities. Finally, the factors that facilitated or hindered the success of the projects are discussed. The chapter ends with a reflection on the perspectives that ALI has opened for the local social services in the province of Pisa.

ALI and social innovation

This chapter analyses ALI through the lenses of social innovation. The concept of social innovation dates back to the nineteenth century and refers to the development of new practices and ideas to tackle societal challenges and improve life conditions of marginalised groups; social innovation is contextually embedded (that is, it must be appraised in its institutional and social context) and dynamic, as it concerns not only objectives but also processes (Jessop et al, 2014; Moulaert, MacCallum and Hillier, 2014; Satalkina and Steiner, 2022). Social innovation is a widespread concept, not only in the scientific literature, but also in public debate and in the reform agenda of European welfare systems (for a review of social innovation in the European Union, see Addarii and Lipparini, 2017) – ALI, which includes innovation in its name, is a perfect example of how this concept sounds appealing to the policy makers. The success of this concept derives from the dual need, on the one hand, to adapt welfare systems for the transition to a post-industrial society and the emergence of new social risks (Taylor-Gooby, 2004; Bonoli, 2005; Armingeon and Bonoli 2006; Bonoli 2007; Häusermann 2010) and, on the other, to make their costs sustainable in light of the constraints on public spending posed by globalisation, especially following the Great Recession, through greater efficiency and the mobilisation of new resources, not only public but also private (Ferrera and Maino, 2014; Fougère et al, 2017).

As often happens with concepts widely diffused in the public and academic debate, definitions of social innovation have flourished through the years: the variety of interpretations of this concept reflects the variety of fields of social innovation, of actors involved, and of approaches to evaluate it (for instance, see Moulaert et al, 2014; Galego et al, 2021). The vagueness and indeterminacy of this concept posed the question of finding one (or more) working definition of social innovation that could be employed in empirical research (Pol and Ville, 2009; European Commission, 2013; Grimm et al, 2013; Campomori and Casula, 2022).

This chapter adopts the approach of Madama et al (2019), who based their definition of social innovation on that of the Bureau of European Policy Advisers (BEPA, 2010), which played a fundamental role in placing the concept of social innovation at the centre of attention for European policy makers (Sabato et al, 2015). According to the BEPA (2010, p 9),

> [s]ocial innovations are innovations that are social in both their ends and their means. [...] Specifically, we define social innovations as new ideas (products, services and models) that simultaneously meet social needs (more effectively than alternatives) and create new social relationships or collaborations.

This definition is particularly restrictive, as it allows to speak of social innovation only if a measure offers a new response to a social need in a more effective and efficient way than existing solutions, and with the objective of renewing or improving the relationships and social skills of the beneficiaries. Madama et al (2019) reworked the BEPA definition to make it less demanding and more able to grasp different levels and intensity of social innovation. For them, it is possible to define as socially innovative a measure that presents at least one process innovation (therefore, relating to the organisational methods and the actors involved) or one product innovation (relating to the services offered and the social needs addressed), which is aimed at objectives such as limiting the need for assistance, improving the level of services offered, reducing costs, or improving quality of life and making beneficiaries more independent. In this sense, ALI shows two potential forms of social innovation.

The first form of social innovation is product innovation and relates to ALI's audience. ALI incorporates the approach to poverty described in the literature on new social risks. The welfare systems of industrial societies were designed to address old social risks – mainly, unemployment and incapacity for work due to illness, disability, or old age – but they have proved to be ineffective against the new risks that emerged in post-industrial society. While old risks tended to manifest themselves in people who were middle-aged or older, new risks emerge early in the working age, and are found in the gap between the labour market, family, and the welfare state – making them particularly difficult to identify for the traditional welfare systems (Ranci, 2010, pp 4–15). The new social risks include difficulties in reconciling work and family time, single parenthood, having a fragile relative, having low-level or obsolete work skills, and poor access to social security mechanisms (Bonoli, 2006, pp 6–8). These risk factors interact in a complex and multidimensional way, determining the conditions of social vulnerability to which people such as women, the young, and people of foreign origins are particularly exposed. ALI aims to tackle these vulnerabilities by making available a series of integrated professional services that act on risk dimensions in order to provide beneficiaries with the tools to follow a path of autonomy in the logic of individual empowerment. This approach to poverty is not innovative in itself: these are well-established concepts in the scientific literature which are slowly also finding application at the policy level – an example of this is the Italian minimum income scheme, the *Reddito di Cittadinanza* (RdC – 'citizenship income'), which, despite its limitations, reflects this same approach.[3] The innovative element of ALI, rather, concerns the attempt to introduce in the province of Pisa a working method for the local social service capable of offering integrated, customisable, and flexible empowerment-oriented services.

This brings us to the second aspect of innovation, which is related to process. Italy is a typical example of southern welfare regime (Ferrera, 1996; Saraceno, 2017) characterised by 'a rather limited intervention model in social assistance, social care and family support' (León and Pavolini, 2014, p 354); this, in the context of the general trend towards the retrenchment of the welfare states of post-industrial Western countries started in the late 1970s (Levy, 2021), determined an under-development of the Italian social assistance policies. In 2001, a constitutional reform assigned to the regions and local authorities the competence over social assistance and introduced the principle that basic levels of social assistance should be guaranteed and defined at the national level; however, these minimum standards were not precisely defined until recently, nor have dedicated funds been allocated to guarantee them. This contributed to scarce investment in social assistance matters at the national level and to a gap between northern and southern regions (Sacchi and Bastagli, 2005; Maino and Neri, 2011; Kapezov, 2015; Pavolini, 2015; Martinelli, 2019). The situation began to change only in recent years, when a minimum income scheme – the RdC – was adopted, national minimum standards of social assistance were defined, and the government allocated significant resources to strengthen the local social services. Against this backdrop, ALI represents an attempt to offer a cutting-edge social service through the involvement of different actors and the mobilisation of financial, human, and professional resources. ALI in fact makes use of €793,165 from the Ministry of Labour and Social Policies and is the result of a co-planning by the public social services – Pisa SdS – and the third social sector – the Arnera, A.FO.RI.S.MA, and Il Simbolo cooperatives. SdS is involved in management, coordination, and monitoring, and the cooperatives implement the individual projects of the participants. Cooperation between public bodies and cooperatives has a double advantage. Management by SdS makes it possible to coordinate and integrate the services provided by the cooperatives so as to offer participants a package that can respond to their conditions and adapt to their needs. The work of the cooperative operators, carried out in close cooperation with the social workers, allows social services to establish more direct and closer relationships with the people they assist, who have tended to see social services as a remote and unresponsive institution.

With its product and process innovations, therefore, ALI represents an experiment in renewing the working methods of the local social services aimed at providing beneficiaries with the tools to follow a path of autonomy with a view to empowerment. Following the most recent lines of scientific literature and of political intervention on the subject, ALI tackles poverty as a complex phenomenon, and acts on the different dimensions of risk that determine social vulnerability – such as foreign origin, single parenthood, relational poverty, unemployment, and psychological fragility – from the perspective of empowering the individual. As regards its governance, the collaboration between the public actor and the third sector organisations has two advantages: it allows local social services closer contact with the beneficiaries of the services, and also enables them to offer an integrated package of services that allows highly customised individual projects. The rest of this chapter is devoted to verifying whether, and to what extent these potential innovations have been realised, and which factors have favoured or hindered their achievement.

Methods and data

The research followed an essentially qualitative approach and is based on two focus groups held in May 2021 and eight interviews held between July and August 2022. In all, 22 people with various roles in ALI were heard. The purpose of the two focus groups, held in the middle of the first round of ALI, was to collect the experiences of the first projects to recount the functioning of ALI, to offer an overview of the types of services and specific services provided, and on the results of the first projects, and to identify the critical issues and virtuous mechanisms that emerged in the first months of the project. The first focus group involved five social workers and a manager, all employed by SdS, and the second focus group involved four cooperative counsellors (who act as case managers, together with the SdS social workers), two social educators, two primary care workers, and a psychologist. The two groups – the first made up of staff from the public social services, the second from staff from third sector organisations – were asked the same questions.

In order to determine what emerged in the focus groups of the previous year, and to evaluate the outcome of the paths at the end of ALI, seven interviews were organised which involved two counsellors, two tutors (who follow the participants during their internships), and three educators. Two methodological observations must be made. First, a social impact assessment would ideally have required the collection of information about what happened to the participants at the end of the project – for example, whether or not they found work, took training courses, or continued to use local social services – in order to make a comparison with the sample of citizens who, despite being eligible, were not selected to participate. Unfortunately, these data were not available, but this does not compromise the outcome of the research in a decisive way. Given the nature of the project and the number of participants, a quantitative evaluation of the results could have been misleading: the participants and their families present important vulnerabilities that are difficult to solve in the few months that the individual projects last. While several participants managed to find employment, thus achieving the highest goal of ALI, for others – as we will see later – the fact of having taken the first steps on a path towards autonomy with the local social services was an important result in itself. Taking a qualitative approach based on interviews with privileged witnesses has therefore made it possible to appreciate the emergence of these mechanisms of activation and autonomy, which would otherwise risk going undetected. Secondly, the interviews involved only the operators of the cooperatives; it was not possible to interview the social workers, as their contracts had expired at the end of the project. An eighth interview was therefore organised to report the perspective of the public local social services and involved an SdS manager and a social worker with coordination functions in the project.

Finally, the research made use of documents provided by the SdS and the cooperatives – in particular, the 'Access and Evaluation Forms', compiled by the social workers of the SdS, which allowed to reconstruct the characteristics of the participants in the projects and the activated services.

The ALI Project in practice

This section reconstructs the ALI Project in its concreteness. First, it covers its most practical aspects: the selection of participants, the design of the personalised projects, and the funding available to ALI. Then, it presents the characteristics of the participants. Subsequently, it discusses the outcomes of the personalised projects and presents some significant cases. Then, it discusses the strengths and, finally, the critical issues of the project.

Operational aspects: selection of participants, personalisation of the projects, funding

The potential participants in the ALI were selected by SdS from among those who, already in charge of the local social services, showed the most suitable characteristics for the project. The social services summoned potential participants for a first interview held by a social worker from the SdS, generally the person in charge of the potential participant, and by a psychotherapist from the project. During this first meeting, the ALI operators described the project and invited them to talk about themselves and explain their needs, desires, and abilities. During the first interview, the social worker filled out an 'Access and Evaluation Form' to report information relating to the psycho-physical health of the individual, the composition of their family unit, and possible elements of personal or family vulnerability. The form involves an assessment of employability[4] and indicates, on the basis of the interview, which possible interventions could be activated.

If the candidates were interested in participating in ALI, they were sent to a second interview, held by the operators of the cooperatives, where they met the case manager that would follow their progress. The purpose of the second interview was to create a relationship between the candidate and the case manager, and to better define the personalised project. In fact, the interventions hypothesised in the first interview do not always turn out to be the most suitable; a deeper knowledge of the candidate can therefore help to improve the personalisation of the project. The objective of the second interview (and of any subsequent interviews, if deemed necessary) is therefore to define the personalised project which is then included on a 'Personalised Individual Project Form' which specifies the objectives of the projects and the interventions activated. The case manager monitors the progress of the individual project, compiling a register of the activities and coordinating with the operators who implement the interventions, and with the social worker who is in charge of the beneficiary. At the end of the project, the case manager draws up a conclusive evaluation that summarises the objectives achieved, the skills acquired, the critical issues that emerged, and the resources that were activated.

The services made available include:

- internships;
- training courses (forklift training, Italian for foreigners, HACCP, and workplace safety);[5]
- home educational services for minors;

- basic home care;
- psychological support;
- orientation to local services (for example, relations with schools, municipalities, and management of personal files with the public services).

The type of activities proposed by the project reflect ALI's approach to the autonomy of socially vulnerable people. In spite of its name, in fact, ALI not only offers services directly aimed at entering the labour market, but also interventions that address the social, personal, and family obstacles that limit the autonomy of an individual. This approach to poverty, albeit with well-known (and perhaps inevitable) limits, also characterises the RdC.[6]

The total allocation for ALI amounted to €793,165; the beneficiary and manager of the funding was the SdS. Every three months, the cooperatives reported on the activities of the project and were reimbursed by the SdS for the expenses incurred. As previously mentioned, ALI was divided into two rounds. The first round, from October 2020 to December 2021, made use of the Poverty Fund (intended for RdC recipients) and the National Operational Programme (NOP) for Social Inclusion (intended for social marginality in the broad sense and co-financed by the European Social Fund). This made it possible to involve not only RdC recipients in ALI, who are mainly Italian,[7] but also families being cared for by social services, many of whom do not have Italian citizenship. The NOP for Social Inclusion funds ran out in the second round, and consequently, only RdC recipients could be involved in ALI. As we will see, this led to a change in the composition of ALI participants, with consequences for the individual projects and their outcomes.

Characteristics of the participants and activated projects

The first round of ALI involved 144 people, while the second one 63,[8] for a total of 207 people involved in the project. Tables 8.1, 8.2, 8.3 and 8.4 show, respectively, the gender of the participants, their country of origin, their age groups, and the composition of families.

The tables show how the participants of the first round of ALI reflect the definition of new social risks. The participants were mainly women; people

Table 8.1: Gender of participants

| | First round | | Second round | |
	Number	%	Number	%
Male	59	41	22	44
Female	85	59	28	54

Source: Authors' elaboration on data provided by SdS

Table 8.2: Country of origin

	First round		Second round	
	Number	%	Number	%
Italy	65	45	32	64
Other country	79	55	18	36

Source: Authors' elaboration on data provided by SdS

Table 8.3: Age ranges

	First round		Second round[9]	
	Number	%	Number	%
<= 24	17	12	2	4
25–34	26	18	7	14
35–44	37	26	14	29
45–54	33	23	18	37
55+	31	21	8	16

Source: Authors' elaboration on data provided by SdS

Table 8.4: Number of family members

	First round[10]		Second round	
	Number	%	Number	%
1	35	25	24	48
2	28	20	9	18
3	27	20	7	14
4	23	17	3	6
5	13	9	2	4
6	12	9	5	10

Source: Authors' elaboration on data provided by SdS

of foreign origin were more numerous than Italians; people who lived alone were the relative majority but, overall, families composed of two or more members were more numerous. The age groups most represented are those between 35 and 44 years old and between 45 and 54 years old, with an average age of the participants equal to 42 years.

The change in the composition of participants between the first and second edition is evident when the data is compared. Women remain the majority,

Table 8.5: Services activated for the individual projects

	First round	Second round	Total
Internship	43	12	55
Forklift training	21	19	40
Italian for foreigners	27	13	40
HACCP course	46	17	63
Safety in workplace course	68	39	107
Home educational services for minors	47	19	66
IT training	Not active	29	29
Soft skills	Not active	9	9
Basic home care	5	4	9
Psychological support	34	12	46
Orientation to the local services	17	12	29

Source: Authors' elaboration on data provided by SdS

but their percentage drops to 54%, and the average age of the participants rises to 45. The change in the participants emerges more clearly in their country of origin – Italians are now the absolute majority – and in the composition of the family unit, where people who live alone rose from a quarter in the first round to almost half in the second. The percentage of single mothers with children is also significant: this was 26% (37 participants) in the first round, compared to 18% (eight participants) in the second round.

Table 8.5 shows the services activated for the individual projects. Note that each individual project can include more services. Internships are the service most requested by the participants. The operators of the cooperatives contact the firms which offer the internships; participants are supervised by a counsellor, which oversees the correct behaviour of the intern and of the firm. The realisation of the internships was hindered by the outbreak of the COVID-19 pandemic, which caused many of them to be postponed or cancelled. Home educational services for minors and basic home care are two services which sometimes overawe the participants: participants often perceive them as an invasion of their private space and as a criticism to their lifestyles. However, these perplexities tend to disappear as the intervention is implemented and the participants become aware of their usefulness. Psychological support consists in a series of meetings with a psychotherapist; it is meant to alleviate situations of discomfort but is no substitute to the specialised mental health service: in the most serious cases, the psychotherapist has sent the participants to the specialised service. The orientation to the local services illustrates the various services present in the territory to the participants. Finally, ALI offers a series of training courses – two of which (IT training and soft skills) could not be activated because of the pandemic.

Outcomes of the paths and significant cases

The interviews and focus groups reported that the outcomes of the individual projects were generally positive, however, it is necessary to clarify what is meant by a positive outcome, bearing in mind the aims of ALI, the characteristics of the participants, and the duration of the courses. ALI is aimed at people already in the charge of social services, with different levels of social unease. As reported by an SdS manager, 'social need is not like health need, where a need is met with a prescription that solves the problem'. In fact, these situations require work for many months, even years, and cannot always be resolved in the relatively few months of ALI's projects. ALI's goal of providing the tools to initiate a path of autonomy is therefore achieved with varying degrees of intensity, depending on the case. Sometimes the projects ended when the participant was hired by the workplace that had offered the internship, or at another workplace; in these cases, ALI achieved its highest aspiration, that of finding a job for the participant. The projects can also end positively without resulting in the participant acquiring a job, however, for example with the completion of a training course, or with the achievement of other objectives such as obtaining a school diploma. As stated by a tutor, 'it is considered positive if the project activates individuals. The goal is to change attitudes towards the condition of social hardship, and to instil the idea that there is a path towards improvement and possibly autonomy'. The individual projects that succeed in activating this mechanism of autonomy are considered successful by the operators.

The most significant individual projects are those in which the different activated services interact to operate on the different social risk profiles of the participants and their families – a classic example is that of the foreign participants who followed the Italian course and were helped in their everyday life and in carrying out internships. Two cases are particularly significant. The first is from a foreign family residing in Italy for many years, recounted by a counsellor.

> The family was composed of father, mother and four children – two minors and two adults, a male and a female. The family was socially integrated: the children studied here and speak perfect Italian, but their mother hardly speaks it. The father is a worker with extremely precarious temporary contracts of very short duration. The breadwinners were the father and the eldest son. The adult daughter took care of the underage siblings, enrolling them in school and keeping in touch with the teachers; the

mother, who did not speak Italian, could not even interface with the services, and limited herself to cooking and cleaning. We also activated the intervention of school educational support and socialization for the children and placed the adult daughter in a fashion store through an internship, where she was then hired and later became shop manager. We have also activated services for the rest of the family. The mother took the Italian course and started to leave the house alone, while the father took the forklift course and the workplace safety course. (Counsellor 1)

The personalised project addressed the various aspects that determined the vulnerability of the family. The school educational support was activated for the children, thus freeing the adult daughter and the mother from the onus of taking care of them. This created the framework conditions for the empowerment of the two women: the daughter could do an internship which resulted in her hiring, while the mother could attend the Italian course which made her more autonomous in her everyday life.

The second case is that of an Italian family recounted by an educator.

The family consisted of mother, father of foreign origin, and three children. The family were evicted from their home in the middle of the project; the children had many personal difficulties, one with ADHD, another with language problems. The mother had always been tied to the house and was frustrated because she could not relate to her children. She used ALI's psychological support and began meeting more frequently with the social worker, who managed to visit her at home and to find her an emergency apartment following the eviction. An ALI operator was assigned to the child with ADHD, I provided parenting support to the mother, who had to take care of the other daughters. Initially, my role was to play with the children while the mother took time for herself. She then took advantage of my presence to be with the children more and learnt to play with them. The children then started asking their mother to play and do things together. In the meanwhile, I assisted the mother in her relations with the school: at first, I accompanied her to meetings with the teachers; at the end of the school year, she was able to deal with the teachers and the school on her own. Eventually, both parents found a job thanks to our assistance. (Educator 1)

This is another case where ALI project addressed the different vulnerabilities of the family – the mother's need for psychological support and the difficult relations with the children and their school. Thanks to the personalised project, the mother managed to become more autonomous, find time for herself, and improve her relations with the children and with the school. The project resulted in both parents finding a job.

These cases are particularly significant because they demonstrate how ALI's approach – which acts on the various social risk factors to create the conditions for a path to autonomy – has led to directly observable results. There have been cases, however, where the paths were interrupted, or the participants withdrew their availability, as we will see in the section relating to the criticalities of the project.

Strengths

The strengths that emerged in the focus groups and interviews include the accurate reading of the participants' needs, the personalisation of the individual projects, and their flexibility. The situations of the participants are carefully analysed during the two interviews in which the individual paths are defined: this differentiates ALI from the traditional working method of the social services, which, given the short intervention times, and the need to respond to a person's primary needs, tends to a less accurate reading.

Closely related to personalisation is the question of the flexibility of the projects. The counsellors of the cooperatives constantly follow the development of individual paths, and this allows them to adapt them according to needs. An emblematic example, reported in the focus groups, is that of a young female adult in a family unit in particularly disadvantaged conditions: the original project was envisaged as focusing on the father, but later the operators realised that it would be more useful to focus on the young female adult. Following an internship, she was then hired by a company and now contributes significantly to the sustenance of the family.

The relationship created between ALI operators and participants is another strength. ALI means that participants have a network of professionals at their disposal, ready to respond quickly to their needs. This point is emphasised by an educator, according to whom quick answers are particularly important in the relationship with the participants:

> Quick responses to needs are essential. Often, when a request is made to the social services, an eternity goes by, because the social worker has so many cases and is unable to see a family more than once a month, or to contact the other professionals who work with the family. With ALI, instead, we were in constant contact with social workers, through e-mails, meetings, and periodic reports. We met every week and updated ourselves on the progress so far. Participants had a network of professionals at their disposal, who looked after them and were able to respond promptly to their

needs and questions. This has increased trust in the services for many families and has allowed us to continue monitoring them. This is the best thing ALI could offer. (Educator 2)

ALI also enabled the social services to get to know the participants better, to 'enter' problematic families, and to observe difficulties that otherwise would have remained hidden. Services such as basic care, or the educational service for minors, are often used to 'probe' the situation experienced by the family unit. Since the conditions of need do not always emerge in the interviews with ALI operators or with the social workers, the educators who deal with this service also have a role in identifying the possible further needs of the family, so as to prevent situations and difficulties remaining hidden or degenerating. As reported by an educator:

School support is often used to control the family and domestic situation with a view to prevention, to bring out further possible problems. This kind of intervention has saved many situations that risked ending up with a report to the family court[11] due to the situation of minors. (Educator 3)

In this sense, ALI's preventive intervention allows to tackle problematic situations involving children before they degenerate and force the judiciary authority to order the foster custody of the minors.

Critical issues

The ALI project was not without its difficulties. A first group of problems involves the relationship between the operators and the participants. The operators involved in the focus group indicated three problematic dynamics. The first relates to the initial resistance of participants, who did not always willingly accept interventions such as home care or education for minors, which was considered a criticism of their lifestyle and an invasion into their private sphere. A second problem arose from the fact that participants were not always fully aware of their condition of need – for example, in relation to the education of children or hygiene in the home. As a result, ALI interventions were not always recognised as useful, and the family becomes unresponsive. As reported by an educator, 'the cultural level of families intersects with economic needs. Families who recognise the importance of cultural growth and education appreciate school support for minors. Conversely, educational support is less appreciated by families with a lower level of education.' A final difficulty involved the dynamic of exchange that some participants establish with ALI. Some participants were, in fact, interested in the project, thinking that it would allow them to obtain in return, to obtain more quickly, or not to lose benefits given by the social services, such as shopping vouchers or a subsidy for the payment of bills or rent. In some cases, after having expressed their willingness to participate in the first interview (the one with the social worker), some participants withdrew from the second (with the cooperative operators), thus abandoning the project. Other cases involved an exchange mechanism, whereby the participant agreed to continue in the project only in exchange for concessions from the social services. A counsellor reported on these cases:

> In one case for the home education service for children, the mother said she did not need it, and that she only accepted because she needed help with the rent. She wanted a bigger apartment and agreed to the home education service, but since the social worker had not found them a larger apartment, she wanted to finish the project. In another case, the education service was fine, and the child was satisfied, but the mother wanted to stop it because the social worker had not responded for a month. Continuing to accept the service, according to the mother, would have meant sending a message to the social worker that everything was fine; by refusing the education, she could signal that there was a problem. The emergency was resolved when we explained that her child would be negatively affected, and that this was not a way to solve the issue. (Counsellor 2)

If these difficulties led to the interruption of progress in some cases, they were overcome in other cases as the paths proceeded, and the participants realised the usefulness of ALI.

A second type of problem related to the services offered. In the interviews, some operators complained about the limited variety of the types of jobs offered in internships. Others, similarly, complained about the limited variety of the professional training courses offered, and suggested that ALI should be able to purchase other training courses, in addition to those already offered, for interested participants. One interviewee observed a tendency to assign training courses automatically, simply because they are available, and regardless of a participant's interests.

The second round of ALI presented some critical issues. The first related to its limited duration, meaning that individual projects had to be shorter. Some individual projects which would have taken longer were interrupted at short notice, prompting negative reactions from the participants. An educator offered this example:

> I followed a young male adult who at some point had interrupted his path. It was going well, albeit in a fluctuating way. When

he learned that in a month and a half the project would be interrupted, he had an emotional breakdown: everything he had relied on in the last year ended. He changed the way he approached us. He was more and more oppositional, he increased the absences from the internship, and finally he interrupted the path saying that it did not make sense to continue it. (Educator 4)

A final critical issue was the high turnover of SdS social workers. Although the workers of the cooperatives – both those who acted as case managers and those who operated the interventions – remained relatively stable, the same was not true of social workers in the SdS, some of whom were hired with temporary contracts. This meant that some of ALI's potential, in terms of both learning and of relationships with the participants, was lost.

Facilitating and hindering factors

Overall, ALI proved that its multidisciplinary approach to poverty can be effective in empowering the participants. This section proposes a reflection on the factors that may facilitate or hinder the success of the projects. The aim is not just to evaluate the experience of ALI, but to draw some insights for similar measures and policies.

According to the interviewees, one factor in ALI's success was the presence of a professional network that could make a timely response to the requests and needs of the participants. This allowed an accurate reading of the need, the provision of flexible and personalised services, and the creation of a closer relationship between participants and the local social services. From this point of view, the management role of the public actor must be emphasised. As pointed out by an SdS executive:

> The idea was to integrate the project with institutional activity. Until now there were very valid projects, even better than ALI, but in which the public social services were marginal. Public service, instead, should be the cornerstone of the welfare system. In ALI, the public social services became the central node, offering direction and control. The success of ALI is the success of the public social services. (SdS executive)

In this sense, the cooperation between the public actor and the third sector organisations appears the key to the success of ALI. The public social service alone could have never implemented personalised and flexible individual projects like those of ALI. The third sector organisations, on the other hand, needed the guiding role of the public actor, which coordinates the projects and integrates the various services present in the territory in a consistent package. This brings us to a first potentially hindering factor: the fact that the kind of services offered depend on the supply in the territory. This was particularly evident in the case of the training courses and of the internships. Some interviewees argued that the offer of training courses should be more diverse, whereas others observed that the jobs proposed for the internships should be more differentiated.

A second determining factor for the success of ALI is the careful selection of participants. Participants in the first round of ALI were selected from a shortlist of people already assisted by the local social service. The selection process identified potential participants whose vulnerabilities suited the type of services offered. This contributed, according to the interviewees, to the overall success of the projects. Conversely, an inaccurate selection of participants can hinder the success of projects. This emerged in particular in the second round when, according to some interviewees who participated in both rounds, some people with unsuitable profiles were included in the project. This was due to the fact that, for the second round of ALI, only RdC recipients could be involved in the project. In some cases, the vulnerabilities were severe and would have required specialised services (for example, addiction services, psychiatric care); in others, the participant's main need was to find a job. In other words, in these cases the vulnerabilities of the participants did not match the profiles ALI is targeting. This has had negative consequences on the work of operators and on the outcome of individual projects.

A third determining factor was the time available to conduct individual projects. Firstly, ALI operators need time to familiarise with the participants and create a bond of trust with them; secondly, the given the nature of the vulnerabilities of the participants, bringing about a change in their lives requires time. The relevance of this factor emerged, once again, in the second round, which lasted less and during which some individual projects had to be concluded suddenly, causing a negative reaction from the participants.

Finally, a factor that remains in the background, but which was fundamental in the success of the ALI project, was the availability of financial resources. A project such as ALI, which offers a package of qualified and customisable professional services, is more demanding than the low-threshold services usually offered by the local social services. The question of financing becomes all the more pressing when the social services in Pisa, having finished the ALI project, are preparing to translate its experience into its ordinary operating methods.

Conclusion

This chapter described and analysed the experiences of the two rounds of the ALI project. Our analysis indicates that, overall, ALI succeeded in achieving its goal of offering an integrated, personalised, and flexible service package that can provide participants with the tools they need to initiate a path of autonomy. ALI's approach proved effective in tackling the various aspects that determine social vulnerability, when the participants were accurately selected, and the individual projects had enough time to induce a change in the participants. In particular, ALI can be particularly defined as a socially innovative measure, as it brings both product and process innovation.

Product innovation regards ALI's approach to social vulnerability. ALI offers a series of services to address the new social risks that determine social vulnerability in post-industrial societies. Ideally, an analysis of the social impact of ALI interventions would have required a period of observation of the participants to collect data on how their life has changed at the end of the courses. The lack of this data, however, did not prevent conclusions from being drawn about the effectiveness of ALI's tools. The focus groups and the interviews with social workers and cooperative operators made it possible to verify that ALI was able to activate a mechanism of change in the participants, through the logic of individual empowerment. Apart from some critical issues, ALI's tools proved effective, if applied to the right participants and with the right timing. Process innovation – that is, at the organisational level – has been fundamental in ALI's success. On the one hand, the role of the public actor – Pisa SdS – must be highlighted: the organisational role of the SdS allowed to organise the third sector organisations present in the territory in order to offer a structured and articulated package of services aimed at addressing the different aspects of social vulnerability. On the other, coordination of the cooperatives allowed the creation of a network of professionals able to respond promptly to the needs of the participants, and to strengthen the relationship between users and the local social service.

ALI was conceived as an experiment by Pisa SdS, aimed at renewing the operating methods of the local social services. The services offered by ALI are personalised and flexible and it would be impossible, because of budget and personnel limitations, to extend them to the entire public assisted by the local social services. As mentioned by an SdS manager during an interview, one way to integrate the ALI experience into the ordinary operating modes of the social services could be to reorganise the work by differentiating, on the one hand, a low-threshold social secretariat, which users can contact for emergencies or urgent needs (for example, help with paying bills or rent); and, on the other hand, a high-intensity service, structured on the ALI model, aimed at families who were already charges of the social services. Despite its experimental nature and the relatively small number of participants, ALI therefore indicates a possible path of renewal for local social services in Italy. This is all the more significant when the huge investments made possible by Next Generation EU open a window of opportunity to renew European welfare systems.

While the lessons that can be drawn from the ALI experience primarily concern Italy, they are relevant to other countries as well. ALI is a tale of how a local public actor managed to harness the resources present in the territory to provide a modern and integrated package of services. In a context where local welfare systems emerge as a consequence of the transformations of the national welfare states and various actors become increasingly more involved in policy design and implementation (Bode, 2006; Johansson and Panican, 2016; Oosterlynck et al, 2020; Notarnicola et al, 2022), and where the integration of social care services is a priority of many Western countries (see for instance Wodkis et al, 2020; European Commission, 2022), ALI represents an example of how the local public actor can play a decisive role in mobilising the third sector organisation and become a promoter of social innovation.

Notes

[1] The Società della Salute ('health agencies') are the provincial public agencies that administer healthcare and social policies in Tuscany region.

[2] This work deepens and develops ALI's social impact assessment report delivered by the authors to SdS in August 2021. We would like to thank all the participants to the interviews and focus groups. In particular, we would like to thank Maria Atzeni (SdS), Barbara Marchi (SdS) and Serena Voliani (Arnera).

[3] The *Reddito di Cittadinanza* consists of a money benefit linked to the right and duty to undertake personalised projects of social or labour-market inclusion. See Grasso (2020) for an account in English of the RdC.

[4] The assessment of employability consists of assigning a score to an individual's characteristics in the following areas: personal conditions, family conditions and networks, economic situation, education, training and skills, communication skills, language skills in Italian, IT and digital skills, stability of employment contracts, transversal skills and autonomy of movement. Past work experience, skills, possible difficulties in work contexts, and professional interests and aspirations are indicated.

[5] Originally, the following courses were also planned, which could not be provided due to the COVID-19 pandemic: green maintenance, furniture assembly and restoration. Basic and advanced IT training and soft skills training were activated in ALI's second round.

[6] See, for example, Baldini and Gori (2019).

[7] One of the conditions of access to the RdC is a ten-year stay on Italian soil for foreigners.

[8] Data was only available for 50 participants in the second round.

[9] One missing value.

[10] Six missing values.

[11] In Italy, the juvenile courts have the task of child protection and have duties of family courts.

References

Addarii, F. and Lipparini, F. (2017) *Vision and Trends of Social Innovation for Europe*, Luxembourg: Publication Office of the European Union.

Armingeon, K. and Bonoli, G. (eds) (2006) *The Politics of Post-Industrial Welfare States. Adapting Post-War Social Policies to New Social Risks*, New York: Routledge.

Baldini, M. and Gori, C. (2019) 'Il Reddito di Cittadinanza', *Il Mulino*, 2: 269–77.

BEPA. (Bureau of European Policy Advisers). (2010) *Empowering People, Driving Change: Social Innovation in the European* Union , Luxembourg: Publication Office of the European Union.

Bode, I. (2006) 'Disorganized welfare mixes: voluntary agencies and new governance regimes in Western Europe', *Journal of European Social Policy*, 16(4): 346–59.

Bonoli, G. (2005) 'The politics of the new social policies: providing coverage against new social risks in mature welfare states', *Policy & Politics*, 33(3): 431–9.

Bonoli, G. (2006) 'New Social Risks and the Politics of Post-Industrial Social Policies' in K. Armingeon and G. Bonoli (eds) *The Politics of Post-Industrial Welfare States. Adapting Post-War Social Policies to New Social Risks*, New York: Routledge, pp 3–26.

Bonoli, G. (2007) 'Times matters. postindustrialization, new social risks, and welfare state adaptation in advanced industrial democracies', *Comparative Political Studies*, 40(5): 495–520.

Campomori, F. and Casula, M. (2022) 'How to frame the governance dimension of social innovation: theoretical considerations and empirical evidence', *Innovation: The European Journal of Social Science Research*. Available from: https://doi.org/10.1080/13511610.2022.2036952

European Commission. (2013) *Social Innovation Research in the European Union. Approaches, Findings and Future Directions*, Luxembourg: Publications Office of the European Union.

European Commission. (2022) *Study on Social Services with Particular Focus on Personal Targeted Social Services for People in Vulnerable Situations: Final Report*, Luxembourg: Publications Office of the European Union.

Ferrera, M. (1996) 'The "southern model" of welfare in social Europe', *Journal of European Social Policy*, 6(1): 17–37.

Ferrera, M. and Maino, F. (2014) *Social Innovation Beyond the State. Italy's Second Welfare in a European Perspective*, 2WEL Working Paper Series, n 2/2014, Turin, Luigi Einaudi Research and Documentation Centre.

Fougère, M., Segercrantz, B. and Seeck, H. (2017) 'A critical reading of the European Union's social innovation policy discourse: (re)legitimizing neoliberalism', *Organization*, 24(6): 819–43.

Galego, D., Moulaert, F., Brans, M. and Santinha, G. (2021) 'Social innovation & governance: a scoping review', *Innovation: The European Journal of Social Science Research*, 35(2): 265–90.

Grasso, E.A. (2020) 'The Italian *reddito di cittadinanza* in search of identity: a comparative perspective', *Revue de Droit Comparé du Travail et de la Sécurité Sociale*, 4: 28–41.

Grimm, R., Fox, C., Baines, S. and Albertson, K. (2013) 'Social innovation, an answer to contemporary societal challenges? Locating the concept in theory and practice', *Innovation: The European Journal of Social Science Research*, 26(4): 436–55.

Häusermann, S. (2010) *The Politics of Welfare State Reform in Continental Europe. Modernization in Hard Times*, Cambridge: Cambridge University Press.

Jessop, B., Moulaert, F., Hulgård, L. and Hamdouch, A. (2014) 'Social innovation research: a new stage in innovation analysis?', in F. Moulaert, D. MacCallum, A. Mehmood and A. Hamdouch (eds) *The International Handbook on Social Innovation. Collective Action, Social Learning and Transdisciplinary Research*, Cheltenham: Edward Elgar Publishing, pp 110–30.

Johansson, A. and Panica, A. (eds) (2016) *Combating Poverty in Local Welfare Systems*, London: Palgrave MacMillan.

Kapezov, Y. (2015) 'Italian social assistance in the European context: residual innovation and uncertain futures', in U. Ascoli and E. Pavolini (eds) *The Italian welfare state in a European perspective: A comparative analysis*, Bristol: Bristol University Press, pp 101–32.

León, M. and Pavolini, E. (2014) '"Social investment" or back to "familism": The impact of the economic crisis on family and care policies in Italy and Spain', *South European Society and Politics*, 19(3): 353–69.

Levy, J.D. (2021) 'Welfare retrenchment' in D. Béland, S. Leibfried, K.J. Morgan, H. Obinger and C. Pierson (eds) *The Oxford Handbook of the Welfare State* (2nd edn), Oxford: Oxford University Press, pp 767–84.

Madama, I., Maino, F. and Razetti, F. (2019) 'Innovating LTC policy in Italy from the bottom: Lombardy and Piedmont confronting the challenge of inclusive local care environments', *Investigaciones Regionales/Journal of Regional Research*, 44(2): 125–41.

Maino, F. and Neri, S. (2011) 'Explaining welfare reforms in Italy between economy and politics: external constraints and endogenous dynamics', in *Social Policy & Administration* 45(4): 445–64.

Martinelli, F. (2019) 'I divari Nord-Sud nei servizi sociali in Italia. Un regime di cittadinanza differenziato e un freno allo sviluppo del Paese', *Rivista economica del Mezzogiorno* 33(1): 41–79.

Moulaert, F., MacCallum, D. and Hillier, J. (2014) 'Social innovation: intuition, precept, concept, theory and practice', in F. Moulaert, D. MacCallum, A. Mehmood and A. Hamdouch (eds) *The International Handbook on Social Innovation. Collective Action, Social Learning and Transdisciplinary Research*, Cheltenham: Edward Elgar Publishing, pp 13–24.

Moulaert, F., MacCallum, D., Mehmood, A. and Hamdouch, A. (eds) (2014) *The International Handbook on Social Innovation. Collective Action, Social Learning and Transdisciplinary Research*, Cheltenham: Edward Elgar Publishing.

Notarnicola, E., Berloto, S. and Perobelli, E. (2022) 'Social innovation in social care services: actors and roles in the innovation process', *Public Management Review*, 24(2): 182–207.

Oosterlynck, S., Novy, A. and Kapezov, Y. (eds) (2019) *Local Social Innovation to Combat Poverty and Exclusion: A Critical Appraisal*, Bristol: Bristol University Press.

Pavolini, E. (2015) 'How many Italian welfare states are there?', in U. Ascoli and E. Pavolini (eds) *The Italian Welfare State in a European Perspective: A Comparative Analysis*, Bristol: Bristol University Press, pp 283–306.

Pol, E. and Ville, S. (2009) 'Social innovation: buzz word or enduring term?', *The Journal of Socio-Economics*, 38(6): 878–85.

Ranci, C. (2010) 'Social vulnerability in Europe', in C. Ranci (ed.) *Social Vulnerability in Europe. The New Configuration of Social Risks*, London: Palgrave MacMillan, pp 3–24.

Sabato, S., Vanhercke, B. and Verschraegen, G. (2015) *The EU Framework for Social Innovation – Between Entrepreneurship and Policy Experimentation*, ImPRovE Working Paper, 15/21, Antwerp: Herman Deleeck Center for Social Policy – University of Antwerp, Social Policy Committee.

Sacchi, S. and Bastagli, F. (2005) 'Italy–striving uphill but stopping halfway: the troubled journey of the experimental insertion income', in M. Ferrera (ed.) *Welfare State Reform in Southern Europe. Fighting poverty and social exclusion in Italy, Spain, Portugal and Greece*, New York: Routledge, pp 65–109.

Satalkina, L. and Steiner, G. (2022) 'Social Innovation: A Retrospective Perspective', *Minerva*, 60(4): 567–591.

Saraceno, C. (2017) 'Southern European welfare regimes: from differentiation to reconvergence?' in P. Kennett and N. Lendvai-Bainton (eds) *Handbook of European Social Policy*, Cheltenham: Edward Elgar Publishing, pp 218–29.

Taylor-Gooby, P. (ed.) (2004) *New Risks, New Welfare: The Transformation of the European Welfare State*, Oxford: Oxford University Press.

Wodchis, W.P., Shaw, J., Sinha, S., Bhattacharyya, O., Shahid, S. and Anderson, G. (2020) 'Innovative policy supports for integrated health and social care programs in high-income countries', *Health Affairs*, 39(4): 697–703.

9

Inequality within equalities: an institutionalist examination of equalities interest groups engagement in a third sector-government partnership

Amy Sanders

Introduction

This study applies a feminist institutionalist lens to examine the impact on equalities[1] organisations of an innovation of third sector engagement in policy making. It considers how the equalities third sector is shaped by the institution of a third sector-government partnership and it is particularly concerned with the interorganisational relationships within the equalities third sector. The case study is the Third Sector-Welsh Government partnership which is set out in legislation. This places a statutory requirement on Welsh Government to uphold the interests of the third sector in its policy making. The partnership encompasses the Third Sector Partnership Council and a series of Ministerial Meetings which are attended by third sector representatives from 25 thematic networks, eight of which are equalities themes. In this chapter, policy actor accounts are examined to consider which equalities organisations are advantaged or disadvantaged by the formal and informal facets of the institution of this partnership and this is used to consider how the partnership shapes the equalities third sector.

The chapter begins with an analysis of extant literature on organisational interrelationships, and it draws from different strands of literature concerned with equalities theory and voluntary sector studies. It then provides some theoretical and contextual background to demonstrate the significance and nature of the case study partnership. This is followed by an account of the study itself, including how it is underpinned by an analytical framework with a feminist institutionalist lens, the research methods and analytical approach that were used. The substantial part of this chapter is dedicated to the research findings and the discussion of their theoretical implications. This first addresses the informal institutional discourses around collaboration and competition and how these relate to the formal structures of the Partnership. It then progresses to consider other informal institutional norms around policy influence and their implication for the hierarchy of (in)equalities. The analysis reveals how 'race' equality organisations experience institutional disadvantage through the informal discourses and formal partnership structures.[2] The chapter concludes with consideration of the implications for how we understand interorganisational relations within the equalities sector and the implications for policy practices and future research.

The relationship between equalities categories

Examining the relative importance of different equalities categories within policy making can enable us to identify whether some categories deserve wider protection (Krizsan et al, 2012: 2). The literature on the hierarchy of (in)equalities can inform this examination. It recognises that this hierarchy is shaped by resource variation whereby certain equalities groups 'fare better than others' in the allocation of resources (Nott, 2005: 124). The hierarchy also responds to political salience, recognising variance in the degrees of attention and support that different equalities groups garner from politicians (Verloo, 2006; Hancock, 2007). Relatedly, Hancock (2007: 68) describes how pluralism leads to an 'Oppression Olympics' in which groups compete to be seen as the most oppressed. This, has led scholars to ask who has 'ownership' over the equalities policy agenda and which equality demands are rejected (Engeli and Mazur, 2018: 119). The literature tends to focus on which strands are most advantaged. Thus, a gap in the literature is a consideration of those groups that are disadvantaged in institutional settings. Yet, the relationship between equalities organisations is a relatively underexplored area. Consequently, Lombardo and Verloo (2009) call for more research into the dynamics behind the alliances, competition and hostility between different equalities representative groups.

Intersectionality theory can inform our understanding of the interorganisational relationships within equalities. Intersectionality rejects linear understanding that prioritises one protected characteristic and recognises that social identities interact to create complex experiences between and within groups (Crenshaw, 1991; Chaney, 2011; Hankivsky and Cormier, 2011; Winker and Degele, 2011). On the one hand, intersectionality theorists have called for marginalised people to form collaborations (Crenshaw, 1991: 1299; Cho et al, 2013). A recent British example was put forward by Dabiri (2021), who recommended coalitions in recognition of the intersections between 'race' and class in preference to allyships which she related to white saviourism. While collaboration may be associated with intersectionality, it has been conceded that competition between equalities organisations might be found within intersectional practices (Verloo, 2006). For example, Bassel and Emejulu (2010: 520) argue intersectionality can 'inadvertently' promote competition between different groups vying for power in institutional spaces. Similarly, Krizsan et al (2012) maintain that competition is likely when some equalities strands are trying to level-up with more dominant strands.

While this suggests competition is a by-product of intersectionality, an alternative perspective is to recognise competition between equalities groups as a particular form of intersectionality. An often-forgotten facet of Crenshaw's (1991) own intersectionality account is the distinction between 'structural intersectionality', which recognises when one identity category amplifies the disadvantage experienced by another, and 'political intersectionality' which recognises where one identity category can obfuscate or marginalise the disadvantage experienced by another's political strategies. The example Crenshaw (1991: 1252) offers of political intersectionality is when some feminist writings fail 'to interrogate "race" [which] means that the resistance strategies of feminism will often replicate and reinforce the subordination of people of colour'. Political intersectionality is frequently neglected (Verloo, 2006). It is useful in the context of this study because political intersectionality introduces the notion of some equalities strands being advantaged or disadvantaged in relation to others in a way that suggests a form of competition between equalities strands.

Intersectionality theory has been driven forward by Black feminists in Northern America and there has been less scrutiny of the intersections between 'race', gender and class within British academia (Young, 2000; Christoffersen, 2019). The contemporary and historical contexts of place are important for understanding these intersections between equalities categories (Young, 2000). The British context has been obscured by the dominance of the American Civil Rights movement (Eddo-Lodge, 2018; Williams, 2022). One example of how the national context is relevant can be seen with the impact of UK's Equality Act 2010 on intersectionality, since it has embedded a 'logic of separation' through regarding protected characteristics as largely being separate rather than relational (Bassel and Emejulu 2010). Additionally, British scholars have observed how white feminism continues to obscure the experience of Black feminists in the UK more than the USA (Young, 2000; Eddo-Lodge, 2018). A shifting UK political discourse on the relationship between whiteness and working class has also been scrutinised, that fails to interrogate implications for anti-racist approaches (Eddo-Lodge, 2018; Bhambra, 2017). Furthermore, at a different scalar level, Welsh scholars have recognised the multiple identities that interact within Wales (Williams, 2022; Shahwar, 2022). Thus, there is an imperative to understand the relationship between different equalities categories within the specific place context.

The literature on intersectionality and hierarchy of (in)equalities can usefully be brought together with the analysis of interorganisational relations which is found in civil society literatures, since equalities organisations tend to be third sector organisations. Here, it is in the context of the relationship between third sector organisations and government in which different notions of collaboration and competition are explored. This relationship between government and the third sector is described in governance theory where the boundaries between the public, private and voluntary sectors are blurred in both the provision of public services and in policy making (Rhodes, 1997; Stoker, 1998; Newman, 2001). This setting has significant implications for the study of interest mediation, which is pertinent for understanding how equalities organisations advance equalities issues with government (Chaney, 2011).

As with intersectionality theory, within civil society literature, consideration is given to collaboration and competition between organisations. There is a broad literature on the requirement for collaboration and consensus in the third sector and social movements to display unity when seeking to influence government policy (Tilly, 2005; Peters, 2014; Dean, 2017; Lowndes and Skelcher, 1998). However, scholars concerned with service delivery have identified that competition for delivering contracts can undermine collaboration between third sector organisations (Lowndes and Skelcher, 1998; Chapman et al, 2010; Davies, 2011; Egdell and Dutton, 2016). Earlier understandings of competition between organisations developed in the arena of pluralism and agenda-setting theory, in which there is a perceived battle for power when plural actors seek to influence policy (Dahl and Lindblom, 1953) and thus interests compete to shape the policy making agenda (Cobb et al, 1976). Note that 'agenda' here refers to 'the list of subjects' towards which governments pay serious attention (Kingdon, 2011: 3). Thus, competition may be seen in policy making agenda setting as well as service delivery contract allocation. These differing notions of competition and collaboration within state-third sector relations, which have tended to be dealt with discretely in civil society literature, can be used to inform our understanding of interorganisational relations within the equalities field.

In the equalities field, scholars have also recognised that governance settings are important for understanding the relationship between equalities groups. For example, Krizsan et al (2012: 22) argue that the degree of 'interaction, convergence and competition' between equality categories is shaped by how the state engages with those equality groups. One example of this is the tension that might arise between giving voice to those who represent groups or directly to those marginalised people. This has been examined elsewhere (Sanders, 2022). Intersectionality theorists have also identified the multiple sub-categories within any equalities category that might be obscured by those that represent one equalities category (McCall, 2005; Hancock, 2007).

Thus, it has been shown that both equalities and civil society literatures address concerns about collaboration and competition against the backdrop of interest mediation with government. Civil society scholars apply these ideas to organisational interrelationships, but equalities theorists apply them to the relationship between equalities categories. However, there is a growing impetus within the field of voluntary sector studies to apply a critical lens to understandings of the sector and recognise such organisations are sites of struggle in terms of racism, sexism and other forms of exclusion and discrimination (Feit et al, 2017; Feit and Sandberg, 2022). This study aims to be an example of this in bringing these strands together. Attention now turns to the case study partnership, through which these differing notions of interorganisational relations in the context of the equalities organisations are explored.

The case study partnership

There are some excellent examples of how equalities theorists have examined interest mediation at multiple levels of governance. For example, Krizsan et al (2012) did a comparative institutional analysis across European countries to consider how equalities interest groups engaged with governments. However, fewer equalities scholars have focused specifically at the sub-state level to examine a broad notion of equalities interest mediation (Hankivsky et al, 2019), with a few notable exceptions (for example, Hankivsky et al, 2019; Chaney, 2011; Parken, 2010). Therefore, devolution provides 'a window of opportunity' for sub-state analysis of equalities groups' policy influence (Donaghy, 2004: 52; Chaney, 2011). This study seeks to address this gap by applying its focus to equalities interest mediation at a sub-state level.

Both partnerships and networks feature in governance literature (Newman 2001). While informal networks have been subjected to substantial scrutiny (for example, Stoker 1998; Rhodes 2007), less attention has been given to partnerships, which have more formal structures and procedures (Lowndes and Skelcher 1998). Therefore, it is apposite to examine how third sector organisations engage with the executive through a partnership. Devolution in Wales embraced a partnership approach (Heley and Moles, 2012). The case study partnership is just one example of this. It is the formal, statutory partnership between Welsh Government and the third sector, which is set out in legislation, specifically, the Government of Wales Act (GOWA) (1998: s114; superseded by GOWA 2006: s74). It requires the Welsh Government to uphold the interests of the sector and publish a Third Sector Scheme which will outline how the government will consult and assist the sector. It formed part of a partnership approach that was seen in the wider UK strategy of New Labour and the political discourses of Blair's Third Way (Dicks et al, 2001). The UK's Third Way rhetoric was also mirrored by international theorising about third sector-government relations (Salamon and Toepler, 2015). Consequently, third sector-government partnerships are of growing global concern.

Yet, the embedding of a civil society partnership in legislation particularly put the voluntary sector at the centre of Welsh politics (Dicks et al, 2001). Thus, the singular nature of this partnership is its legal grounding (Birrell, 2009; Dicks et al, 2001). This makes it a 'revelatory case' (Yin, 2014: 48), rendering Welsh devolution a key locus to explore contemporary third sector-government relations.

It is also appropriate to examine how equalities organisations are engaged within this partnership because Welsh Government made a commitment to have 'due regard to the principle that there should be equality of opportunity for all people' under the same legislation that created the statutory partnership. (GOWA 1998: s.120, 2006, s.77) This equalities clause is evidence that devolution provided a critical juncture for the advancement of equalities in Welsh policy making (Minto and Parken, 2020). The commitment to 'all people' means that Welsh Government has adopted a multi-strand equalities approach which makes Wales a valuable context for examining broader equalities engagement (Parken, 2010). These developments should be understood in the context of the impetus for a new politics founded on inclusion which dominated Welsh pro-devolution rhetoric (Chaney and Fevre, 2001). Given these pioneering developments, it is appropriate to examine how such a partnership is being used to advance equalities.

An overview of the partnership structure is as follows: it includes the Third Sector Partnership Council (TSPC) and a series of ministerial meetings addressing different cabinet portfolios. These are managed by Wales Council for Voluntary Action (WCVA), the representative body of the Welsh third sector. The third sector representatives who attend these meetings are drawn from 25 thematic third sector networks. Of these, eight are directly concerned with an equalities category (gender, sexuality, youth, children and families, older people, disability, religion and ethnic minorities), while other thematic networks are concerned with multiple equalities categories. The collective partnership mechanisms of the TSPC, ministerial meetings and thematic third sector networks will henceforward be referred to as 'the Partnership'.

Consideration is now given to how the Partnership was examined in this study.

About this study

The aforementioned analysis brought together the equalities literature on intersectionality and hierarchy of (in)equalities with diverse strands of literature concerned with collaboration and competition in voluntary sector studies. An analytical framework was developed that brought together these literatures using an overarching lens of feminist institutionalism. Feminist institutionalism is concerned with how formal and informal institutional configurations can promote or frustrate equality (Mackay, 2011). This study broadens feminist institutionalism to scrutinise how wider equalities relations are impacted by an institution. This leans on intersectionality theory (Crenshaw, 1991) to justify this wider view of equalities. A wider equalities lens can draw on advances in feminist theory. Where feminist institutionalists seek to identify how gendered power relations are constructed or maintained by institutions (Mackay et al, 2010; Mackay, 2011), this broader analysis of equalities allows an examination of the power relations between equalities categories within an institution. This approach acknowledges the iterative, dynamic nature of institutions, wherein the equalities third sector seeks to influence government policy making, but the institution also impacts on the equalities third sector itself. This allows for a scrutiny of how some equalities organisations might be institutionally advantaged or disadvantaged. This analysis of extant literature led to the development of the research question: 'how is the equalities sector shaped by the institution of the third sector–government partnership?'

In adopting a feminist institutionalist lens that is informed by intersectionality, it is important to address some related ethical considerations. Intersectionality originated with a focus on the intersections between 'race', gender and class (Crenshaw, 1991). There has been some concern either that it has subsequently been coopted by white feminists within gender studies which has obscured the Black female scholars who advanced it, or that it has been mobilised to look at a broader range of equality categories, which are relationally opposite to the original concerns of intersectionality (Christoffersen, 2019). Certainly, this latter critique could be levelled at this study's broad interpretation of equalities and I must be reflexive on the former critique, given that I can be racialised as a white feminist scholar. Prominent British theorists concerned with anti-racism have rejected essentialist, exclusivist approaches that place the onus on people with lived expereince instead calling for a coalition of scholars to critically engage with the intersectional processes of hierarchical construction (Dabiri, 2021; Young, 2000). This paper is a response to this call. The nuance of these ethical considerations has been well explored by Christoffersen (2019) and I share her positioning as a reflexive researcher who is critical of appropriations of intersectionality, while acknowledging that the criticism of complicity can be validly applied to this study. This uncomfortable reflexivity cannot and should not be easily resolved (Christoffersen, 2019: 417).

Another concern is that some interpretations of intersectionality suggest that analysis of the hierarchies of equalities is flawed because it reinforces the essentialism that intersectionality seeks to overcome (Young, 2000). However, there are multiple forms of intersectionality, including an analysis of the intersections within a category (intra-categorical intersectionality) (McCall, 2005). Furthermore, as has been shown with the previous discussion of political intersectionality, it is possible to use intersectionality to understand how one equalities category can obfuscate another (Crenshaw, 1991). Thus, this study maintains that an analysis of the relationship between equalities organisations in the context of the hierarchy of (in)equalities is consistent with intersectionality theory.

Moving from ethical considerations to data collection, this study used semi-structured, elite interviews as its primary data collection method. Purposive sampling was utilised to identify 41 policy actors from Welsh Government, WCVA and the Equalities Third Sector Organisations. These interviews were recorded and then transcribed. The analytical framework informed the nature of the research questions and interview schedule. It also shaped the initial coding framework that was deployed using NVivo software. This coding framework was iteratively developed throughout the analysis. The data were analysed using discourse analysis. Given the variety of discourse analysis approaches (Potter, 2004), it is worth noting that this study follows the problem-orientated discourse analysis described by Wodak (2001: 69). In this, the specific research questions are used to identify how these discursive devices and rhetorical and interactional strategies are relevant (Goodman, 2017).

Findings

Informal institutional discourses on collaboration and competition

In interviewees' accounts of the Partnership's informal norms, the equalities organisations commonly described themselves as working well together, as this excerpt typifies:

> 'Thinking about ... all the different interactions I've had with other equalities organisations, I feel like, obviously we all fight our corner for our cohort of people we're representing ... but I feel that we're quite united in what we want to see ... I think we're all united and we're all fighting for equality.' (Participant 32, Equalities Organisation)

The sense of unity across the equalities third sector demonstrated here resonates with the calls from intersectionality theorists for oppressed or marginalised people to form alliances and coalitions (Crenshaw 1991: 1299; Cho et al, 2013). Furthermore, the equalities policy actors described working collaboratively to effectively influence government, as was captured by this interviewee: "The reasons we work so much in coalition or alliances or networks is because ... many voices saying the same thing are much stronger than just one voice, saying the same thing" (Participant 41, Equalities Organisation). This chimes with the civil society literature that recognises the value of collaboration for presenting a unified voice (Tilly, 2005; Dean, 2017).

In addition to references to the informal norm of collaboration within policy actors' accounts of the partnership, there was also considerable discourse about competition between equalities representatives. Some participants described competing to get an item on the agenda, as seen here:

> 'Our role was knowing what [our] sector are concerned about and presenting that, and fighting for our bit of air space ... Where everybody is trying to represent their bit ... you're trying to wrestle with somebody who wants to talk for fifteen minutes about [something else].' (Participant 37, Equalities Organisation)

The terms *'fighting'* and *'wrestling'* conveys the competitive nature of their Partnership engagement. One equalities interviewee described the competition as an inevitable consequence of "a pluralistic model" in which "you've got government at the centre and you've got all these different influences trying to get their say" (Participant 40, Equalities Organisation). These informal discourses are concerned with equalities organisations competing to influence the agenda both in terms of the literal Partnership agenda but also the associated government priorities, as described in agenda-setting theory (Kingdon, 2011).

In addition to the competition to set the Partnership agenda, accounts of competition for funding were also present and these dominated accounts of interorganisational relations. For example, this WCVA interviewee stated: "In funding, they [organisations] might compete but in terms of getting their message across, they do work together" (Participant 10, WCVA). This excerpt is typical of interviewees' accounts of collaboration which foreground funding competition. As noted, it is well-documented in the third sector literature that funding leads to competition between organisations. However, this funding competition was not directly linked to the Partnership. Although Partnership representatives get a small stipend, known as the Partnership Capacity Fund, organisations did not tend to compete for this. Interviewees' accounts revealed it was not seen as a sum worthy of competition between organisations, since "the funding pot isn't big enough to make it worth fighting for" (Participant 8, WCVA). In any case, the Partnership representatives were supposed to be selected through an "election" (Participant 7, WCVA). Thus, any tendency for funding-competition between equalities organisations was external to the Partnership stipend.

However, it should be noted that the relationship between funding-competition and competition to be a representative organisation cannot easily be disaggregated. Interviewee accounts revealed there are many other funds allocated by Welsh Government unrelated to the Partnership. Partnership representatives were recipients of funds administered by the Welsh Government's Equalities Unit, the Health and Social Services division, the Housing Department and Education Department. Additionally, there were also references made to contracts to deliver services from various Welsh Government departments. These sources of Welsh Government money allocated via a competitive process fuelled the discourse around competing equalities organisations. For example:

> 'They [Welsh Government] try to develop various mechanisms through funding, where they've ... said one organisation to represent all race, one organisation to represent all disability, one organisation to represent all women ... [They could have said] "We want you to come together ... as a third sector and work in a joined way". But instead, they have pitted everyone [against each other] because of that money, and because they want one person to represent.' (Participant 30, Equalities Organisation)

This excerpt reveals that funds administered by other Welsh Government departments were seen to have caused animosity between equalities organisations. Although such competition was associated with other Welsh Government funds, the Partnership's ethos of one representative for each network fuelled the perception that Welsh Government expected there to be only one lead organisation for each identity category. As this participant explained; "the concept of being a national representative organisation for even just a protected characteristic is flawed ... That loses the plurality that is actually really important" (Participant 28, Equalities Organisation). Welsh Government's role in generating this competition between equalities organisations was criticised, as one interviewee explained:

> 'The way that Welsh Government has almost acted as a kind of kingmaker and the way that they appoint so-called lead bodies for "race" or gender or so on, is, in itself, divisive ... I think they are kind of acting as the crowning people and then obviously that's not going to go down well with other groups.' (Participant 33, Equalities Organisation)

This notion of the 'kingmaker' is crucial to understanding the conflicts between equalities organisations. It is a different form of competition than is usually identified by the interest group scholars.

However, the notion of having one representative per strand is discussed in equalities literature. Squires (2005: 375) argued against single representatives for an equalities strand, because it can essentialise or reify the identity, thereby 'obscuring intra-group divisions and inter-group commonalities'. Similarly, Mansbridge (1999: 636) maintained that a variety of representatives are needed to provide the heterogeneous, 'complex and internally contested perspectives'. Yet the cost of having such representative structures to interorganisational relations and the association with public funding allocation is less well understood. Here, the interview data shows the selection of representative is tied with funding allocation, and this is how interorganisational animosity is created.

In the earlier account, there was competition between equalities 'strands' over agenda items. However, here, in competing to be known as the one representative for their identity category, the competition is between organisations within an equalities strand. Other researchers have called for the elimination of funding structures that create competition between equalities strands (Hankivsky et al, 2019), but these findings reveal how funding creates complex relationships between organisations within strands. This study shows the competition between strands to get items on the agenda is an expected consequence of pluralism. However, the competition within strands to be seen as the one representative is perceived by interviewees as much more divisive. This is illustrated by this quote: "It's basically Game of Thrones, but with the TSPC" (Participant 8, Equalities Organisation). From a feminist institutionalist perspective, the latter form of competition is a consequence of the formal institutional structure of the Partnership, which laid the foundation for one equalities organisation per identity category, and this was then perceived to underpin the Welsh Government funding criteria.

According to the interviewees, the equalities organisations that were impacted most directly by this were the 'race' equality organisations. As this official described: "there has been quite a lot of disharmony between BME (Black and Minority Ethnic) organisations" (Participant 19, Welsh Government). There are "historical reasons" (Participant 21, Welsh Government) why "race" representation has been particularly contentious in Wales. This historical context refers to when the mantle of representation had passed from "the Black Voluntary Sector Network Wales," to a '"Communities First ... umbrella body" and then "the All Wales Ethnic Minorities Association"' (AWEMA) (Participant 6, WCVA). The latter organisation became discredited for management impropriety, which led to a vacuum that needed to be filled. Consequently, Welsh Government funding for a lead 'race' representative is cited by multiple policy actors as the cause of considerable tension between 'race' equality organisations.

Thus, the Partnership's formal structures have led to competition to become the recognised representative for Welsh Government, not only in the Partnership but in the wider sphere of Welsh Government-funded programmes too and this has particularly disadvantaged 'race' equality organisations. The final analysis of this chapter consider how other informal institutional norms of the Partnership impact on the equalities interorganisational relations.

Informal institutional factors shaping the equalities hierarchy

When interviewees were asked about which equalities organisations dominated policy influence, they tended to shy away from identifying the most influential equalities organisations within the Partnership, replying with answers like "You will probably get a different answers from whoever you ask" (Participant 22, Welsh Government). Interviewees' failure to identify equalities organisations advantaged in the Partnership makes it difficult to consider whether any equalities identity strands do have a privileged position. However, one equalities strand was clearly identified as disadvantaged in the informal Partnership discourses. Consistent with the previous findings, 'race' equality organisations were disadvantaged by the informal institutional norms and discourses in the ways that will now be detailed.

Policy actors across Welsh Government, WCVA and other equalities third sector organisations often alluded to the tensions among 'race' equality organisations. The funding tensions were resented by some equalities organisations, as described here: "Some of the equality meetings will get over-dominated by BME issues ... BME groups want everything to be funded for BME" (Participant 40, Equalities Organisation). Furthermore, others felt that this made them far from ideal as collaborative partners, as this quote reveals: "Race organisations, you get involved with at your peril to be honest" (Participant 38, Equalities Organisation).

Chapman et al (2010) have previously described how certain third sector representatives might be seen as 'troublesome' by public sector officials but here we see this labelling of 'race' equality organisations as 'troublesome' could also be reinforced by other equalities organisations. Where feminist institutionalists have previously recognised informal discourses can marginalise gender representatives (Mackay and Krook, 2011), here discourses of other Partnership actors, including other equalities organisations, can marginalise 'race' equality organisations.

There were other informal institutional norms of the Partnership that acted against 'race' equality organisations. The quality that dominated the policy actors' responses to questions about how they achieved policy influence through the Partnership, was the necessity to "represent themselves professionally" (Participant 17, Welsh Government). Moreover, professionalism was equated with good behaviour in the policy actor accounts, whereby representatives were expected to be "polite and reasonable" (Participant 32, Equalities Organisation). Examples of behaviour to be avoided were given, such as: "Don't be rude to the minister" (Participant 23, Equalities Organisation) and avoid "colouring your reputation in ministerial eyes" (Participant 21, Welsh Government). Officials described inappropriate behaviour from the past such as entering meetings late, using laptops or taking phone calls during ministerial meetings. These officials' accounts did not identify a particular group of organisations but attributed such behaviours to the third sector generally.

However, one interviewee observed how such expectations about professionalism and behaviour had impacted 'race' equality organisations, as seen here:

> 'There has always been excuses as to why it's not working from the Welsh Government perspective [like] "we don't really think that this is being done professionally" … They probably don't think that they ("race" equality representatives) are professional enough to be able to engage at that level. It is snobbery really.' (Participant 30, Equalities Organisation)

The previous account from a 'race' equality organisation interviewee indicates the impact on an organisation's perception of Welsh Government, who interpreted such criticisms as being specifically directed at 'race' equality organisations. Correspondingly, an interviewee from another organisation within the 'race' equality sector felt that this scrutiny of 'race' equality organisations' behaviour stretched back to the historic scandal of management impropriety (discussed previously), as explained here:

> 'The sadness for many people was that organisations pulled back from a lot of "race" equality. And we sensed that we were punished for being BME-led … Everywhere we went, people were like "You've got to see [good] governance". "You've got to check accountability". … and you just get this patronising sense of "Prove you're trustworthy" … It's shocking. And I think it's institutional racism actually.' (Participant 34, Equalities Organisation)

This interviewee relates scrutiny of professional practices to the charitable scandal that led to a loss of trust in 'race' equality organisations. The questioning of third sector professionalism against the backdrop of charitable scandals is a contemporary feature of the UK media (Zimmer and Pahl, 2018). Voluntary sector scholars have detailed the impact on the trust in the sector of such discourses (Milbourne and Cushman, 2013; Aiken and Taylor, 2019). Notably, charity scandals were dominating the headlines at the time of the interviews. This impacted how Welsh Government interacted with the sector, as this participant stated: "One organisation that hits the press for the wrong reason can impact on so many other organisations … As a government … we need reassurance that that's not going to happen again"

(Participant 18, Welsh Government). Scholars' accounts of this faltering trust in the third sector's professionalism attribute it to the third sector as a whole. However, the previous excerpts demonstrate that some 'race' equality organisations perceived this lack of trust in organisational management was directed at them.

Another set of qualities that third sector representatives should display according to institutional discourses was clarity and brevity. Thus, interviewees explained "presentation skills are really important" (Participant 6, WCVA) and organisations need to "put across a reasoned argument" which is "evidence-based [with a] mix between actual empirical evidence and some stories that bring it to life" (Participant 5, WCVA). The demand for brevity was related to the ministers, as these officials explained, "Cabinet Secretary interest in things can switch" (Participant 9, WCVA) and the third sector need to know how not to "turn off a minister's attention" (Participant 21, Welsh Government).

Again, such an institutional norm was deemed problematic by one 'race' equality representative:

> '[Welsh Government] don't tend to want to know about how passionate you are about a topic. [laughs] They just want a bog-standard presentation that is clean cut and is very clinical in a sense. Not too much effusive, passionate, sweating, and preaching. They just want to hit the nail on the head ... When you're dealing with people from diverse backgrounds, we express ourselves differently and I think there has to be a freshness in the way that Welsh Government come to the table with ethnic minority groups. Not to impose their style of working.' (Participant 34, Equalities Organisation)

This account demonstrates that Welsh Government's expectation on third sector organisations' communication style has the potential to structurally discriminate against 'race' equality organisations.

This finding should be compared with feminist theorists' accounts of the tendency to see male behaviour as the norm which can lead to gendered discrimination (Celis and Lovenduski, 2018; Krook and Mackay, 2011; Squires, 2005). Here we see a related obstacle for 'race' equality organisations, in which the norms that define how they were expected to communicate and evidence their claims has cultural discrimination underpinning it.

Another tool for achieving policy influence in Welsh Government and the third sector accounts was the importance of utilising informal relationships. As this official explained: "100%–98% of our relationships are informal" (Participant 12, Welsh Government). Interviewees frequently cited these informal relationships as an effective way to advance equalities policy interests, as seen here:

> 'Not at the meetings, not at the formal thing, the real work should be done in between [with] people on both sides working together to make things happen ... The [Partnership] meetings then are kind of a formal overlay ... but the real hard work should be done outside of the meetings.' (Participant 1, Welsh Government)

As this excerpt illustrates, informal relationships are viewed as an acceptable and vital method for achieving policy influence.

However, one interviewee from a 'race' equality organisation expressed great discomfort at the notion of developing such informal relationships:

> 'I don't like this highly personalised approach where it's all about just getting that minister to agree with you ... You can see that people are playing that game. And sometimes I think we should be playing that game, but I don't really want to. It's not something that we do naturally. But people do cosy up to ministers and politicians a lot ... It all seems a very elitist exercise ... It just seems very anti-democratic to me. You're not meant to be just sucking up to powerful people.' (Participant 33, Equalities Organisation)

Given the additional scrutiny that the 'race' equality organisations felt themselves to be under, which was detailed earlier, it is unsurprising that they showed caution in developing relationships that might be deemed improper. However, as has been shown, other policy actors across Welsh Government, WCVA and equality organisations viewed it as an acceptable influencing tool. Therefore, yet again, this 'race' equality organisation was disadvantaged because it was not adopting claims-making tools that other equality organisations were successfully deploying.

Feminist theorists refer to the homosocial capital that is born out of interpersonal relationships (Celis and Lovenduski, 2018). Though they were describing gender inequality, these concepts apply here to other equality organisations' ability to build informal relationships. Here, it is the 'race' equality organisations that lacked the opportunity to build these informal interpersonal relations. Other equalities organisations were able to utilise the informal relationships which therefore gave 'race' equality organisations a disadvantage in influencing policy.

Conclusion

In the foregoing discussion, a feminist institutionalist lens was used to explore how the Partnership's formal institutional structure and informal institutional discourses and norms have shaped the equalities third sector with respect to their interorganisational relations. The analysis reveals different notions of collaboration and competition coexisting and influencing interorganisational relations. The one equalities strand demonstrably disadvantaged in the Partnership was 'race' equality. 'Race' equality organisations are found to face structural disadvantage in the formal institutional structures of thematic networks and in informal institutional discourses on competition and policy-influencing norms. These institutional factors led to intra-strand tensions, resulting in the tarnishing of their reputation, and they were viewed as the deviant case in the equalities portfolio. These factors undermined their trust in Partnering with each other and Welsh Government. Furthermore, 'race' equality organisations have not adopted the claims-making strategies that other equalities organisations have applied in their policy influencing. Thus, informal institutional practices utilised within the institution of the Partnership by other equalities organisations have disadvantaged 'race' equality organisations, which should be recognised as a form of political intersectionality.

While much of the literature around the hierarchy of (in)equalities refers to the 'Oppression Olympics' and tends to focus on which identity categories are leading in securing dominance in the political agenda (Hancock, 2007), this study's approach differs by identifying the institutional factors that disadvantage certain equality identity categories. Therefore, it makes a new contribution to knowledge by drawing attention to the existence of disadvantaged categories in the hierarchy of (in)equalities in the context of sub-state partnerships. A future implication for research is to recognise that a broad approach to understanding equalities strategies should consider which equalities strands face institutional disadvantage.

Another contribution this study makes to knowledge is in demonstrating how theory developed by feminist scholars can be extended to a broader equalities context. It has also shown that informal factors alongside formal structures are important for the relative position of different equalities strands. The feminist institutionalist lens of this study has shown that some equalities organisations face structural disadvantages borne out of informal norms and discourses, even where they are given representation within the formal institutional structures. One area for further theoretical development is to consider the implication for equalities strategies to apply equality of opportunity considerations to equalities organisations' engagement in such governance mechanisms.

A limitation of this study has been that it restricted its scope to exploring the significance of one sub-state partnership. This sub-state level of analysis has been useful because it addresses a key gap in the literature concerning the relationship between the equalities third sector and state policy actors at a devolved level of government. However, there is scope for a future study to explore the ways that other tiers of governance might influence the interrelationships of the third sector. Another area ripe for further examination is a comparative study of how other sub-state institutional structures shape the equalities third sector and the interrelationship between equalities organisations or even how these might change over time.

Further work could be done in relating hierarchies of (in)equalities with political intersectionality, particularly in relation to COVID-19. The pandemic has created competing equalities agendas as some equalities groups are especially vulnerable to COVID-19, while others represent people who experience greater disadvantages from social distancing policies or the economic impact of the pandemic and now the Ukraine war. Understanding which issues gain political salience is pivotal to examining the impact on hierarchies between equalities categories and equalities interorganisational relationships.

The particular disadvantage experienced by 'race' equality organisations needs to be scrutinised further, especially with recent political discourses around #BlackLivesMatter to examine variable practices for inclusion of 'race' equality organisation in state-third sector relations.

While this account reveals multiple institutional facets that have disadvantaged 'race' equalities organisations in this partnership with Welsh Government, caution should be shown in apportioning blame. It must be remembered that Wales has shown innovation in advancing equalities by embedding the equalities clause in legislation. The 'race' equality organisations are given a formal position through which they can influence government policy making through this partnership. Moreover, it should be noted that 'race' equality organisations have previously been described as being in tension with other equality strands in Britain (Krizsan et al, 2012). Thus, these institutional disadvantages cannot be assumed to be limited to this Welsh setting. Additionally, a feminist institutionalist lens requires us to accept that informal institutional norms and discourses can subvert formal equalities commitments (Chappell and Waylen, 2013). Lessons for practice can be learnt from such an analysis. Since data collection, Welsh Government sought to address structural inequality with the 2022 publication of Welsh Government's 'Anti-Racist Wales Action Plan'. This recognises disadvantage is embedded in organisations' policies, processes and ways of working. However, it focuses on individuals' experiences of racism, neglecting the disadvantages faced by 'race' equality organisations. Yet it is evidence that Welsh Government continues to reflect on how to advance 'race' equality.

Wider lessons can be drawn to inform practice in other state-third sector settings. One recommendation for practice is that governments should avoid structuring future funding allocation in a way that implicitly suggests one organisation has been designated as the leading representative organisation within that field. Additional support could be offered for 'race' equality organisations to redress any particular disadvantage these organisations have faced. For example, training in policy influencing practices could be made available. Due consideration should be given to how government expectations for brevity, clarity and professionalism can be exclusionary. Instead, innovative mechanisms should be developed that enable equalities organisations to communicate with governments in alternative ways that celebrate cultural diversity. This could also be tied in with innovative ways to build in direct participation of stakeholders into such governance mechanisms.

To conclude, it is evident that through accepting that certain equalities organisations might face disadvantages in institutional structures, this provides new recommendations for practice in promoting equality of opportunity for equalities organisations' engagement in governance. It also opens up new scope for theorising equalities policy making. In this study it has enabled us to contribute to the hierarchy of (in)equalities literature and identify a form of political intersectionality, hitherto neglected by intersectionality scholars.

Notes

[1] Equalities organisations refers to those third sector organisations that seek to represent the interests of particular constituencies facing disadvantage or discrimination with respect to, for example, gender, 'race', religion, age, disability, sexuality, class and so on. (Sanders, 2022). The plural 'equalities' is an established trend in equalities theory in recognition of the many facets of equality (Chaney, 2011). There are multiple identity categories, to which it might refer and also, intersectionality theory reminds us that there are a multitude of sub-categories that can be found within and across identity categories (Hancock, 2007).

[2] The term 'race' is in quotation marks to recognise that it is a social and legal construction (Obasogie, 2015). This position is derived from critical 'race' theory and the insights on 'racialism', which refers to the erroneous presumption that racial identity objectively exists (Crenshaw et al, 2018, p. 916). 'Race' equality is used in preference to 'BAME' (Black, Asian and minority ethnic) which has been critiqued as a synonym for 'not-white' that pathologises racialised people rather than racism itself (Adebisi, 2019).

References

Adebisi, F.I. (2019) 'The Only Accurate Part of 'BAME' is the 'and' ...'. Available from: https://folukeafrica.com/the-only-acceptable-part-of-bame-is-the-and/ [Accessed 6 June 2020].

Aiken, M. and Taylor, M. (2019) 'Civic action and volunteering: the changing space for popular engagement in England', *Voluntas: International Journal of Voluntary and Nonprofit Organizations*, 30(1): 15–28.

Bassel, L. and Emejulu, A. (2010) 'Struggles for institutional space in France and the United Kingdom: intersectionality and the politics of policy', *Politics & Gender*, 6(4): 517–44.

Bhambra, G.K. (2017) 'Brexit, Trump, and "methodological whiteness": on the misrecognition of race and class', *The British Journal of Sociology*, 68(1): 214–32.

Birrell, D. (2009) *The Impact of Devolution on Social Policy*, Bristol: Policy Press.

Celis, K. and Lovenduski, J. (2018) 'Power struggles: gender equality in political representation', *European Journal of Politics and Gender*, 1(1–2): 149–66.

Chaney, P. (2011) *Equality and Public Policy – Exploring the Impact of Devolution in the UK*, Cardiff: University of Wales Press.

Chaney, P. and Fevre, R. (2001) 'Ron Davies and the cult of inclusiveness: devolution and participation in Wales', *Contemporary Wales*, 14(1): 21–49.

Chapman, T., Brown, J., Ford, C., Baxter, B., (2010) 'Trouble with champions: local public sector–third sector partnerships and the future prospects for collaborative governance in the UK', *Policy Studies*, 31(6): 613–30.

Chappell, L. and Waylen, G. (2013) 'Gender and the hidden life of institutions', *Public Administration (London)*, 91(3): 599–615.

Cho, S., Crenshaw, K. and McCall, L. (2013) 'Towards a field of intersectionality studies: theory, applictions, and praxis', *Signs: Journal of Women in Culture and Society*, 38(4): 785–810.

Christoffersen, A. (2019) 'Researching intersectionality: ethical issues', *Ethics and Social Welfare*, 12(4): 414–21.

Cobb, R., Ross, J.K. and Ross, M.H. (1976) 'Agenda building as a comparative political process', *American Political Science Review*, 70(1): 126–38.

Crenshaw, K. (1991) 'Mapping the margins: intersectionality, identity politics, and violence against women of colour', *Stanford Law Review*, 43(6): 1241–300.

Crenshaw, K., Gotanda, N., Peller, G., Thomas, K. (2007) '"Introduction," Critical Race Theory: The Key Writings that Formed the Movement', *The New Press*, May 1996. *The Canon of American Legal Thought*, 887–925, doi:10.23943/9780691186429-023 10.1515/9780691186429-023

Dabiri, E. (2021) *What White People can do Next: From Allyship to Coalition*, Dublin: Penguin.

Dahl, R.A. and Lindblom, C.E. (1953) *Politics, Economics and Welfare*, New York: Harper.

Davies, S. (2011) 'Outsourcing, public sector reform and the changed character of the UK state-voluntary sector relationship', *International Journal of Public Sector Management*, 24(7): 641–9.

Dean, R.J. (2017) 'Beyond radicalism and resignation: the competing logics for public participation in policy decisions', *Policy and Politics*, 45(2): 213–30.

Dicks, B., Hall, T. and Pithouse, A. (2001) 'The National Assembly and the voluntary sector: an equal partnership?', in Chaney, P., Hall, T. and Pithouse, A. (eds) *New Governance – New Democracy?: Post-Devolution Wales*, Cardiff: University of Wales Press, pp 102–25.

Donaghy, T.B. (2004) 'Mainstreaming: Northern Ireland's participative-democratic approach', *Policy and Politics*, 32(1): 49–62.

Eddo-Lodge, R. (2018) *Why I'm No Longer Talking to White People about Race*, London: Bloomsbury.

Egdell, V. and Dutton, M. (2017) 'Third sector independence: relations with the state in an age of austerity', *Voluntary Sector Review*, 8(1). Available from: Doi: 10.1332/204080516x14739278719772

Engeli, I. and Mazur, A. (2018) 'Taking implementation seriously in assessing success: the politics of gender equality policy', *European Journal of Politics and Gender*, 1(1–2): 111–29.

Feit, M.E., Blalock, A.E. and Nguyen, K. (2017) 'Making diversity count: critical race theory as a lens on the present and future of nonprofit education', *Journal of Nonprofit Education & Leadership*, 7(1).

Feit, M.E. and Sandberg, B. (2022) 'The dissonance of "doing good": fostering critical pedagogy to challenge the selective tradition of nonprofit management education', *Public Integrity*, 24(4–5): 486–503.

Goodman, S. (2017) 'How to conduct a psychological discourse analysis', *Critical Approaches to Discourse Analysis across Disciplines*, 9(2): 142–53.

Hancock, A-M. (2007) 'When multiplication doesn't equal quick addition: examining intersectionality as a research paradigm', *Perspectives on Politics*, 5(1): 63–79.

Hankivsky, O. and Cormier, R. (2011) 'Intersectionality and public policy: some lessons from existing models', *Political Research Quarterly*, 64(1): 217–29.

Hankivsky, O., de Merich, D. and Christoffersen, A. (2019) 'Equalities "devolved": experiences in mainstreaming across the UK devolved powers post-Equality Act 2010', *British Politics*, 14(2): 141–161 Available from: Doi: 10.1057/s41293-018-00102-3: xocs:firstpage xmlns:xocs=""/

Heley, J. and Moles, K. (2012) 'Partnership working in regions: reflections on local government collaboration in Wales', *Regional Science Policy & Practice*, 4(2): 139–53.

Kingdon, J.W. (2011) *Agendas, Alternatives, and Public Policies*, Boston, Mass: Longman.

Krizsan, A., Skjeie, H. and Squires, J. (2012) *Institutionalizing Intersectionality: The Changing Nature of European Equality Regimes*, Basingstoke: Palgrave Macmillan

Krook, M.L. and Mackay, F. (2011) 'Introduction: gender, politics, and institutions', in Mackay, F. and Krook, M.L. (eds) *Gender, Politics and Institutions: Towards a Feminist Institutionalism*, Basingstoke, New York: Palgrave Macmillan.

Lombardo, E. and Verloo, M. (2009) 'Institutionalizing intersectionality in the European Union?: policy development and contestations', *International Feminist Journal of Politics*, 11(4): 478–95.

Lowndes, V. and Skelcher, C. (1998) 'The dynamics of multi-organizational partnerships: an analysis of changing modes of governance', *Public Administration*, 76(2): 313–33.

Mackay, F. (2011) 'Conclusion: towards a feminist institutionalism', in Mackay, F. and Krook, M.L. (eds) *Gender, Politics and Institutions: Towards a Feminist Institutionalism*, Basingstoke, New York: Palgrave Macmillan, pp 181–96.

Mackay, F., Kenny, M. and Chappell, L. (2010) 'New institutionalism through a gender lens: towards a feminist institutionalism?', *International Political Science Review/Revue internationale de science politique*, 31(5): 573–88.

Mansbridge, J. (1999) 'Should Blacks represent Blacks and women represent women? A contingent "Yes"', *The Journal of Politics*, 61(3): 628–57.

McCall, L. (2005) 'The complexity of intersectionality', *Signs: Journal of Women in Culture and Society*, 30(3): 1771–800.

Milbourne, L. and Cushman, M. (2013) 'From the third sector to the big society: how changing UK government policies have eroded third sector trust', *Voluntas: International Journal of Voluntary and Nonprofit Organizations*, 24(2): 485–508.

Minto, R. and Parken, A. (2020) 'The European Union and regional gender equality agendas: Wales in the shadow of Brexit', *Regional Studies*, 55(9): 1550–1560 Available from: Doi: 10.1080/00343404.2020.1826422. 1–11

Newman, J. (2001) *Modernising Governance New Labour, Policy and Society*, London: Sage.

Nott, S. (2005) 'Securing mainstreaming in a hostile political environment', *International Journal of Discrimination and the Law*, 8(1–2): 121–40.

Obasogie, O.K. (2015) *The Constitution of Identity*, Hoboken, NJ: John Wiley & Sons, Inc, pp 337–50.

Parken, A. (2010) 'A multi-strand approach to promoting equalities and human rights in policy making', *Policy & Politics*, 38(1): 79–99.

Peters, G. (2014) 'Is governance for everybody?', *Policy and Society*, 33(4): 301–306

Potter, J. (2004) 'Discourse analysis as a way of analysing naturally occuring talk', in Silverman, D. (ed.) *Qualitative Research: Theory, Method and Practice*, (2nd edn), London: Sage Publications, pp 200–21.

Rhodes, R.A.W. (1997) *Understanding Governance: Policy Networks, Governance Reflexivity and Accountability*, Buckingham: Open University Press.

Rhodes, R.A.W. (2007) Understanding governance: ten years on. *Organization studies* 2007, *28*, 1243–1264, doi:10.1177/0170840607076586.

Salamon, L.M. and Toepler, S. (2015) 'Government – nonprofit cooperation: anomaly or necessity?', *Voluntas: International Journal of Voluntary and Nonprofit Organizations*, 26(6): 2155–77.

Sanders, A. (2022) 'Elite or grassroots? A feminist institutionalist examination of the role equalities organisations play in delivering representation and participation', *Voluntary Sector Review*, 13(1): 1–24.

Shahwar, D. (2022) 'Identity as place: constructing a Welsh identity through nature', in Chetty, D., Muse, G., Issa, H., et al (eds) *Welsh [Plural]*, London: Repeater Books, pp 35–46.

Squires, J. (2005) 'Is mainstreaming transformative? Theorizing mainstreaming in the context of diversity and deliberation', *Social Politics: International Studies in Gender, State & Society*, 12(3): 366–88.

Stoker, G. (1998) 'Governance as theory: five propositions', *International Social Science Journal*, 50(1): 17–28.

Tilly, C. (2005) 'Introduction to Part 11: invention, diffusion, and transformation of the social movement repertoire', *European Review of History: Revue europeene d'histoire*, 12(2): 307–20.

UK Government. (1998) *Government of Wales Act 1998. Section 114.*

UK Government. (2006) *Government of Wales Act 2006. Section 74.*

Verloo, M. (2006) 'Multiple inequalities, intersectionality and the European Union', *European Journal of Women's Studies*, 13(3): 211–28.

Welsh Government. (2022) 'Anti-Racist Wales Action Plan'. Available from: https://www.gov.wales/anti-racist-wales-action-plan

Williams, C. (2022) 'Knowing our place: Cynefin, the curriculum and me', in Chetty, D., Muse, G., Issa, H., et al (eds) *Welsh [Plural]*, London: Repeater Books, pp 197–213.

Winker, G. and Degele, N. (2011) 'Intersectionality as multi-level analysis: dealing with social inequality', *The European Journal of Women's Studies*, 18(1): 51–66.

Wodak, R. (2001) 'What CDA is about; a summary of its history, important concepts and its developments', in Wodak, R. and Meyer, M. (eds) *Methods of Critical Discourse Analysis*, London: Sage.

Yin, R.K. (2014) *Case Study Research: Design and Methods*, Los Angeles London: Sage.

Young, L. (2000) 'What is Black British feminism?', *Women (Oxford, England)*, 11(1–2): 45–60.

Zimmer, A. and Pahl, B. (2018) 'Barriers to third sector develoment', in Enjolras, B., Salamon, L.M., Henrik Sivesind, K., et al (eds) *The Third Sector as a Renewable Resource for Europe: Concepts, Impacts, Challenges and Opportunities*, Cham: Palgrave Macmillan.

Part III

Policy developments

10

Homelessness and the coronavirus

Hilary Silver[1]

Introduction

It is often assumed that the US is a 'welfare laggard' compared to European welfare states. But in one social policy area, the US is a leader: policies to address homelessness. In fact, the evidence-based Housing First approach not only became the federal government's best practice, but is now also being advocated, piloted and adopted in many European countries (Padgett, Henwood and Tsemberis 2015). Yet the reasons for American leadership in this domain ironically reflects its laggard status in anti-poverty policies. The severe inadequacy of housing subsidies, income supports, child care and active labour market policies, coupled with the lack of universal health care, contribute to America's persistently high level of homelessness, necessitating specialised interventions for the unhoused.

The onset of the coronavirus pandemic in March 2020 exacerbated the problem on both sides of the Atlantic and led to policies specifically targeted at this disadvantaged population. This paper discusses social policy responses to COVID-19 aimed at people experiencing or at-risk of homelessness. It presents the pre-pandemic arrangements in the US and parts of Europe in order to explain subsequently why special procedures were called for after the coronavirus began to infect large numbers of residents. The main areas of policy response are then comparatively analyzed, identifying similarities and differences in the ways Americans and Europeans responded to the risks of COVID-19 for the homeless. It concludes that the crisis induced a breakthrough in existing arrangements as progressive reforms were instituted on an emergency basis. Whether these will endure as emergency measures expire remains an open question.

Literature review

'Homelessness' is a relatively recent social policy construct in the West. The increase in people living outdoors and on the streets of American and European cities dates to the 1980s shift in welfare states towards neo-liberalism, including in housing policies. Privatisation of public housing through sales to tenants and private investors, curtailing renovation and new construction, and outright demolition reduced the stock of deeply affordable places to live (Silver, 1991). Gentrification of center city single-room occupancy (SRO) hotels compounded the shortage (Snow and Anderson, 2003). Rent controls and tenant protections were lifted. Any remaining housing subsidies were reoriented to the supply side, giving individuals housing allowances or vouchers if they could find a landlord willing to accept them. Waiting lists for assistance piled up to the point that many cities stopped taking names.

At the same time, vulnerable populations in need of subsidised housing increased. In the US, deinstitutionalisation of mental and rehabilitation hospitals did not produce the hoped for community homes to integrate the ill and disabled into society. Deindustrialisation took a toll on local jobs, forcing the unemployed to migrate in search of work. The end of wars demobilised veterans suffering from trauma. Women's and gay rights allowed the abused to flee violent unloving households, despite the material consequences. Decolonisation and the ending of guest worker programmes increased the number of migrants seeking housing. Welfare reform reduced the safety nets available for single parent families, and activation programmes provided very low minimum incomes. Destitute people encountered a rental housing market beyond reach.

Cities were the first to confront the growing numbers of unhoused. Since the reformed subsidised housing programmes were already on the books, new national legislation was not forthcoming. Neoliberal policies had also strapped urban budgets, and municipalities, especially in the US and UK, were experiencing fiscal crises of their own. So initially, in the late 1980s, the charitable sector stepped into the breach. Churches and nonprofit organisations, some already operating emergency care facilities, expanded their facilities for the newly unhoused and began advocating for public intervention. When government finally responded, it was with an entirely independent bureaucracy instead of an expansion of existing social housing programmes. The 'homelessness' industry was established.

In the United States (US), the first federal reaction was the Stewart B. McKinney Homeless Assistance Act, enacted in 1987 and renamed the McKinney-Vento Homeless Assistance Act in 2000. Most funds went to local nonprofits sheltering and assisting the homeless through an often-non-governmental Continuum of Care clearinghouse agency. In 2009, Congress passed the Homeless Emergency Assistance and Rapid Transition to Housing (HEARTH) Act to consolidate the separate homelessness programmes at the US Department of Housing and Urban Development (HUD) and to make the system of homeless assistance more performance-based. It funds programmes, outreach, shelter, transitional housing, supportive services, short- and medium-term rent subsidies, and permanent housing for people experiencing homelessness and in some cases for people at risk of homelessness. Jurisdictions receive funding for the Emergency Solutions Grants (ESG) programme through a formula, allocating resources to Continuums of Care (CoC). Over the next decade, as randomised control trials accumulated evidence of what worked to stabilise people in housing, HUD moved from a system that primarily funded emergency shelters and temporary transitional housing to a 'best practice' model of Housing First (Evans et al, 2021).

Much of Europe, however, lacks national-level policies for homelessness per se, or even national-level data on the distribution, nature, and extent of homelessness services that do exist. Regional, municipal, and city level information is 'often not aggregated to national or pan-European level. Accurately assessing the scale, disposition, and range of homelessness services across Europe, or within many European countries, is not possible at present' (Pleace, 2019, p 12). In some countries, like Germany, there is no national strategy to tackle homelessness per se, and despite the 2021 coalition government's plan to end homelessness by 2030, the federal government has so far left data collection and service provision to the states and nonprofits. Elsewhere, as in the British 'Supporting People' programme, homelessness services and social services for vulnerable adults generally are not clearly distinguished or are earmarked to various problem groups. Migrant housing is addressed with migrant integration programmes. Domestic violence, runaway youth, substance abuse, ill health – these all receive support under the more comprehensive welfare states of Europe. Liberal welfare regimes tend to focus on general housing policies and a rights-based approach in statutory definitions of homelessness, while social democratic regimes focus on the most marginal groups for social services and interventions (Benjaminsen et al, 2009). Denmark, Finland and France have well-funded integrated homelessness strategies, while in other countries, 'homelessness services centre on emergency shelters and, to varying degrees, on single site transitional housing'.

The European Social Fund (ESF) partly finances local initiatives for the homeless via member states. But homelessness per se was and mostly still is the domain of charities. Bundesarbeitsgemeinschaft Wohnungslosenhilfe e.V. (BAG W), The Federal Association for the Support of the Homeless in Germany, the umbrella organisation of non-profit homeless service providers, and not the government, provides annual homelessness estimates, but the first national count took place in January 2022. In France, about 80% of the shelter directors are nationally represented by the *Fédération des acteurs de la solidarité* (FAS) who, with housing ministry funds, have housed some 280,000 people from January 2018 to 30 June 2021 (*Le Figaro*, 2021). In turn, national associations have formed a European Union (EU) level network, *Fédération Européenne d'Associations Nationales Travaillant avec les Sans-Abri* (FEANTSA), or the European Federation of National Organisations Working with the Homeless, which receives financial support from the European Commission for the implementation of its activities. After decades of lobbying, in June 2021, for the first time in the EU's history, all the EU member states signed the European platform to combat homelessness, a binding agreement to eradicate homelessness by 2030 (FEANTSA, 2022).

This abbreviated policy history should not imply, however, that all localities have adopted a compassionate approach to homelessness. At the same time as the nonprofit sector addresses homelessness by default, some municipalities have adopted policies that chase away and criminalise unavoidable practices of people experiencing homelessness. Prohibitions on loitering, panhandling and other activities often aim deliberately to force these unfortunates to move elsewhere, especially out of public view. Encampments are razed and violators arrested, adding to suffering. Irrationally, prison ends up costing the public more than housing would have (National Law Center on Homelessness and Poverty, 2019).

Homelessness contributes to health care costs, too. The homeless have more chronic health conditions, and need continuous primary care, but structural barriers, including lack of health insurance and financial difficulties, make them more likely to use hospital emergency departments, at great expense. Hospital discharge planning is suboptimal and contributes to high re-admission rates (Liu and Hwang, 2021). The relationship of poor housing and poor health is reciprocal and mutually reinforcing. Those suffering from physical and mental disabilities may find it difficult to maintain housing and may turn to self-medication. Those already unhoused may find it difficult to stay clean and healthy or to recover from medical treatment on the streets and become sick again.

Permanent supportive housing has thus been found to be a cost-effective, harm-reduction solution to chronic homelessness among those with multiple disabilities. The evidence is the basis for Housing First programmes. They eliminate barriers to shelter while offering, but not mandating, case management services. Once healthy and stable in housing, people are more capable of addressing other life challenges. The approach has dispersed from the US to Canada, Finland and additional European locations. There are clear elements of convergence towards a Housing First approach across the different welfare state regimes, and homeless policies are increasingly aimed at prevention through targeted, individualised and tailor-made interventions (Benjaminsen et al, 2009; Williams, 2020).

The scale of homelessness is difficult to compare across countries (OECD, 2021). Although the definition of homelessness varies across government agencies, the US has two federal methods for counting homelessness: point-in-time (PIT) counts including the unsheltered, and counts of those who used shelter services during a full year. These are reported in the two-part Annual

Homelessness Assessment Reports to Congress (HUD 2022a). Homeless children are also counted by the schools. In contrast, the absence of an official definition or clearinghouse for homeless policies of the 27 member states of the EU impedes any systematic comparison with the US or one another. One European parliament resolution referred to 700,000 homeless people who have to sleep in shelters or on the street on any given night in the EU, as an increase of 70 % in the past ten years (Van Sparrentak, 2020).

FEANTSA has devised a classification scheme (European Typology of Homelessness and Housing Exclusion (ETHOS)) to facilitate comparison of the extent of homelessness within Europe. It is the basis for its annual Overview of Housing Exclusion in Europe, published together with the Fondation Abbé Pierre. The sixth edition from 2021 reported that 4% of Europeans have been homeless at least once in their lifetime. The latest FEANTSA (2022) data show wide national variations, depending on measurement and timing. England recognised 67,820 households as legally homeless, a fall of 4.4% in 2020 once the pandemic began, and on 30 September 2021, 96,060 people were living in temporary accommodation, a 1.5% increase compared to 2020 and a 20% increase since 2017. In Italy, 1.9 million people used the services of Caritas Italiana in 2020, and homeless service users decreased from 20% in 2019 to 16% in 2020 (22,527). According to the Foundation Abbé Pierre, 300,000 people were sleeping rough, in homeless accommodation, or asylum seeker accommodation in France in 2022, or twice as many as in 2012.

The OECD (2021) has also attempted to estimate the extent of homelessness across countries, building on the ETHOS framework. The latest figures for 2020 included data collected during at least part of the COVID-19 pandemic, adding complexity to cross-country comparison, depending upon when in the year a point-in-time census was taken and if unsheltered, doubled up and others were included in the count. Different countries also introduced emergency measures to protect the homeless and housing insecure that year that varied in duration. Taking all this into account, the OECD found that in nearly all countries, less than 1% of the population is reported as homeless. Nevertheless, all official statistics probably underestimate the extent of homelessness (Busch-Geertsema et al, 2014).

The pandemic

The onset of the COVID-19 pandemic in March 2020 impelled governments to take emergency measures to protect their populations from what was a very contagious deadly disease. Critical care facilities were being overwhelmed. Hospitalisations and fatalities made it clear that certain sub-populations were especially vulnerable to infection. These included people living in institutions and group quarters, where it was difficult to self-isolate and stay clean. In addition to nursing homes, prisons, and migrant accommodations, homeless shelters and encampments became targets of urgent intervention. Indeed, there were cluster outbreaks among staff and residents of homeless shelters (Mosites et al, 2020).

Although there was considerable geographic variation in COVID-19 prevalence, evidence accumulated that people experiencing homelessness were at higher risk of coronavirus infection, hospitalisation, critical care and death than the general public, due to chronic health conditions, age, racial identity, congregate living, and lack of hygiene and severe illness common among the hospitalised (Calabro, Patton and Saadian, 2020, p 1; Cha et al, 2021; Leifheit et al, 2021; Tsai and Wilson, 2020; Silver and Morris, 2023). In Los Angeles County, the COVID-19 mortality risk of people experiencing homelessness rose to nearly three times that of the general population, and even higher than deaths from drug overdose, traffic injury, suicide and homicide (Nicholas et al, 2021).

The immediate lockdowns due to the pandemic also induced a sharp rise in firm and school closures and unemployment. Consequently, housing insecurity among low-income renters rose, and evictions and homelessness were expected to rise (Schuetz, 2020). As of January 2021, nearly one in four of the 43 million renter households in the US reported having missed at least one rent payment during the pandemic (Reed et al, 2021). In the fall of 2021, 4.6 million, or 33% of adults, lived in households not current on rent or mortgage where eviction or foreclosure in the next two months was either very or somewhat likely (U.S. Census Household Pulse Survey, October 2021). Eurofound's EU PolicyWatch Database likewise found that in April–May 2020, 6% of Europeans reported being at risk of having to leave their current home within the following three months due to their inability to pay rent. That percentage fell to 4.8% in June–July 2020 but rose again to 5.4% in February–March 2021.

The dip coincided with the institution of progressive policies to house the homeless or those at risk of homelessness. The first reactions were local and state/regional, as on the ground responses were most immediate. But local capacity was limited, so national and even European assistance measures, mostly financial and regulatory, ensued. These included de-densifying and improving emergency shelters, relocating people to individual housing units, and extensive outreach to rough sleepers and ending sweeps of encampments. At the same time, as unemployment burgeoned, policies were established to prevent new homelessness. The US enacted Emergency Rental Assistance (ERA) and eviction moratoriums. The most widely adopted measures in Europe were temporary bans on rental evictions and repossessions, as well as emergency supports to compensate for loss of income due to the pandemic and limiting the cutting off of energy supplies (FEANTSA, 2022, p 37). Subsequently, attention turned from urgent to more long-term policies, such as subsidising housing units and increasing the supply of housing. These measures are discussed next.

USA

In the US, where unsheltered homelessness exceeded sheltered homelessness for the first time in 2020, the US Centers for Disease Control (CDC) (2022) recognised that there is a high prevalence of certain medical conditions associated with severe COVID-19 among people experiencing homelessness. The agency issued 'Interim Guidance on People Experiencing Unsheltered Homelessness' as well as 'Interim Guidance for Homeless Shelters'. The difference in advice reflected the fact that outdoor settings may allow physical distancing, but may not provide protection from the environment, adequate access to hygiene and sanitation facilities, or connection to services and healthcare. The CDC called for temporary housing sites for shelter decompression, isolation sites for COVID-positive people, quarantine sites for people who are awaiting testing and their results, or who were exposed to COVID-19, and immediate protective housing for people at increased risk for severe illness. It recommended housing in individual rooms (such as hotels/motels) with separate bathrooms, and called for planning housing opportunities after people leave these temporary sites.

In March 2020, the Federal Emergency Management Administration (FEMA) recognised that providing non-congregate shelter including hotels for people experiencing homelessness is a powerful public health response to combat the spread of COVID-19. In February 2021, FEMA expanded the available reimbursement for communities providing non-congregate housing to 100%, while requiring a 25% match for congregate shelter facilities. It agreed to retroactively fund these costs back to January 2020, and extended a September 2021 cutoff date to March 2022. Nevertheless, FEMA can only fund hotel rooms temporarily, impeding their conversion to permanent units.

Hotel placements were common in areas with tourist economies hit by the pandemic. For example, King County, WA, that includes Seattle, counted some 12,000 homeless people in January 2020. When COVID-19 arrived, the county reduced shelter capacity and leased hotel rooms and small efficiency units through January of 2021. An assessment by the University of Washington found that moving over 800 homeless people from shelters to hotels reduced the spread of COVID-19 and increased rates of exit to permanent housing (Brey, 2020b; Eckart, 2020). At the same time, more people moved to encampments (Brownstone, 2021). The county proposed health and safety and access standards for when homeless encampments could and could not be removed, but the county council rejected them. 'Tiny house' villages were established to provide collective services – from case management to WiFi internet, hygiene services and communal kitchens – and to connect people formerly sleeping rough to permanent housing. Seattle committed more than a third of the $128 million the city received from the stimulus package to alleviate homelessness.

California also instituted a programme to move people from the streets to hotel rooms. Dubbed Project Roomkey, it was a county-operated programme to rent some 15,000 hotel, hostel, and motel rooms to house homeless individuals at higher risk of infection with two goals: to reduce transmission of COVID-19 by enabling social distancing and isolation and to lessen the financial toll that minimal tourism was having on the lodging industry. Initially, FEMA provided 75% of the funds, topped up by the state, until the agency decided to fully reimburse state and local governments for the costs. Project Roomkey had difficulty procuring all the hoped for hotel rooms because of staffing limitations, not in my back yard (NIMBY) opposition, and lack of hotel participation, but since the COVID-19 pandemic began, it sheltered more than 42,000 people experiencing homelessness (California Housing and Community Development, 2021). As of June 2021, the 33,141 of the 42,000 people who had exited Project Roomkey ended up in the following destinations: 6,710 to permanent housing, 3,355 to temporary housing, 1,691 to institutional settings, 7,962 to congregate shelter, 5,288 became unsheltered and the whereabouts of 8,135 were unknown or died (California Department of Social Services, 2021).

In March 2020, CDC interim guidelines instructed cities that, unless housing units are available, 'do not clear encampments during community spread of COVID-19. Clearing encampments can cause people to disperse throughout the community', which 'increases the potential for disease spread'. It called for outreach to provide the unsheltered with information, contact tracing, testing, and later, vaccination; for hygiene facilities and masks to be distributed in encampments; and if individual housing options are not available, ending camp clearances and allowing tents and encampments to remain where they are to prevent dispersal throughout the community, breaking connections with service providers, and raising the potential for infectious disease spread. Continuation of substance use treatment and other health and social services was advised.

Unfortunately, sweeps of encampments continued during the pandemic (Wiltz, 2020). As people lost jobs, homes, and sought to socially distance rather than go to shelters, many tent cities grew in inhabitants. To be sure, a few cities (for example, LA, Alexandria, Echo Park Lake) built tiny house villages for homeless residents, while others relocated encampments to sites where hygiene and distancing were possible. But despite the CDC guidelines, cities in California, Washington, Texas, Minnesota, New York and other states razed encampments, ironically justified with public health and safety concerns about human waste, discarded needles and garbage and labelled as hot spots for outbreaks of hepatitis A, typhus and tuberculosis.

Public spaces were also cleared. New York City instituted COVID-19 rules that prohibited people from staying in a subway station for more than an hour or after a train is taken out of service, and banned carts more than 30 inches long or wide. When the pandemic eased and the system resumed service, ridership remained low, for which the continuing presence of mentally ill homeless people in the subway was blamed. In November 2022, the new Mayor Eric Adams directed the police and emergency medical workers to forcibly hospitalise people they deemed too mentally ill to care for themselves (Newman and Fitzsimmons, 2022).

Finally, as vaccines became available, efforts were made to vaccinate the homeless. The effort faced many challenges. The jabs had to be free of charge, even for the uninsured. Accessibility was important, as the homeless often lack reliable information, transportation to get a shot, and the technology to schedule and record the vaccination. One strategy was bringing vaccines directly to shelters, places where people were already used to being tested, where vaccine hesitancy could be addressed, and where records could be kept. Pop-up vaccination tents on city streets also appeared. The National Alliance to End Homelessness reports that mobile vans helped vaccinate the unsheltered. The CDC issued interim guidance on 2 Feb. 2021 on the logistics of vaccinating people experiencing homelessness, but did not recommend that states prioritise them. Indeed, at least 20 states did not include people living in homeless shelters in their vaccine distribution plans (Van Less, 2021). Few state plans even mention homeless people not in shelters. Some states that did prioritise shelter residents in early plans changed tack, moving them further down the priority list. Some (North Carolina, Colorado) placed shelter staff before shelter residents.

The pandemic coupled with public health advice provided a political opening for tenant groups and housing advocates long agitating for a 'Right to the City', preservation of subsidised housing and against displacement. They mobilised and won moratoriums on evictions, rent freezes, or additional rental assistance.

Measures were taken to prevent a surge in new homelessness. Given estimates that evictions would lead to significant increases in COVID-19 infections (Nande et al, 2021; Leifheit et al, 2021), some 44 states instituted eviction bans of varying length and eligibility requirements at some point in the pandemic. Then Congress enacted an eviction moratorium as part of the Coronavirus Aid, Relief, and Economic Security Act (CARES). When it expired after 120 days, the CDC instituted its own nationwide eviction moratorium effective 4 September 2020 and renewed several times until its sunset in late August 2021. It covered nearly all renters with annual incomes of less than $99,000 a year (or $198,000 jointly) who experienced a substantial income loss due to the pandemic. However, after several landlord lawsuits, the Supreme Court struck it down, arguing that the CDC had exceeded its authority. Federal authorities scrambled, and while the Biden administration unsuccessfully tried to extend the ban by executive order, states were advised to intervene in eviction proceedings, ask courts to delay if a tenant had applied for Emergency Rental Assistance (ERA), and support legal representation and ERA application assistance.

State and local governments are indeed constitutionally authorised to impose eviction moratoria and other measures to ensure public health. But as states lifted quarantines, closures and other public health mandates, their emergency measures began expiring. By August 2021 many state and local eviction bans had expired. Benfer et al (2021) estimated 13 states and Washington, DC still had eviction moratoria that protected some renters facing eviction, while four other states had some alternative protections, such as requiring landlords to provide information to renters about rental assistance programmes before eviction, requiring mediation processes, or providing extended eviction notices to give renters more time to pay rent or find other housing. Eight local jurisdictions in states without eviction moratoria also protected some renters facing eviction, and three local jurisdictions in states with eviction moratoria offered even greater protections for renters (Liptak and Thrush, 2021). This left 53% of renter households living in states and localities at risk of eviction (Davis and King-Viehland, 2021).

In response to the economic fallout of the COVID-19 pandemic, Congress enacted the CARES Act on March 27, 2020, a $2.2 trillion economic stimulus. The $1,200 checks with President Trump's signature were sent to most households, propping up consumer demand. The $600 bonus unemployment benefits and the Paycheck Protection Program for small businesses to keep workers on the payroll expired, and investigations of their misallocation are underway. These benefits hardly reached the unsheltered, who rarely pay taxes, are often jobless, and lack bank accounts, internet access, and addresses for debit cards. Shelters and outreach teams were enlisted to get benefits to the homeless. Some of them used the money for rental deposits.

The Emergency Rental Assistance (ERA) programme was intended to prevent homelessness due to rent arrears and eviction. States, local governments, and other jurisdictions received two rounds of funding through existing or newly created rental assistance programmes to assist with unpaid rent and utility expenses of low-income households affected by the economic consequences of the COVID-19 pandemic. ERA1, passed in late December 2020, provided up to $25 billion under the Consolidated Appropriations Act, 2021, and ERA2, enacted under President Biden in March 2021, provided up to $21.5 billion under the American Rescue Plan Act (ARPA). The $1.9 trillion ARPA included $5 billion to fund approximately 70,000 emergency housing vouchers and the provision of services in 626 communities to assist individuals and families who are experiencing or at risk of homelessness, fleeing or attempting to flee domestic violence, dating violence, sexual assault, stalking, or human trafficking, or recently homeless and in need of rental assistance to prevent homelessness or housing instability.

The US Department of the Treasury was responsible for the ERA funds, but aside from Public Housing Authorities, most states and localities had no administrative capacity for distributing the money to eligible people. At first, the expenditure of the funds to landlords and, if they are noncooperative, their tenants was extremely slow, with just $5.1 billion of the $46.5 billion distributed by July 2021, just as the federal eviction moratorium was about to expire. Some landlords refused to accept the payments, preferring to file for eviction, and tenants found it difficult to provide the required documentation for the notoriously complicated online applications. In response, Treasury relaxed its rules and threatened to reallocate unspent funds to get the money out the door. There was huge variation across states in the disbursement of ERA funds, with NY, TX, CT, OR, MN and NJ having obligated all their allocations by fall and halting new applications.

In early 2022, Treasury reallocated $1.1 billion in the first round of reallocations, including $875.5 million in voluntarily returned funds and $239.9 million in recaptured funds. However, after Treasury allowed funds to bypass laggard states to go directly to big cities, jurisdictions like New York – that after a slow start, quickly burned through its allocation and hoped for more – did not receive all of the expected reallocations (Nova, 2022). Treasury continued reallocations of undrawn ERA2 funds through much of 2022, but the Department announced in December 2022 that Grantees had drawn down and obligated their ERA2 funds at higher rates, obviating a final undrawn funds assessment until at least June 2023, if ever. The creation of state and local government rental assistance infrastructure enabled over 7 million unique household rental assistance payments of ERA1 (CARES) and ERA2 (ARPA) funds, committing over 90% of funds allocated through 30 September, 2025.

The ARPA also included the Coronavirus State and Local Fiscal Recovery Funds (SLFRF) programme, allocating $350 billion to state, local, and tribal governments to flexibly support their response to and recovery from COVID-19, to be obligated by December 2024. These funds can, but need not be used to address housing-related needs, from assisting households with rent, mortgage, utility and relocation costs to supporting affordable housing development, permanent supportive housing, and other efforts to improve access to stable, affordable housing for individuals who are homeless and impacted by the pandemic. The Urban Institute's analysis of the recovery plans of 29 cities found that only four places had no housing-related uses. The most common planned expenditure in 57% of the cities was to expand or rehabilitate the affordable housing stock, and the next most common was homelessness prevention and alleviation (53%), especially through means to mitigate the risk of COVID-19 exposure. Only about a third of cities planned to use the funds for eviction prevention, perhaps because the ERA was already available (Reynolds, Elder and Tajo, 2021).

Building on the CARES Act, the ARPA is the basis for the Biden Administration's *House America: An All-Hands-on-Deck Effort to Address the Nation's Homelessness Crisis* (2021), a joint initiative of HUD and the U.S. Interagency Council on Homelessness (USICH). The latter federal agency coordinates the federal response to homelessness of 19 agencies, state and local governments, and the private sector to use housing resources efficiently and effectively. The multi-agency, multi-sector, multi-level partnership aims to spend ARPA funds for 70,000 housing vouchers and $5 billion for HOME Investment Partnerships - American Rescue Plan (HOME-ARP), together with other emergency resources, to address the crisis of homelessness through a Housing First approach, rehousing 100,000 households and adding at least 20,000 new affordable housing units (USICH, 2021). *House America* recognises that:

> The pandemic only made homelessness worse, and created additional urgency to address the crisis, given the heightened risks faced by people experiencing homelessness. At the same time, COVID-19 slowed re-housing activities due to capacity issues and impacts on rental market vacancies. *House America* recognizes that it will take government working at all levels and local collaboration to address this crisis.

Europe

In Europe, the main measures applied in the early months of the pandemic were similar to those in the US, although documentation is more uneven. According to OECD (2020) and the International Union of Tenants (2021), interventions included: eviction bans; postponement, suspension or temporary reduction of rent payments; rent freezes; reforms to financial support schemes; mortgage forbearance; foreclosure bans; utility payment moratoriums and assured continuity of service; reforms of or housing subsidy schemes; and emergency support for homeless people in particular. Eviction bans were most common, found in 12 of the 13 European countries examined (OECD, 2021).

For example, the onset of the pandemic in March 2020 led the government of the United Kingdom to ban repossessions, freeze local rates, increase Housing Benefit (HB) and Universal Credit to cover 30% of market rents, and like in the US, fund local authorities in England and Wales to offer emergency accommodation and other support to rough sleepers. Evictions in England were suspended for the pandemic, to resume in 2021. From 1 June to 30 September 2021, landlords had to give tenants a four month notice period, except for those with serious rent arrears and anti-social behaviour. Under the 'Everyone In' plan, 33,000 homeless people would be temporarily sheltered in individual accommodation, hotels, and hostels between March and November 2020. The government claimed over 90% of rough sleepers in England had been offered emergency accommodation by mid-April 2020, and nearly 15,000 people had been provided emergency accommodation by local authorities by May (Wilson, 2021).

The pandemic changed British homeless support services in some notable ways. Night shelters closed, and people placed in hotels and other emergency accommodation had difficulty accessing food since there were no cooking facilities, or benefits were denied when people could not meet certain conditions. Face-to-face assessments for health and disability-related benefits and Jobcentres' appointments also stopped (Groundswell, 2020).

In 2021, the UK government provided £310 million to councils through the Homelessness Prevention Grant, augmented by a further £65 million when the Department for Levelling Up, Housing and Communities (DLUHC) announced in October a £65 million support package to local authorities 'helping to prevent homelessness and support families get back on their feet.' These funds supported low-income vulnerable renters in arrears due to the pandemic, on top of a £500 million Household Support Fund announced in September 2021 to help vulnerable households with the cost of food, energy, water and other essentials and the £400 billion support package for the economy.

On the Continent, there was much variation in emergency responses to the pandemic. Some countries like France, Germany, and Italy decreed eviction moratoriums, but they were unevenly enforced. Germany imposed a federal freeze on evictions for rent arrears caused by a tenant's income loss due to the pandemic, but it was only in effect from April to June 2020. It gave tenants a long period to repay rent arrears, but in the early stage of the pandemic, the amount of back rent was not very high. At the state level, there was more variation in responses. Baden-Wurttemberg and Schleswig-Holstein provided additional funding for municipal governments to finance more temporary accommodation, while in Hamburg, charities gave a large amount of money (almost €450,000) to a voluntary organisation to rent hotel rooms for people experiencing street homelessness. Frankfurt, Düsseldorf and Berlin also provided temporary accommodations in hotels; Berlin rented some 200 beds in hostels, with no more than two people per room.

Although the districts of Berlin are legally obliged to accommodate homeless people, the State of Berlin received additional ESF funds of €36.8 million from 'REACT-EU' of which €11 million flowed into COVID-19 homeless assistance for 2021–22. The Senate Social Administration promised to offer homeless people 24/7 accommodation with care and advice, given that these corona pandemic accommodations have shown many homeless people's lives improve if they live in safe accommodation, are fed and advised there and can come to rest. However, the State of Berlin's corona 'cold aid' ended on 30 June 2021. Around 500 homeless people who were housed in hostels and hotels were sent back to the streets unless they could qualify for other aid programmes. For example, residents evacuated from their camp on *Rummelsburger Bucht* in February were housed in the A&O Hostel on Boxhagener Strasse. Their stay was extended to 30 June only because of the vaccination campaign for homeless people. While they received offers for social housing assistance, it was always clear that the hostel 'was only a temporary accommodation and a time-limited offer' (*Time*, 2021).

Politically motivated squatting was long tolerated in Berlin, but homeless encampments like *Rummelsburger Bucht* and especially camps of migrant Roma households, are increasingly unwelcome. For example, Berlin-Lichtenberg district council voted against a Safe Place pilot project of Karuna, a homeless association that was assembling a tiny house settlement on a meadow with a repair café and community garden. It was designed to avoid undisciplined homeless camps, prevent drug use and show the public that homeless people should be able to live independently, with supervision of social workers. Although approved and funded by the Berlin State Senate before the pandemic, the district opposed it (Klages, 2021).

Meanwhile, Berlin sought to address its shortage of affordable housing with a five-year rent freeze, but the courts ruled it unconstitutional. In 2021, the city voted to take over a private social housing company in order to control rents, another questionable policy. The new 'traffic-light' Social Democratic Party (SPD)-led government is planning its national action plan to end homelessness by 2030.

In Italy, some regions drew on the European Social Fund to offer subsidies to unemployed tenants or encouraged landlords to lower rents during the pandemic. In August 2021, a new national decree went into effect in Italy to allocate rental subsidies for the poorest to regions on an urgent and simplified basis.

In France, some 43,000 emergency shelter places were created from the first lockdown in March 2020. It is estimated that over 200,000 experiencing homelessness were housed in shelters or hotels (*Le Figaro*, 2021). The French Housing Ministry broke with its older 'management by thermometer' policy that closed emergency shelters when the weather warmed up. Instead, it announced in May 2021 that the emergency shelter places established in response to COVID-19 will stay open until March 2022 when it will move to a multi-year budget to support both emergency shelters and Housing First ('*Logement d'abord*') (*Le Figaro*, 2021). However, by the end of the five-year

(2018–2022) plan for Housing First and the fight against homelessness, more than 300,000 people were homeless, more than 4 million poorly housed, the shelters were permanently congested, and social housing was underutilised by homeless households. Undocumented people and those evicted from camps and squats are left to fend for themselves (Fondation Abbé-Pierre, 2022).

Encampments in Europe, including migrant settlements, are seen as 'squats' and criminalised. Efforts to improve them are rare. Roma encampments are often targeted for sweeps. In Italy, despite the suspension of evictions during the early pandemic, local authorities in Rome and Turin carried out forced evictions of Roma. Amnesty International (2020) noted that after the COVID-19 pandemic began, refugees and asylum-seekers in Greece were granted only 30 days from their legal recognition to leave migrant accommodation to seek housing on the private rental market.

At the same time, for public health, vaccinations of the homeless proceeded. In Germany, adult refugees of all ages living in group homes or refugee centers were considered high priority and got their shots around the same time as people aged 70 and older. In France, where the government has said it would give undocumented migrants a temporary social security number for vaccination, advocates for migrants worried that lack of access to the internet and information about the process would hamper inoculations (McCann, 2021). In contrast, although the British government said that people could get vaccinated regardless of their immigration status, some undocumented migrants were denied registration at local doctors' offices. Likewise, the Italian government has said that people have a right to get vaccinated no matter their legal status, but in practice, many undocumented migrants and homeless people have been overlooked because they lacked a social security number to book an appointment on their online platforms.

The pandemic persisted

The policies put in place at the outset of the pandemic were mostly short-term. Some protections expired, some ran out of money, but some are still coming on line, intended to increase housing in the long run. On both sides of the Atlantic, the pandemic jumpstarted proposed solutions to long-lasting and structural problems in the public and affordable housing sectors.

As mentioned, the expiration of eviction moratoria in many locales led to predictions of a 'tsunami' of mass displacement and homelessness. Even as rents have increased, though, these fears have yet to be confirmed (Kasakove 2021a, b; Kasakove and Thrush, 2022; Siegel and O'Connell, 2021). Eviction filings have been well below pre-pandemic levels, with the exception of a few areas of the US. This may be because of local protections, or legal help, or preemptive moves prior to an eviction to avoid ruining one's credit rating. Some people may have saved their stimulus checks, taken out loans, or worked out payment plans. The slow rollout of ERA funds may also be working at last, but that effect will be short-lived unless more vouchers are allocated. Besides, eviction filings continued throughout the pandemic. Some were removed from their homes because of reasons other than nonpayment or because they were unaware of the moratorium. Finally, eviction statistics are notoriously unreliable, and 'informal' evictions may be uncounted. The federal government began assessing legal and community 'Innovations in State and Local Eviction Prevention' to ensure that eviction practices do not return to their prepandemic norms (HUD, 2022b).

The Federal Emergency Management Agency's reimbursement of costs associated with sheltering people in individual rooms was slated to run through the end of the year, but on November 9, 2021, President Biden extended payments through the end of March 2022. This gave localities time to find a different source of funds to purchase the hotels and repurpose them as permanent housing. In fact, there is growing pressure for cities to convert hotels and now, underused office buildings to residential uses (Padgett and Herman, 2021), even by taking them through eminent domain (Roy et al, 2020). Some jurisdictions, like King County, are already attempting to purchase the hotels outright to use as permanent housing for the formerly homeless.

Not all places have been willing to convert hotels to housing. As the economy re-opened, especially in tourist spots, authorities began relocating formerly homeless residents in order to book paying guests in the hotels. The most publicised case was in New York City. Because New York's right to housing legally required it to shelter everyone, it already had experience with housing the homeless in hotels. In 2016, 12% of the city's homeless were already placed in hotels at great public expense, leading to efforts to house them elsewhere. There was also an earlier wave of resistance to bringing back the infamous SRO units that were upgraded in the 1980s. Thus, to many New Yorkers, placing the most vulnerable in hotels for the pandemic seemed regressive. In addition, while FEMA had reimbursed the city for the emergency hotel rooms since April 2020, it decided to stop after Gov. Andrew Cuomo lifted a statewide emergency order as of 24 June. Mayor Bill DeBlasio called for removing some 8,000 residents living in hotels back to shelters by 1 July 2021 (Newman, 2021b).

The policy was controversial for the start. On one side, the placement of the homeless in hotels in posh neighbourhoods led to resident and business owner complaints about harassment, theft, drug use and disorder spilling out to the street. On the other side, neighbours defended the hotel policy as a version of Housing First, enabling people to stabilise and get their lives on track. The supportive neighbours even filed a lawsuit to prevent relocating disabled residents when the hotel contract expired. The suit argued that health problems and disabilities should exempt some people from being relocated to congregate facilities, especially with the Delta surge underway. New York State was among the last to distribute emergency rental assistance as well, so that alternative funding was not yet available. However, the city prevailed, pointing to its pandemic protocols to determine which homeless people should be assigned to large shelters, single hotel rooms, or double-occupancy rooms. The lawsuit ruled that people had no right to a hotel room, just to some form of shelter.

Housing advocates and Eric Adams, the new Mayor of New York, wanted to turn vacant hotels into permanent housing for the homeless (Newman, 2021c). It would be more humane and economical, as it costs the city an annual average of $56,000 for each person in the shelter system, but $36,000 to place the same person in supportive housing (Chen, 2021). However, previous efforts of nonprofit developers to buy and convert some of the city's more than 700 hotels into housing ran afoul of regulatory and zoning rules and private sector competition. Some of the targeted hotels were more easily remade into transient shelters. Finally, as the pandemic eased, conservative governors of Texas and Florida began putting more than 23,000 migrants on busses to New York, overwhelming the city's homeless system. Huge tents had to be constructed in peripheral areas to house the newcomers, although gradually the last residents were relocated to downtown hotels (Stack, 2022).

In contrast, California, the state with the highest number of unsheltered homeless people in the country and a severe lack of affordable housing, is actively converting hotel rooms to permanent housing. Its Project Homekey builds on the pandemic experience of Project Roomkey, and recognises that converting hotels into permanent housing for people experiencing homelessness reduces the cost of an additional unit to one-third that of building from scratch (Brey, 2020a). Since hotel stays plummeted during the pandemic, owners also had a greater incentive to sell.

For years, California has tried to increase the supply of affordable housing. Governor Newsom promised in 2019 to build 3.5 million homes by 2025, but there has been little progress since. In July 2021, Governor Newsom signed the $100 billion California Comeback Plan that included $10.3 billion for affordable housing and $12 billion over two years towards moving tens of thousands of people off the streets. The new homelessness funding includes $5.8 billion to add 42,000 new housing units through Project Homekey, $3 billion of which is dedicated to housing people with the greatest health needs. The plan allocates $150 million to stabilise participants in existing Project Roomkey hotels and $50.6 million to local governments that assist people in moving out of unsafe, unhealthy encampments and into safer, more stable housing. The plan includes greater accountability requirements on cities and counties for results in return for Homeless Housing, Assistance and Prevention grants (HHAP), support for more Accessory Dwelling Units and upzoning to increase housing density (Dougherty, 2021). The first round of Project Homekey funding housed over 8,000 individuals in over 6,000 housing units, and its second round will create up to 14,000 new, long-term housing units.

But the most important change for the long-term prospect of ending homelessness in the US is to increase the supply of deeply affordable housing and to subsidise rent-burdened households. While ARPA provided a start on the backlog of progressive housing proposals, the Biden Administration's Build Back Better Act had included billions of federal dollars for capital investments to preserve public housing, capitalisation of the National Housing Trust Fund, and a huge expansion in the number of housing voucher allowances. Of the $22.1 billion provided for vouchers, $7.1 billion was set aside for people experiencing or at risk of homelessness and survivors of domestic violence and trafficking.

Unfortunately, the bill was shelved, even after it was scaled back in the final House of Representatives version. The annual budget stalled, endangering a once in a generation opportunity to build more affordable housing and make homelessness a short, episodic experience at best. Advocates have turned to using the rest of the ARPA funds and preserving the state and local administrations built to distribute ERA to make the emergency rental assistance programme permanent.

Europe

At the level of the EU, the Coronavirus Response Investment Initiatives initially redirected Cohesion Policy and the EU Solidarity Fund to where it was most needed for the short term emergency. The EU Council also agreed on a longer-term investment plan, the Recovery and Resilience Facility (RRF), consisting of €723.8 billion in loans and grants, and an injection of an additional €17.5 billion for the ESF from Recovery Assistance for Cohesion and the Territories of Europe (REACT EU). Altogether, NEXT GENERATION EU will provide some €800 billion for recovery from the pandemic, including for some housing.

Europe has also begun long term planning to end homelessness in the post-pandemic period. On 21 June 2021, EU institutions, member states, cities and civil society launched the European Platform to Combat Homelessness. Under the Portuguese EU Presidency, they signed the Lisbon Declaration on the European Platform on Combatting Homelessness committing to the following shared objectives:

- no one sleeps rough for lack of accessible, safe and appropriate emergency accommodation;
- no one lives in emergency or transitional accommodation longer than is required for successful move-on to a permanent housing solution;

- no one is discharged from any institution (for example, prison, hospital, and care facility) without an offer of appropriate housing;
- evictions should be prevented whenever possible and no one is evicted without assistance for an appropriate housing solution, when needed;
- no one is discriminated against due to their homelessness status.

The new platform also represents a concrete deliverable of the European Pillar of Social Rights Action Plan.

Housing First projects pioneered in America are now considered best practices in Europe. The RFF housing funds were unevenly distributed. Italy, which received the largest share, proposed to finance some 250 Housing First interventions as well as more social housing to reduce marginalisation and social degradation.

Conclusion

The shock of the coronavirus pandemic induced significant changes in the treatment of people experiencing homelessness on both sides of the Atlantic. Policies that progressives had advocated for years were at the ready to avoid a disaster among this vulnerable population. The action was most dramatic in the US, which had been at the forefront of designing and assessing programmes to end homelessness, and whose Housing First approach influenced policy for the unhoused across the ocean.

An important caveat of the comparative discussion here is that, in fact, there is considerable variation in social policies across the American states, just as there is across the EU member states. The contrast in the literature between Anglo-American liberal and European social democratic models is a caricature of what are in fact many detailed, context-dependent differences. Nevertheless, in this particular policy area of addressing widespread homelessness, the US has led, partly because it has such an underdeveloped welfare state to begin with.

In the initial months of the crisis, when countries around the world shut down and quarantined much of the population, the unhoused and people dwelling in emergency shelters were recognised as especially at risk of COVID-19. In the US and across Europe, congregate facilities were de-densified, in some cases by opening additional shelter spaces and day shelters to allow for social distancing, in other cases, by commandeering hotel rooms made vacant by the economic shutdown. Outreach to rough sleepers and encampments aimed to protect the vulnerable, either by bringing facilities and services to tent cities or encouraging people to accept housing. Despite efforts to prevent dispersal of the homeless, some places closed shelters down entirely, adding to street living, and then, razed or relocated tent cities.

Next, to prevent a large inflow into homelessness, authorities mandated bans on evictions and foreclosures, while expanding rental assistance of various kinds so any arrears could be paid after the economy resuscitated. However, these proved to be temporary measures, and were difficult to execute at short notice.

Surprisingly, in the longer run, high rates of COVID-19 infections and deaths among homeless people stayed much lower than expected throughout 2020, in London, the US, and other settings globally (Guise et al, 2022). In Los Angeles County, for example, COVID-19 contributed to an increase in deaths during the pandemic, but drug overdose was the main driver of the homeless mortality surge. To be sure, the coronavirus and related closures of care facilities may have indirectly contributed to the stressors increasing drug use, overdoses and other health problems in the homeless population (County of Los Angeles 2022). Similarly surprising was that the expected 'eviction tsunami' did not materialise, possibly because governments responded promptly to the warnings (Demsas, 2022). Numbers of filings have gradually crept up, but expanded legal services and emergency rental assistance appear to be helping people avoid removals.

As the pandemic ended its third year with the impact of new coronavirus variants uncertain, longer-term measures came into effect. Some places began to convert hotels to housing. Others dedicated stimulus funds to affordable housing construction or permanent rent subsidy programmes in line with Housing First principles. The EU embarked on putting the Platform into effect. Whether these longer-term solutions to homelessness will ultimately end homelessness remains to be seen, but the pandemic has clearly focused renewed public attention on the need for everyone to have a safe, secure home.

Note
[1] I am grateful for the contributions of Laura Colini and Rebecca Morris to this paper.

References
Amnesty International. (2020) *Affordable Housing For All: Key to Building a Resilient Post-COVID-19 World*. Available from: https://www.amnesty.org/en/latest/news/2020/10/affordable-housing-key-to-resilience-post-covid/

Benfer, E.A., Koehler, R. and Alexander, A.K. (2021) *Covid-19 Eviction Moratoria & Housing Policy: Federal, State, Commonwealth, and Territory*. Available from: https://statepolicies.com/policy-by-topic/economic-precarity/housing/

Benjaminsen, L., Dyb, E. and O'Sullivan, E. (2009) 'The governance of homelessness in liberal and social democratic welfare regimes: national strategies and models of intervention', *European Journal of Homelessness*, 3: 23–51.

Brey, J. (2020a) 'California's Project Homekey turns hotels into housing at a third of the cost of building new', *Next City*, 29 September. Available from: https://nextcity.org/urbanist-news/californias-project-homekey-turns-hotels-into-housing

Brey, J. (2020b) 'Repurposing hotels helped contain Covid-19 spread, study shows', *Next City*, 9 October. Available from: https://nextcity.org/daily/entry/repurposing-hotels-helped-contain-covid-19-spread-study-shows

Brownstone, S. (2021) '57 people from one Seattle homeless encampment got hotel rooms last year. More than 1/3 likely went back to the streets', *The Seattle Times*, 24 August. Available from: https://www.seattletimes.com/seattle-news/homeless/57-people-from-one-seattle-homeless-encampment-got-hotel-rooms-last-year-more-than-1-3-likely-went-back-to-the-streets/

Busch-Geertsema, V., Benjaminsen, L., Filipovič Hrast, M., and Pleace, N. (2014) *Extent and Profile of Homelessness in European Member States – A statistical update. European Observatory on Homelessness*, Brussels: EOH.

Calabro, A., Patton, N. and Saadian, S. (2020) 'Housing Is Healthcare', Washington, DC: National Low Income Housing Coalition. Available from: https://nlihc.org/sites/default/files/FEMA_Housing-Is-Healthcare.pdf

California Department of Social Services. (2021) *Issue Brief – Project Roomkey – Outcomes to Date and Looking Ahead*. Sacramento: California Department of Social Services. Available from: https://www.cdss.ca.gov/Portals/9/FEMA/Issue-Brief-Project-Roomkey.pdf

California Housing and Community Development. (2021) Homekey: A Journey Home, 2021 Legislative Report, 1 April.

Cha, S., Henry, A., Montgomery, M.P., Laws, R.L., Pham, H., Wortham, J., Garg, S., Kim, L. and Mosites, E. (2021) 'Covid-NET surveillance team, morbidity and mortality among adults experiencing homelessness hospitalized with Covid-19', *The Journal of Infectious Diseases*, 224(3): 425–30. Available from: https://doi.org/10.1093/infdis/jiab261

Chen, S. (2021) 'Is the chance to turn hotels into affordable housing slipping away?' *New York Times,* 3 December.

CNBC. (2022) 'Several states have run out of federal rental assistance.' *CNBC*, 6 January. Available from: https://cnb.cx/3tcO43n

County of Los Angeles Public Health. (2022) *Mortality of PEH in LA County: One Year Before and After the Start of the Covid-19 Pandemic*. April. Available from: http://publichealth.lacounty.gov/chie/reports/Homeles s_Mortality_Report_2022.pdf

Cuellar Mejia, M., Johnson, H. and Herrera, J. (2022) *A Snapshot of Homeless Californians in Shelters*, Public Policy Institute of California Blog Post, 2 March.

Davis, C. and King-Viehland, M. (2021) *With Limited State and Local Protections, the End of the Federal Eviction Moratorium Puts Millions of Renters at Risk*. 30 August. Available from: https://www.urban.org/urban-wire/limited-state-and-local-protections-end-federal-eviction-moratorium-puts-millions-renters-risk

Demsas, J. (2022) 'Why so many COVID predictions were wrong', *The Atlantic*, 7 April. Available from: https://www.theatlantic.com/ideas/archive/2022/04/pandemic-failed-economic-forecasting/629498/

Dougherty, C. (2021) 'Gavin Newsom signs two laws to ease California's housing crisis', *The New York Times*, 17 Sept. Available from: https://www.nytimes.com/2021/09/17/businesoundaom-california-housing-crisis.html?campaign_id=49&emc=edit_ca_20210920&instance_id=40845&noundationia-.today&regi_id=52258932&segment_id=69401&te=1&user_id=03e18edbfb156aca2917f37340442828

Eckart, K. (2020) 'Turning hotels into emergency shelter as part of Covid-19 response limited spread of coronavirus, improved health and stability', *UW News*, 7 October. Available from: https://www.washington.edu/news/2020/10/07/turning-hotels-into-emergency-shelter-as-part-of-covid-19-response-limited-spread-of-coronavirus-improved-health-and-stability/

Evans, W., Phillips, D., and Ruffini, K. (2021) 'Policies to reduce and prevent homelessness: what we know and gaps in the research', *Journal of Policy Analysis and Management*, 4(3): 914–63.

FEANTSA and Fondation Abbé Pierre. (2022) *The Seventh Overview of Housing Exclusion in Europe 2022*. Brussels. Available from: https://www.feantsa.org/public/user/Resources/reports/2022/Rapport_Europe_GB_2022_V3_Planches_Corrected.pdf

Fondation Abbé-Pierre. (2022) 'Logement d'abord, une promesse à tenir', Cahier 3. L'état de mal-logement en France 2022, Annual Report 27. Available from: https://www.fondation-abbe-pierre.fr/sites/default/files/reml_2022_cahier_3_web_logement_dabord_une_promesse_a_tenir.pdf

Groundswell. (2020) *Monitoring the Impact of Covid-19 Fortnightly Homelessness Briefing 3*, May. Available at: https://groundswell.org.uk/wp-content/uploads/2020/05/Covid-19-Fortnightly-Briefing-3-18.05.20.pdf.

Guise, A., Burridge, S. and Annand, P.J., Burrows, M., Platt, L., Rathod, S.D., Hosseini, P. and Cornes, M. (2022) 'Why were Covid-19 infections lower than expected amongst people who are homeless in London, UK in 2020? Exploring community perspectives and the multiple pathways of health inequalities in pandemics,' *SSM – Qualitative Research in Health*, 2022 Dec; 2: 100038. doi: 10.1016/j.ssmqr.2021.100038. Epub 2022 Jan 3. PMID: 35036989; PMCID: PMC8744008.

International Union of Tenants. (2021) '11 Claims by the International Union of Tenants to continue building for each person's right to a safe home in a Post-COVID World', Available at: https://www.iut.nu/wp-content/uploads/2021/09/IUTEUpostcovidclaimsFINAL.pdf

Kasakove, S. (2021a) 'With cases piling up, an eviction crisis unfolds step by step' *The New York Times*, 7 November. Available from: https://www.nytimes.com/2021/11/07/us/evictions-crisis-us.html

Kasakove, S. (2021b) 'As rents rise, so do pressures on people at risk of eviction', *The New York Times*, 18 October. Available from: https://www.nytimes.com/2021/10/18/us/eviction-rising-rent-cost.html?campaign_id=2&emc=edit_th_20211019&instance_id=43192&nl=todaysheadlines&regi_id=7123482&segment_id=72027&user_id=11e222152f3650adbda32b6305ca9654

Kasakove, S. and Thrush, G. (2022) 'Federal rental assistance is running out, with tenants still in need', *New York Times*, 7 January. Available from: https://www.nytimes.com/2022/01/07/us/federal-rental-assistance-evictions.html?campaign_id=2&emc=edit_th_20220108&instance_id=49813&nl=todaysheadlines&regi_id=7123482&segment_id=79071&user_id=11e222152f3650adbda32b6305ca9654

Klages, R. (2021) 'Bezirk votiert gegen pilotprojekt: doch kein "safe place" auf wiese am ring-center in Berlin-Lichtenberg.' *Tagesspiegel*, 30 June. Available from: https://www.tagesspiegel.de/berlin/doch-kein-safe-place-auf-wiese-am-ring-center-in-berlin-lichtenberg-6857062.html

Le Figaro. (2021) 'Sans-abri: le gouvernement annonce une réforme de l'hébergement d'urgence', 9 September. Available from: https://www.lefigaro.fr/actualite-france/sans-abri-le-gouvernement-annonce-une-reforme-de-l-hebergement-d-urgence-20210906

Leifheit, K.M., Linton, S.L., Raifman, J., Schwartz, G. L., Benfer, E. A., Zimmerman, F. J. and Pollack, C. E. (2021) 'Expiring eviction moratoriums and COVID-19 incidence and mortality', *American Journal of Epidemiology*, 190(12): 2503–10. Available from: Doi:10.1093/aje/kwab196

Leifheit, K.M., Chaisson, L., Medina, J.A., Wahbi, R. and Shover, C. (2021) 'Open forum infectious diseases', 8(7). Available from: Doi: 10.1093/ofid/ofab301

Liptak, A. and Thrush, G. (2021) 'Supreme Court Ends Biden's Eviction Moratorium', *The New York Times,* 7 November. Available from: https://www.nytimes.com/2021/08/26/us/eviction-moratorium-ends.html

Lui, M. and Hwang, S. (2021) 'Health care for homeless people', *Nature Reviews Disease Primers*, 7: 5. Available from: https://doi.org/10.1038/s41572-020-00241-2

McCann, M. (2021) 'Entitled to vaccines, undocumented immigrants in U.K. Struggle for access', *The New York Times*, 25 Sept. Available from: https://www.nytimes.com/2021/03/30/world/europe/uk-covid-vaccine-migrants.html?action=click&module=RelatedLinks&pgtype=Article

Mosites, E., Parker, E. and Clarke, K. (2020) 'Assessment of SARS-CoV-2 infection prevalence in homeless shelters—four U.S. cities, March 27–April 15, 2020', *MMWR. Morbidity and Mortality Weekly Report*, 69. Available from: https://doi.org/10.15585/mmwr.mm6917e1

Nande, A., Sheen, J., Walters, E. L., Klein, B., Chinazzi, M., Gheorghe, A. H., et al. (2021) 'The effect of eviction moratoria on the transmission of SARS-CoV-2', *Nature Communications*, 12(1): 2274. Available from: Doi:10.1038/s41467-021-22521-5

National Law Center on Homelessness and Poverty. (2019) *Housing not Handcuffs: Ending the Criminalization of Homelessness in US Cities* Washington: December.

Newman, A. (2021) 'Virus surges in New York City's homeless shelters', New York Times, [online] 23 December. Available from: https://www.nytimes.com/2021/12/23/nyregion/homeless-shelters-covid-cases.html?campaign_id=44&emc=edit_ur_20211224&instance_id=48617&nl=new-york-.today&regi_id=7123482&segment_id=77838&te=1&user_id=11e222152f3650adbda32b6305ca9654

Newman, A. (2021b) 'Eric Adams, N.Y.C.'s likely next mayor, wants to turn shuttered hotels into permanent housing for the homeless', *The New York Times*, 21 September. Available from: https://www.nytimes.com/2021/09/21/nyregion/homeless-shelters-eric-adams.html.

Newman, A. 2021c. '8,000 homeless people to be moved from hotels to shelters, New York says', *The New York Times*, June 16. Available from: https://www.nytimes.com/2021/06/16/nyregion/homeless-de-blasio-hotels.html

Newman, A. and Fitzimmon, E. (2022) 'New York City to remove mentally ill people from streets against their will', *The New York Times*, 29 November. Available from: https://www.nytimes.com/2022/11/29/nyregion/nyc-mentally-ill-involuntary-custody.html?smid=nytcore-ios-share&referringSource=articleShare

Nicholas, W., Greenwell, L., Henwood, B.F. and Simon, P. (2021) 'Using point-in-time homeless counts to monitor mortality trends among people experiencing homelessness in Los Angeles County, California, 2015-2019', *American Journal of Public Health*, 111: 2212-22. Available from: https://doi.org/10.2105/AJPH.2021.306502

Nova, A. (2022) 'Several states have run out of federal rental assistance, CNBC, January. Available from: https://cnb.cx/3tcO43n

OECD. (2020) 'Housing amid Covid-19: policy responses and challenges'. Available from: https://www.oecd.org/els/family/HC3-1-Homeless-pop ulation.pdf

OECD. (2021) *Affordable Housing Database.* Available from: http://oe.cd/ahd

OECD Social Policy Division, Directorate of Employment, Labour and Social Affairs. (2021) *HC3.1. Homeless Population*, May. Available from: https://www.oecd.org/els/family/HC3-1-Homeless-population.pdf

Padgett, D. K., Henwood, B. and Tsemberis, S. (2015) *Housing First: Ending Homelessness, Transforming Systems, and Changing Lives*, New York: Oxford University Press.

Padgett, D.K. and Herman, D. (2021) 'From shelters to hotels: an enduring solution to ending homelessness for thousands of Americans', *Psychiatric Services*, 72 (9): 986–7.

Pleace, N., Baptista, I. and Knutagård, M. (2019) *Housing First in Europe*, Brussels: Housing First Europe Hub. Available at: file:///Users/hsilver/Downloads/20191010HFinEurope_Full-Report2019_final.pdf.

Pleace, N., Baptista, I., Benjaminsen, L. and Busch-Geertsema, V. (2018) *Homelessness Services in Europe*, Brussels: FEANTSA.

Reed, D., Divringi, E. and Akana, T. (2021) 'Renters' experiences during COVID-19', *Federal Reserve Bank of Philadelphia*, 1 March.

Reynolds, K., Elder, K. and Tajo, M. (2021) *How Are Cities Planning to Use State and Local Fiscal Recovery Funds for Their Housing Needs?* 15 November. Available from: https://www.urban.org/urban-wire/how-are-cities-plann ing-use-state-and-local-fiscal-recovery-funds-their-housing-needs

Roy, A., Blasi, G., Coleman, J. and Eden, E. (2020) 'Hotel California: Available from: Hou file:///Users/hsilver/Downloads/20191010HFinEurope_Full-Report2019_final.pdfsing the crisis. UCLA Luskin Institute on Inequality and Democracy', 9 July. Available from: https://escholarship.org/uc/item/0k8932p6

Schuetz, J. (2020) 'How many households can't pay next month's rent? That's a tricky question', Washington, DC: The Brookings Institution. (October 26) Available from: https://www.brookings.edu/research/how-many-hou seholds-cant-pay-next-months-rent-thats-a-tricky-question/

Siegel, R. and O'Connell, J. (2021) 'The feared eviction "tsunami" has not yet happened. Experts are conflicted on why', *Washington Post*, 28 September. Available from: https://www.washingtonpost.com/business/2021/09/28/eviction-cliff-moratorium-rental-assistance/?utm_campa ign=wp_evening_edition&utm_medium=email&utm_source=newslet ter&wpisrc=nl_evening&carta-url=https%3A%2F%2Fs2.washingtonp ost.com%2Fcar-ln-tr%2F34d03ea%2F6153826b9d2fda9d41ecb047%2F5 96a708fade4e20ee3722758%2F8%2F53%2F6153826b9d2fda9d41ecb047

Silver, H. (1991) 'The privatization of housing in Great Britain', in *Privatization and its Alternatives*, ed. W.T. Gormley, Madison: University of Wisconsin Press.

Silver, H. and R. Morris. (2023) 'Homelessness, Politics, and Policy: Predicting spatial variation in COVID-19 cases and deaths', *IJERPH, MDPI*, 20(4): 1–13.

Snow, D. and L. Anderson. (2003) 'Street people', *Contexts* (Winter): 12–18.

Stack, L. (2022) 'Migrant shelter on Randalls Island will close after opening last month', *The New York Times*, 10 November. Available from: https://www.nytimes.com/2022/11/10/nyregion/migrant-shelter-randalls-island-close.html

Time News. (2021) 'Homeless people from Rummelsburger Bucht now also have to leave the hostel', July. Available from: https://time.news/homeless-people-from-rummelsburger-bucht-now-also-have-to-leave-the-hostel/

Tsai, J. and Wilson, M. (2020) 'COVID-19: a potential public health problem for homeless populations', *Lancet Public Health*, 5: e186–e7.

U.S. Bureau of the Census. (2021) Household Pulse Survey, October. Available from: https://www.census.gov/data/experimental-data-products/household-pulse-survey.html

U.S. Centers for Disease Control. (2022) *Guidance on Management of COVID-19 in Homeless Service Sites and in Correctional and Detention Facilities*, updated 29 Nov. Available from: https://www.cdc.gov/coronavirus/2019-ncov/community/homeless-correctional-settings.html?CDC_AA_refVal=https%3A%2F%2Fwww.cdc.gov%2Fcoronavirus%2F2019-ncov%2Fcommunity%2Fhomeless-shelters%2Funsheltered-homelessness.html

U.S. Department of Housing and Urban Development. (2022a) *The 2022 Annual Homelessness Assesssment (AHAR) Report to Congress*, Part 1, Washington, December. Available from: https://www.hudexchange.info/homelessness-assistance/ahar/#2022-reports

U.S. Department of Housing and Urban Development. (2022b) *Reforming the Eviction System During and After the Pandemic*, 20 September. Available from: https://www.huduser.gov/portal/pdredge/pdr-edge-featd-article-092022.html

U.S. Department of Housing and Urban Development and U.S. Interagency Council on Homelessness. (2021) *House America: An All-Hands-on-Deck Effort to Address the Nation's Homelessness Crisis*, Washington. Available from: https://www.hud.gov/house_america

US Department of the Treasury. (2022) 'Emergency Rental Assistance Program', 10 January. Available from: https://home.treasury.gov/policy-issues/coronavirus/assistance-for-state-local-and-tribal-governments/emergency-rental-assistance-program

U.S. Interagency Council on Homelessness. (2021) *Getting It Done: The American Rescue Way*, December. Available from: https://www.usich.gov/resources/uploads/asset_library/Getting_It_Done_the_American_Rescue_Plan_Way.pdf

University of Washington and King County Department of Community and Human Services. (2020) 'Impact of hotels as non-congregate emergency shelters', November. Available from: https://kcrha.org/wp-content/uploads/2020/11/Impact-of-Hotels-as-ES-Study_Full-Report_Final-11302020.pdf

Van Ness, L. (2021) 'States fail to prioritize homeless people for vaccines', *Stateline*, 1 March. Available from: https://www.pewtrusts.org/en/research-and-analysis/blogs/stateline/2021/03/01/states-fail-to-prioritize-homeless-people-for-vaccines

Van Sparrentak, K. (2020) 'Report on access to decent and affordable housing for all (2019/2187(INI))', Committee on Employment and Social Affairs, European Parliament, 8 December. Available from: https://www.europarl.europa.eu/doceo/document/A-9-2020-0247_EN.html.

Walker, A. (2021) 'L.A. built a tiny-house village for homeless residents, and some aren't so sure about it', *Curbed*, 27 April. Available from: https://www.curbed.com/2021/04/tiny-home-village-homeless-los-angeles.html

Williams, I. (2020) 'A reappraisal of contemporary homelessness policy: the new role for transitional housing programmes', *International Journal of Housing Policy*, 20(4): 578–87. Doi: 10.1080/19491247.2019.1663070.

Wilson, W. (2021) *Coronavirus: Support for Landlords and Tenants*, London: House of Commons Library, number 8867, December. Available from: https://commonslibrary.parliament.uk/research-briefings/cbp-8867/

Wiltz, T. (2020) 'Against CDC guidance, some cities sweep homeless encampments', *Stateline*, 28 April.

11

A Cultural Political Economy case study of Singapore's Central Provident Fund: critiquing welfare policy in the reproduction of subordination and inequality

Eve Yeo and Joe Greener

Introduction

Critical and politicised analyses of East Asian social policy have been constrained in social policy analysis due to a tendency toward scholarship focusing on comparative and modelling approaches. The comparative literature claims that the five 'Asian Tiger' countries could be competently categorised as 'developmental welfare states' (Hudson, Kühner and Yang, 2014, p 304). Hong Kong, South Korea, Singapore, Taiwan and Japan were seen in the comparative literature as primarily 'productivist' welfare states where market-oriented advancement is carefully calibrated to coordinate with development through technocratic competency (Holliday, 2000). The argument is that welfare policies in the five East Asian states are aligned to economic growth, possibly due to centralised managerialist bureaucratic competency through semi-authoritarian governance. Singapore, in particular, has been celebrated within this literature, functioning as an exceptional case for both its economic and political stability (for example, see: Ortmann and Thompson, 2020).

Criticising this view from political economy perspective, Hameiri and Jones (2020) argued that analyses of Southeast Asian development tended toward Weberian explanations of the capacity of bureaucratic state apparatuses to direct and orchestrate growth. According to Hameiri and Jones, Weberian explanations of the extensive growth in Southeast Asia focus on the projection of state power through centralised strategic coordination by professionalised administrative workers, with a clear view to nuture capital expansion. The authors contend that this tendency to focus on the 'autonomous' power of technocratic states to achieve development occludes the deeply *political* nature of state formation as the approach is often inadequate for explaining specific class forces and the aggregation of power (Hameiri and Jones, 2020, p 5). Whether countries achieve growth and the progression of these projects to distribute and secure access to welfare benefits across the population, for instance, are an outcome of localised struggle and contestation; the ability of capitalist classes to co-determine economic objectives with Government institutions; and the influence of globally institutionalised forces to adopt supportive or antagonistic positions as growth strategies consolidate and solidify. Comparative models and policy case studies may seem to present 'lessons' for replicability, but this disregards the complex geopolitical context in specific countries.

Analogous critiques of comparative social policy approaches can also be made with their tendency towards categorising and re-categorising 'ideal types'. As Hameiri and Jones point out in relation to comparative perspectives in political economy, there is an inclination toward 'producing endless typologies but very little in the way of explanation of why these regime forms exist and how they operate in practice' (2020, p 10). When research questions and methodologies developed in comparative East Asian social policy perspectives are preoccupied with classifications and comparative models, they fail to confront the forms of oppression meted out through welfare policies, leaving aside political questions around which groups and classes benefit and the capacity of policies to structure unmet need and exclusion (for example, see: Abrahamson, 2017; Aspalter, 2020). There is a need for critical perspectives in East Asian social policy that identify the systemic (re)production of oppression and inequality.

This piece unpacks social policies in Singapore, seeking to problematise assertions of the all-encompassing efficiency and effectiveness of the apparent technocratic social policies. The argument presented here, through an interrogation of the Central Provident Fund (CPF), is that East Asian social policies can be vessels for morally charged, discriminatory and dominating dynamics which are strongly implicated in structuring systems of inequality (see also Greener and Yeo, 2022). Utilising official government websites to map policy discourses and regulations, we follow a Cultural Political Economy (CPE) approach to problematise the regulation of welfare practices and relations in cementing the economic imaginary (Sum and Jessop, 2013). In doing so, we seek to denaturalise technocratic explanations of Singapore to position welfare policies as primary dynamics in the structuring and material routinisation of political economy. Much of the analysis of Singapore has tended toward a kind of celebration of development (Lee and Vasoo, 2008) or a surface level identification of technical problems (Mathew and Lim, 2019). The next section sets out and argues for a CPE approach to Singaporean and East Asian social policy scholarship (Jessop, 2009).

Theoretical framework: the cultural political economy

The CPE approach allows for a critique of welfare practices and an identification of the state-led processes in structuring social life. Sum and Jessop's (2013) CPE approach is harnessed here to critically interrogate welfare policies of Singapore as a crucial aspect in fabricating the everyday economy. CPE insists that bringing the relationship between meaning and practice is required to scrutinise interconnectedness between semiotic and material practices in the constitution of economic objects and subjects (Jessop, 2009; Sum and Jessop, 2013; Sum and Jessop, 2015). Semiosis encompasses the intersubjective processes of sense and meaning-making. We follow Sum and Jessop's preliminary definition of culture as 'the ensemble of social processes by which meanings are produced, circulated and exchanged', and as stressed by the authors, this definition 'indicates the overlap between culture and semiosis and importantly, does not reduce culture to language or discourse' (2013, p viii). CPE's maintains the role of semiosis in *all* areas of social life, and is in fact a response to address shortcomings of both 'hard' structuralist and 'soft' constructivist approaches to critical political economy (Sum and Jessop, 2013, p 22). In following the CPE approach, the chapter identifies the embedding of specific economic practices and logics in cultural significations, subjectivities and social relations that are formed, in part, through social policy's penetration into the fabric of everyday life.

CPE mobilises the concept of *economic imaginaries* to conceive of semiotic systems co-constitutive of material realities. Economic imaginaries are semiotic configurations that help to make sense of social realities as they inform social relations and embed production necessary for the functioning of a capitalist world. For example, Jessop argues that the more official use of term 'economy' has been used to simplify a complicated social world: to connote certain semiotic and material practices that entrench the organisation of economic activities (Jessop, 2005). While what counts officially as the economic realm remains contested, it has been historically constituted to reflect which productive practices and relations are viable, legitimate, elevated and institutionalised. The definition of what the economy really is has consequences for the boundaries of economic practices (Jessop, 2004; Jessop, 2009; Sum and Jessop, 2013). In truth, the entirety of an economy, even within a defined territory, is too complex and unstructured to be governed. Economic imaginaries simplify complex processes into objects that can become governable within or outside the architecture of the state. Economic imaginaries provide entry-points for the management of specified industrious activities amidst the chaotic totality of all economic activities. Through forces such as the state or supranational institutions like the World Bank and the International Monetary Fund (IMF), certain events, relations or practices come to be prioritised, lifting certain practices as central sites of governance, rendering others as tertiary. Economic imaginaries render some relations and dynamics as valuable while others are seen as secondary. Some imaginaries are more dominant than others, as dominant interests seek to entrench or destabilise markets, flows of goods, circuits of capital, socio-technical systems of labouring or intersections of state/family in caring, among a host of other potential economic realities. Concurrently, certain practices, notably caring and women's reproductive labour, are constructed as out of the boundaries of the economy, even when they are central to the functioning of economic relations.

Within wider economic imaginaries rest combinations of definable construals. Where an imaginary is a semiotic system, a construal is a semiotic element. A construal denotes a narrower assertion of a particular meaning. While 'all social construals are equal in the face of complexity, some are more equal than others in their impact on social construction', there are thus some construals that become hegemonic (Sum and Jessop, 2013, p 163). Dominant construals go on to constitute imaginaries. For the purposes of this chapter, we focus on welfare construals as sponsored by the state, to highlight the constitutive role of social policy as an integral aspect in the production and congealing of an economic imaginary which coordinates actions across specific institutional fields. Policy functions as 'important meaning-making instruments as deployed by agents to ... structure social life' (Jessop, 2009, p 339).

Economic imaginaries are a key site of contestation, with a 'central role in the struggle not only for "hearts and minds" but also for the reproduction or transformation of the prevailing structures of exploitation and domination' (Sum and Jessop, 2013, p 165). Social forces will seek to position a dominant imaginary and/or other complementary imaginaries that reproduce hegemony. As argued by Sum and Jessop, 'effective hegemony depends on the capacity of dominant groups to suture the identities, interests, emotions and values of key sectors of subordinate classes and other sub-altern groups into a hegemonic vision and embed this in institutions and policies – leading in turn to their translation into common sense' (Sum and Jessop, 2013, p 201). Where the state's 'suturing' of identities is a crucial aspect of how subjects make sense of inequality, dominant economic imaginaries shape the formation of identities and are partially constitutive of how individuals make sense of one another and their own positionality within the social world. Thus, imaginaries are important components in the shaping of social worlds and subjectivities, and specifically, a critical analysis of which imaginary comes to be reinforced and retained is then an investigation into the formation of hegemony.

Social policies regulate the material access to goods and services while conveying politically charged discourses about who is deserving. Thus, the welfare system is a key means by which the state penetrates economic life, often naturalising inequalities. While some scholars have developed the concept of welfare imaginary as a potential apparatus for building new projects of social policy, we use the term differently. Mary Murphy argues in the Irish context that developing imagination can helps us to think of what kind of society we collectively want to build, and build demands for new social policy consolidation (Murphy, 2021). We use it to understand the central role that a welfare system has in shaping semiotic and material processes in the governing of economic activities for a state-sponsored social order. In the next section, we provide an overview of the CPF, Singapore's foremost welfare system, before going on to reveal two construals on which it is founded.

A Cultural Political economy analysis of the Central Provident Fund: social policy processes in constituting the anti-welfare welfare state

The CPF is a 'forced' savings scheme where government deductions from wages allow individual and familial entitlement to healthcare, housing and education. The CPF rests on and fabricates a series of economic meanings and practices, promoting a host of normative decrees about what is the appropriate citizen in relation to work, finance management, and familial commitment. Rather than being completely benign, rational and technocratic, it arranges a set of exclusionary and inclusionary schemas. We focus on the configuration of two welfare construals at the foundation of the state's welfare project: labour activation and heteronormative familial relations. These semiotic imperatives fashion everyday life in Singapore as these construals constitute the anti-welfare imaginary and are innate to the state's hegemonic project.

The 'anti-welfarist' attitudes of Singaporean state leaders have been noted throughout the development of welfare project in Singapore (Barr and Skrbiš, 2008). In the early years of Singapore's nation building, then-Prime Minister Lee Kuan Yew has remarked that welfarism following post World War II in the developed West has led to people growing increasingly reliant on the state, which he believed made workers unproductive while also punishing successful and wealthy individuals (Lee, 2005). To avoid the imagined problem of welfarism where pensions were provided by the state and paid for by taxpayers, state leaders believed that a system where individuals accumulated their own savings for retirement was the best way forward (Lee, 2000, p 102).

CPF is a private pension scheme initially established in 1955 under the British colonial administration and it was later reformed by the post-independence government. CPF was initially designed as a pension fund, where withdrawals were initially only permitted after an individual turned 55 (Cheong, 2005). In a bid to increase home ownership in Singapore, the

1968 Approved Housing Scheme allowed individuals to utilise savings for housing purchases. Subsequently, as cost of living rose in Singapore during rapid industrialisation, CPF withdrawals were also allowed for healthcare, education and investment in the equity market (Vasoo and Lee, 2001). This makes CPF a comprehensive system covering many subsistence and welfare needs of the mass population.

CPF operates through private, individualised accounts. It is restricted to Singaporean citizens and permanent residents (PR) and accounts are created automatically. CPF savings accrue primarily from non-voluntary deductions from wages. Contribution rates vary based on the employee's income, age and citizenship status. There are also strict rules and regulations regarding the usage of funds to pay for eligible benefits.

Officially, CPF represents the state's approach to social policy, as reflected on the CPF website, where it states that 'Singapore's social policies embody the national philosophy of active government support for citizen self-reliance. This reinforces the values that keep Singapore strong, which are *individual effort and responsibility for the family*' (Central Provident Fund Board, 2022a, emphasis added).

One of the distinctive features of CPF and the welfare system in Singapore is that while there is a huge administrative and governance effort in managing social policy, the state claims that this policy architecture is fundamentally anti-welfare. It is geared toward promoting responsibility and activation, by its own admission. In truth, CPF is an immense welfare apparatus, it has come to be embedded into the everyday lives of the citizenry, and is the central policy tool configuring socio-economic relations. As noted earlier, the CPE approach seeks to see semiosis – for example, the meanings and construction of what is desirable or appropriate, what kind of society 'we are', what is the appropriate identity and behaviour of a given group, and so on – as co-constitutive of material economies (Sum and Jessop, 2013). Within the anti-welfare imaginary, welfare is conceptualised through self-reliance and familial responsibility rather than the social democratic notions of rights. In our case, we are interested in the official state-endorsed view of Singaporean national culture and the embedding of these assertion in the eligibilities and exclusions of social policy. *Economic self-reliance* and *family values* are two construals that constitute the dominant economic imaginary – claims around who should have what, when and why – underpinning the welfare system and the wider political economy.

Welfare Construal 1: Economic self-reliance

As briefly described previously, CPF is tied to the employment status of the individual. Labour in Singapore therefore remains highly commodified (Esping-Andersen, 1990). Labour commodification in Singapore has become naturalised through notions of economic self-reliance, and CPF offers insights into the pro-work emphasis of Singaporean life. Crucially, the construal of economic self-reliance must be contextualised alongside the financialisation of welfare as the dimensions of such financialising policy structure inform how labour remains commodified within Singaporean economic life. Financialisation displaces welfare responsibility onto the subject, and it also accounts for the highly individualised nature of Singaporean welfare.

We refer to financialisation as being concerned with the role of interest-bearing capital (Fine and Saad-Filho, 2016), and it can also be broadly understood as an increasing concern with finance, financial motives, and financial institutions (Epstein, 2005). Funds in CPF accounts are interest-bearing, which are matched by the CPF Board (Government Investment Corporation Private Limited (GIC) 2022). The monies within CPF are invested by the CPF Board in Special Singapore Government Securities (SSGS) that are issued only to CPF Board by the Singapore government. Proceeds from SSGS are managed through the nation's sovereign wealth fund, tying the capital sourced from the people's compulsory savings within financial markets and the global economy. This embedding of funds from CPF into interest-bearing capital as part of Singapore's global financial assets sorely anchors financialisation within the functioning this welfare apparatus.

The financialisation of welfare via CPF establishes the material basis of financialised capital and legitimises the domination of financial capital as a system of accumulation (Martin, 2002). The design of welfare in Singapore cannot be uncoupled from economic relations and processes as access to welfare is predicated on waged labour and the financial market. As a private pension fund that accumulates interests and encourages financial investments, facets of social life become assimilated into the financial sphere through CPF. Financialisation through CPF embed pro-work values with financial accumulation as *economic self-reliance* can only be achieved – according to state-led semiosis – through work and financial responsibility.

While Singaporeans and PR with gainful employment benefit from compound interest across sustained CPF contributions, there are 'losers' of this system. Low-wage employees with monthly earnings above Singapore Dollars (SGD)50 (€30) and lower than SGD500 (€350) will not see their wages subjected to CPF contributions, those earning between SGD500 to SGD750 (€350 to €526) are subjected to very low CPF contributions (less than 1% of their wage) while individuals earning more than SGD750 (€526) will be subjected to much higher CPF contributions. For the self-employed, CPF contributions are not mandatory unless their business income is more than SGD6000 (€4214) a year. This means that gig workers, notoriously precarious, will not benefit from the scheme. Low-wage workers also 'lose out' from attractive interest rates as their CPF funds are limited. CPF clearly privileges higher earning individuals who maintain consistent employment.

The introduction of CPF Investment Scheme (CPFIS) allows individuals to invest CPF funds so as to optimise their retirement funds. There are strict measures in place to 'protect' the funds accrued in CPF for retirement purposes, such as specifying eligibility through a minimal threshold of funds, where only individuals with sufficient funds are allowed to invest. Individuals who have been able to reap returns from their investments are likely to be able to put aside a higher pension and perhaps choose to withdraw cash from their CPF account if and when they are able to. Individuals with certain endowments are most likely the ones who are able to optimise their retirement through this scheme.

To meet retirement needs, CPF requires every subject to buy into the CPF Life annuity scheme through meeting a Retirement Sum (RS) using funds available in their CPF account. This is a scheme that ensures lifelong cash payouts for individuals after their retirement. There are varying retirement sums, ranging from SGD96 000 (€67 432) to SGD288 000 (€202296). The higher the RS, the higher the cash payout will be during the individual's retirement. Individuals who have been able to accumulate sufficient funds in their CPF accounts through long-term gainful employment and investments through CPFIS are able to access significant amounts of cash as compared to individuals who may have struggled from low wage jobs or inconsistent employment. Only individuals who have bought into a private annuity either through cash or CPFIS may be exempted from setting aside a RS.

Furthermore, even though the retirement age in Singapore is 62 years old, the monthly cash payouts will only be made automatically when the individual turns 70 years old, although individuals can opt to receive them earlier at age 65. The gap between the retirement age and cash payouts does point towards the expectations of private savings and even working after retirement, which highlights the inadequacies of CPF as a retirement fund. Where an individual has been able to accumulate sufficient funds by reaching FRS through long-term gainful employment and/or been lucky with their investments through CPFIS, they would be able to access significant amounts of cash during their retirement as compared to less wealthy individuals.

Chua highlights that social policy in Singapore prioritises individual wealth accumulation rather than alleviating poverty (2015). CPF reflects the disciplining force of policy: that subjects need to maintain a consistent level of productivity or risk falling out of the social net. The material mechanisms of CPF works to regulate Singaporean life, and its processes attempt to support a subjectivity aligned with asset or wealth accumulation to facilitate the labouring and active citizen who can expect assistance from the government given they plan carefully and work hard.

As a private pension fund, CPF cultivates investor-subjects through transferring 'overproduced and undercontrolled' risks onto subjects and forcing the internalisation of financial market logics (Belfrage, 2008, p 279). The

CPF website stresses the principle role the account-holder plays in saving, as 'CPF is designed to help Singaporeans support and take care of themselves in retirement', with the state only stepping in to provide targeted assistance (Central Provident Fund Board, 2022b). The emphasis on self-reliance through personal responsibility to 'stay employed and save more for your retirement' encourages specific behaviours for subjects to be self-responsibilised for access to welfare goods. The semiosis of self-reliance within the CPF functions as a regulatory force to moralise economic activity. Where the person is employed and enabled to save through CPF, they are considered to be financially savvy and responsible. This responsibilisation then works to naturalise the individualising and uneven nature of CPF in Singapore, which not only removes culpability of the policy for the increasing inequality in the country or poor social redistribution, but actively places blame at the individual level rather than considering inequality a structural consequence of its welfare regime.

While welfare in Singapore has been characterised as residual and highly conditional (Ng, 2015; Chua, 2015), the restrictive nature of CPF that we highlight here reveals the strategic nature of policy to enforce labour commodification and limit the compossibility of alternative capital-labour relations through semiotic and material moments. As *economic self-reliance* offers the pathway to a 'good retirement', the dimensions of financialisation via the architecture of CPF enable economic governance through the continued commodification of labour and moralisation of finance management. CPF processes are deliberate in privileging a self-reliant, that is, a productive and financialised subject: asset accumulation policies and pro-work values stresses the responsibility of the individual CPF account holder, and the various regulations in place reflects policy effort to discipline subjects into specific forms of employment.

Welfare Construal 2: Family values

Family values is the second welfare construal tangibly achieved through CPF's exclusions and entitlements, and it is perpetuated through hegemonic semiosis. This current section interrogates CPF policy framework with a view to its structuring of familial relations and values. Eligibility to a range of welfare goods is dependent on engaging in heteronormative household practices. The Singaporean family privileged by CPF is semiotically constituted and materialised by state agents and welfare policies. While scholars have described the changing nature of family and its members (Ciabattari, 2017; Treas, Scott and Richards, 2017), the Singaporean family remains very much a heteronormative nuclear household, formed by a marriage between a man and a woman. As a social form, the family normalises patriarchal gender roles and locates family relations as the primary site of social reproduction (Fraser, 2016).

Familial relations in particular have been 'rewarded' by CPF to encourage the formation of a 'proper family nucleus' (Housing & Development Board, 2023). As same-sex marriage is not legally recognised and same-sex couples are not eligible to apply for adoption under Singapore law, familial relations as inscribed within CPF policy specifically refers to relations within the heteronormative nuclear family which excludes alternative or diverse family structures. CPF seeks to embed shared economic responsibility between generations within the nuclear family by ascribing financial benefits to parents and legally recognised partners. Notions of filial piety inform certain aspects of CPF policy where rules often emphasise the financial and physical support of the elderly by their children. While CPF is tied to its account holder, the funds within the account can be used for close family members with the account holder's consent. For example, if an elderly parent does not have sufficient funds in their CPF medical account to cover hospitalisation, their child(ren) will be able to utilise funds in their CPF to cover insufficient funds (Central Provident Fund Board, 2022c). Adult children are also able to support their parents' mortgage using their CPF if their parent(s) are retired or unable to continue financing their mortgage. There are also Top Up schemes, which also offer tax benefits, that implore working children to contribute funds to their parents' CPF account to better support them during their retirement (Central Provident Fund Board, 2022d). Furthermore, other than in housing and healthcare, parents are also able to support their children's tertiary education using funds through the CPF Education Loan Scheme.

Accumulation of CPF funds start young. Children that are born as Singaporean citizens are given a Child Development Account (CDA) that is a part of the Baby Bonus scheme designed to support parents with the cost of raising a child. While money in the CDA can only be used for educational and healthcare expenses, unused funds will eventually be transferred to the child's CPF when they turn 31. From the state's perspective, this acts to strengthen the family unit, increasing reliance on the nuclear family (Loke and Sherraden, 2009). The design of CPF ensures firstly that direct family members are able to become the core financial support, rather than cultivating a reliance on the state for medical, housing or educational costs. There is a Proximity Housing Grant that seeks to encourage married children to stay near their parents and the 1995 Maintenance of Parents Act allows elderly Singaporeans to take legal action against their children who fails to support them financially. These are overt indications that there is a responsibility of elderly parents by their children.

In recent decades women's participation in the labour market has increased significantly which has conflicted significantly with the pro-natalist stance of the state. To deal with the contradictions between economic production and social reproduction, domestic and care work is often outsourced to cheap female foreign domestic workers. The employers of domestic foreign workers are required to pay a Foreign Worker Levy which was introduced to regulate the number of foreign workers, but only wives or mothers are allowed to apply for a Foreign Worker Levy Relief. Singaporean women are treated as implicitly responsible for the delegation of work in the private sphere as a direct employer of their domestic workers given that they are the ones who are eligible for the tax relief. Despite women's increased participation in the labour market, welfare policy does not seek to challenge traditional gender relations, and instead rely on labour immigration which displaces care roles onto exploited migrant women.

The state believes that the nuclear family is 'the basic building block of society' (Ministry of Social and Family Development, 2023). As highlighted previously, the family unit is therefore not only a social construction utilised by welfare policy for moral regulation, but also an economic modality through which social resources can be allocated and claimed. Within CPF websites and brochures, CPF transfers and cash top-ups are often encouraged to be made for 'loved ones' in pamphlets and videos so that their 'loved ones' would meet the RS or have higher monthly pay-outs (Central Provident Fund Board, 2017; Central Provident Fund Board, 2019). 'Loved ones' refer namely to spouses, elderly parents or siblings, and points quite specifically to heteronormative familial relations, since as previously highlighted, gay marriage is not legal and adoption for LGBTQ+ couples remain illegal. With the selective constitution of family as 'loved ones' across state-led semiosis to signify familial responsibility, it is the nuclear family that enables shared obligations where 'love' is subordinated to calculation and utility. The mobilisation of familial love to encourage subjects to beef up CPF accounts for their recognised family members should problematise the notion of 'loved ones', since relationships that are not state-sanctioned do not get to enjoy this sharing of CPF monies. Research conducted by Sayoni, a charity for queer women and transmen revealed that individuals were unable to utilise their CPF account for their partners as their relationships are not recognised by the state (Sayoni, 2018). Queer formations of families are rejected social forms by the state, and they do not get to share the familial benefits that are designed into CPF. These are specific material consequences of CPF, but the semiosis of 'loved ones' as an encouragement between the family that has been allowed to exist and flourish serves to deny the existence of love that exist within queer families and other alternative forms of collectivities. Through CPF processes, the nuclear family is constructed as an economic object with which the state organises access to welfare goods.

In a White Paper that sought to define the national values of Singapore, the family is considered 'fundamental building block out of which larger social structures can be stably constructed … within which human beings most naturally express their love for parents, spouse and children, and find happiness and fulfilment (Parliament of Singapore, 1991, p 3). As such the semiosis of family values indicates CPF as the central arena on which individuals should pursue wealth and happiness. CPF regulations highlight that policy processes determine eligibility and access to claims based on an individual's membership to a state-determined family nucleus. When the semiosis of the nuclear family is utilised to necessitate the exclusion of queer subjectivities and legitimise restricted access to welfare goods, this configuration of familial relations serves to hinder meaningful debates and potential struggles over redistribution as the valuation of the nuclear family within the welfare regime harbours heteronormativity as moralistic to establish queerness as undesirable, naturalising differentiation of the citizenry to legitimise the subordination or exclusion of certain sexualities and forms of intimacies.

Discussion

This chapter has focused on two distinct welfare construals as they represent enduring semiotic constellations on which policy frameworks rest and, by consequence, the very fabric of daily life. Our conception of the anti-welfare imaginary rests on Jessop's formulation of the CPE – that the stasis and transformation of economies rests on an interaction between symbolic and discursive realms with the co-determinate arena of the corporeal and substantial economy, including the built environment, technological forces of production and the socio-technical organisation of labour (Jessop, 2004). For Jessop, whether an economy is likely to re-organise or stabilise, is dependent on the 'social, material, and spatio-temporal relations among economic and extra-economic activities, institutions, and systems and their encompassing civil society' (2004, p 166). The development, imposition and reproduction of what Jessop describes as economic 'construals' is central when considering these economic relations. The manner in which certain circuits of value are legitimised as of primacy concern (for example, is it the financial or the industrial sector, which markets within these arenas are of central importance for governance and policy), which inequalities in power and wealth are justified, or the dominant explanation for economic crises arise are all examples of areas where construals operate in the economic realm. To be successful they must be embedded in social reality. They must go some way to allow people to understand economic realities and make decisions about subsistence.

The two construals move on to constitute the anti-welfare imaginary of Singapore. Welfare realities are avenues through which subjects themselves understand their economic lives through *individual effort* and *responsibility for the family*. The anti-welfare imaginary is harnessed to understand the stability of social policy in Singapore around two main discursive and symbolic construals. These construals, then, can be considered as a set of assumptions that favour and stabilise certain welfare-orientated relations and their associated identities and practices. They transform the problem of welfare into a set of identifiable manageable units. In other words, rendering individuals, families, households and non-citizen migrant labour as governable objects in order to secure reliable reproduction of the citizenry. Importantly, these are not merely discourses pushing the appropriate way one should behave or what is the state-desired identity. They are structured welfare policies, organising access to benefits and economic advantages while excluding and rendering marginal certain other actors and life-pathways. The anti-welfare imaginary is thus the semiotic scaffolding on which welfare provision is built. They prioritise certain arenas of care and wellbeing while offering rationales for those who are deserving and those undeserving. They also offer explanations for what a welfare state is, why it is in crisis and why there is a need for reform. Consistently the imaginary terrain structures the actual forms of welfare delivery that are retained, rejected and transformed in the face of socio-political and economic alteration.

The shorthand for these two constellations of signification offers a way into the main semiotic ensemble of the Singaporean welfare state, which could be competently argued to be, firstly, *a set of norms pushing hard work and self-reliance*, and secondly, *those construals pushing familial piety and conservative family values*. These habitually reproduced official discourses materially shape life practices through CPF processes where certain identities and behaviours related to responsible financial planning cover against uncertainty while encouraging productive employment, and the co-ordinating of care through the nuclear family. CPF regulates the everyday life, and the privileging of certain choices reproduces how responsible citizen-subjects should act, where subjects are increasingly taking on a role of the investor-consumer as their lifestyles are increasingly commodified so that financialised products can be enlivened and bodies more easily governed (French and Kneale, 2009).

We argue that the idea of anti-welfarism epitomises the manner in which CPF arranges class inequality. As Ruth Lister (2003) argues, while notions of rights have been key to understanding citizenship during the heyday of social democracy, political systems increasingly foreground obligation, active work and duty. Citizenship can be described as a set of rights which 'enables people to act as agents' (Lister, 2003, p 37). What rights can be accessed and on what terms is always a contested terrain. Singapore's post-independence history is defined by a historical commitment to defining citizenship in terms of obligation. Despite the fact that the state has concerned itself with an almost incomparable administrative and economic effort in centrally administrating the necessary arrangements for meeting needs, it is still able to claim that it is anti-welfare because obligations are asserted through discourse far more than rights. This also arguably means that the inequalities that are perpetuated through the various welfare policies come to be seen as acceptable. To reiterate, because CPF largely facilitates greater rewards for higher earning families and offers very little in the way of de-commodification, it generally supports, rather than mitigates, inequality. Semiotically this inequality is a justifiable reflection of what the state views as an authentic meritocratic system where hard work and capability rise to the top. The provision of housing, healthcare and retirement are not guaranteed outside of paid work or self-directed economic activity.

Welfare is governed tightly around the formation of the family unit and imposing shared responsibilities between family members. The upshot of this has been that the Singaporean system since independence has preferred to establish a series of rules concerning familial support, assistance within the family unit and migrant domestic worker migration over and above, for instance, the development of community care. The instigation of say, sheltered housing, residential care, or communal forms of support have been greatly restrained when compared to other welfare states.

As we noted more extensively in a recent paper (Greener and Yeo, 2022), CPF works to create a series of oppressive outcomes for certain groups. For instance, the compulsion to form heteronormative households constructs sexuality in a narrow fashion. Even in light of the recent repealing of laws banning homosexuality, the priorities given to heterosexual couples makes accessing housing for LGBTQ+ individuals difficult. Faced with the fact that CPF orientates toward a form of privatised planning of care and reproduction within the family nucleus, many households have inevitably turned to migrant domestic workers. This is perhaps the most glaring failure of Singapore's welfare system: the care needs of many dependents – children, the elderly and disabled people – are met through highly exploited and lowly paid migrant domestic workers from the Philippines, Indonesia, Myanmar and other poorer nations (Ye, 2016).

The CPF system also crafts and replicates social stratification through the configuration of productive and reproductive relations (Greener and Yeo, 2022). As described, it delivers greater benefits to wealthier families and individuals due to its 'get what you saved for' principle. Perhaps most significantly, it guarantees virtually no support outside of paid employment and thus acts according to what Claus Offe saw as the central dynamic of social policy in capitalism: proletarianisation, or the 'transformation of dispossessed labour into active wage-labour' (Offe, 1984, p 93). CPF delivers no assistance to unemployed people, but retirement incomes are almost entirely determined by previously saved monies. In 2018, the employment rate for over 65s was 26.8% (Liew, 2019). Others have argued that the CPF system fails to deliver liveable subsistence standards for many in retirement with many older people forced back into the labour market or left dependent on their family (Ng, 2011; Ng et al, 2019).

Tremewan (1994), recounting the history of housing policy in Singapore argues that while Singapore's public housing programme offered significant improvements in the standard of wellbeing, it also isolated the family from its previous embedding in dense communitarian networks. Indeed, the relocation from village contexts to large housing estates from the 1960s onwards was also a significant victory for the wider PAP project orientated toward eliminating or nullifying potential opposition elements. With the end of the Kampung came the end of the organic social ties and solidarities that existed there. Although the country looks significantly different to the industrialising period Tremewan was discussing, the current system maintains this principle of a clearly bounded family as the primary object of social control. As Hochuli, Hoare and Cunliffe (2021) argued recently, political life in many parts of the developed world have been defined as a period of de-politicisation. Politics, for them, is defined as contestation and struggle aimed at overturning unequal social orders. Herein lies one of the central enduring features of CPF. Just as its original orientation was to break up potentially counter and pro-labour forces, it lasts as a depoliticising technology maintaining a series of hierarchies around class, gender and race. Critically, by calibrating a series of benefits – such as access to property or healthcare – as well as ineligibilities, it also effectively mitigates from serious contestation even as it maintains high levels of inequality.

Semiotically the two construals – those relating to self-directed economic activity and the family – are continually framed as the primal and natural justifications for the welfare system. As Piketty notes, 'every human society must justify its inequalities' (2020, p 1), the state's 'suturing' of welfare relations results in the legitimating of unequal hierarchies that exist within the labour market and non-state sanctioned relationships.

Conclusion

The purpose of this chapter has been to map out the contours of the dominant economic imaginary through Singapore's welfare project to identify the ways in which economic processes come to be reproduced. Policy processes relating to paid economic activity and the family constitute the 'common sense' of Singaporean society, helping to naturalise a series of hierarchies. The approach taken here considers the significance of using economic imaginaries in understanding social systems. The manner in which a dominant political and ideological system understands itself continually frames and fashions the very policies and their associated daily practices that are at the heart of welfare practices. Focusing on these imaginaries assists in asking questions around who is seen as valuable and worthy of support and what groups are seen as undeserving. The point being that the semiotic assertions around the purposes of welfare pervade and influence the conjunctural development of policy.

Arguably, conventional previous approaches to understanding social policy in East Asia have sought to take a less critical stance and reproduce a naturalised technocratic myth around the innate of benefits of so-called developmentalist or productivist social policies without examining the contestable and arguably contentious politics they rest on.

References

Abrahamson, P. (2017) 'East Asian welfare regime: obsolete ideal-type or diversified reality', *Journal of Asian Public Policy*, 10(1): 90–103.

Aspalter, C. (2020) *Ideal Types in Comparative Social Policy*, UK: Routledge.

Barr, M.D. and Skrbiš, Z. (2008) *Constructing Singapore: Elitism, Ethnicity and the Nation-building Project*, Denmark: Nias Press.

Belfrage, C. (2008) 'Towards "universal financialisation" in Sweden?', *Contemporary Politics*, 14(3): 277–96.

Central Provident Fund Board (2017) CPF #ICanAdult – Are your parents ready to retire? *CPF in One Bite* [online video]. Available from: https://www.youtube.com/watch?v=ApEqjDvaVio [Accessed 1 May 2020].

Central Provident Fund Board. (2019) *CPF Transfers and Cash Top-ups: Learn how You can Grow Your CPF Savings or that of Your Loved Ones to get Higher Retirement Payouts,* Singapore: Central Provident Fund Board.

Central Provident Fund Board. (2022a) *The CPF Story.* Available from: https://www.cpf.gov.sg/member/who-we-are/the-cpf-story [Accessed 14 Sep 2022].

Central Provident Fund Board. (2022b) *CPF Overview.* Available from: https://www.cpf.gov.sg/member/cpf-overview [Accessed 14 Sep 2022].

Central Provident Fund Board. (2022c) *Healthcare Financing: Using your MediSave Savings for Yourself and Loved Ones.* Available from: https://www.cpf.gov.sg/member/healthcare-financing/using-your-medisave-savings [Accessed 14 Sep 2022].

Central Provident Fund Board. (2022d) *Growing Your Savings: Retirement top-ups for Loved Ones, Employees and Others.* Available from: https://www.cpf.gov.sg/member/growing-your-savings/saving-more-with-cpf/top-up-to-enjoy-higher-retirement-payouts/top-ups-for-loved-ones-employees-and-others [Accessed 14 Sep 2022].

Cheong, C. (2005) *Saving for Our Retirement: 50 Years of CPF*, Singapore: Published for Central Provident Fund Board by SNP Editions.

Chua, B.H. (2015) 'Singapore: growing wealth, poverty avoidance and management', in Bangura, Y. (ed.) *Developmental Pathways to Poverty Reduction*, Springer, pp 201–29.

Ciabattari, T. (2017) *Sociology of Families: Change, Continuity, and Diversity*, UK: Sage Publications.

Epstein, G. A. (2005) *Financialization and the World Economy*. USA: Edward Elgar Publishing.

Esping-Andersen, G. (1990) *The Three Worlds of Welfare Capitalism*, USA: Princeton University Press.

Fine, B. and Saad-Filho, A. (2016) 'Thirteen things you need to know about neoliberalism', *Critical Sociology,* 43(4–5): 685–706.

Fraser, N. (2016) 'Contradictions of capital and care', *New Left Review,* 100(99): 99–117.

French, S. and Kneale, J. (2009) 'Excessive financialisation: Insuring lifestyles, enlivening subjects, and everyday spaces of biosocial excess', *Environment and Planning D: Society and Space,* 27(6): 1030–1053.

Government Investment Corporation Private Limited (GIC). (2022) *Does GIC invest money from the Central Provident Fund (CPF)?* Available from: https://www.gic.com.sg/who-we-are/faqs/ [Accessed 07 Mar 2022].

Greener, J. and Yeo, E. (2022) 'Reproduction, discipline, inequality: critiquing East- Asian developmentalism through a strategic-relational examination of Singapore's Central Provident Fund', Global Social Policy, 22(3): 483–502.

Hameiri, S. and Jones, L. (2020) 'Theorising political economy in Southeast Asia', in Carroll, T., Hameiri, S. and Jones, L. (eds) *The Political Economy of Southeast Asia: Politics and Uneven Development Under Hyperglobalisation* (4th edn), Switzerland: Palgrave Macmillan, pp 3–34.

Hochuli, A., Hoare, G. and Cunliffe, P. (2021) *The End of the End of History: Politics in the Twenty-First Century*, UK: Zero Books.

Holliday, I. (2000) 'Productivist welfare capitalism: Social policy in East Asia', *Political Studies*, 48(4): 706–723.

Housing & Development Board. (2023) *Eligibility Check – Buying an HDB Flat and Applying for an HDB Housing Loan.* Available from: https://services2.hdb.gov.sg/webapp/BP13EligCheck/BP13PEssentialOcc.jsp. [Accessed 08 Jan 2023].

Hudson, J., Kühner, S. and Yang, N. (2014) 'Productive welfare, the East Asian "model" and beyond: placing welfare types in greater China into context', *Social Policy and Society*, 13(2): 301–15.

Jessop, B. (2004) 'Critical semiotic analysis and cultural political economy', *Critical Discourse Studies*, 1(2): 159–74.

Jessop, B. (2005) 'Cultural political economy, the knowledge-based economy and the state', in Barry, A. and Slater, D. (eds) *The Technological Economy*, London and New York: Routledge, pp 142–64.

Jessop, B. (2009) 'Cultural political economy and critical policy studies', *Critical Policy Studies*, 3(3–4): 336–56.

Lee, J. and Vasoo, S. (2008) 'Singapore: social investment, the state and social security', in Midgley, J. and Tang, K.-l. (eds) *Social Security, the Economy and Development*, London: Palgrave Macmillan UK, pp 269–86.

Lee, K.Y. (2000) *From Third World to First: The Singapore Story: 1965–2000*, USA: HarperCollins.

Lee, K.Y. (2005) '37th Jawaharlal Nehru Memorial Lecture', New Delhi

Liew, M. (2019) 'Seniors at work: the new norm for ageing in Singapore', *Asean Today*. Available from: https://www.aseantoday.com/2019/02/seniors-at-work-the-new-norm-for-ageing-in-singapore/ [Accessed 1 Sep 2022]

Lister, R. (2003) 'Investing in the citizen-workers of the future: transformations in citizenship and the state under New Labour', *Social policy & Administration*, 37(5) 427–43.

Loke, V. and Sherraden, M. (2009) 'Building assets from birth: a global comparison of child development account policies', *International Journal of Social Welfare*, 18(2): 119–29.

Martin, R. (2002) *Financialization of Daily Life*, USA: Temple University Press.

Mathew, M. and Lim, L. (2019) 'Social equity in Singapore', in Johansen, M. (ed.) *Social Equity in the Asia-Pacific Region: Conceptualizations and Realities*, Cham: Springer International Publishing, pp 215–33.

Ministry of Social and Family Development. (2023) *Family Protection and Welfare*. Available from: https://www.msf.gov.sg/policies/Strong-and-Stable-Families/Supporting-Families/Family-Protection-and-Welfare/Pages/default.aspx [Accessed 08 Jan 2023].

Murphy, M. (2021) 'A new welfare imaginary for the island of Ireland', *Irish Studies in International Affairs*, 32(2): 532–57.

Ng, I.Y.H. (2015) 'Being poor in a rich "Nanny State": developments in Singapore social welfare', *The Singapore Economic Review*, 60(03). 1550038.

Ng, K.H. (2011) 'Review essay: prospects for old-age income security in Hong Kong and Singapore', *Journal of Population Ageing,* 4(4): 271–93.

Ng, K.H., Teo, Y.Y., Neo, Y.W., Maulod, A. and Ting, Y. T. (2019) *What Older People Need in Singapore: A Household Budgets Study*, Singapore: ScholarBank@NUS Repository. Available from: https://scholarbank.nus.edu.sg/handle/10635/157643

Offe, C. (1984) *Contradictions of the Welfare State*, London: Hutchinson.

Ortmann, S. and Thompson, M.R. (2020) *China's 'Singapore Model' and Authoritarian Learning*, UK: Routledge.

Parliament of Singapore (1991) *Shared Values*. White Paper.

Piketty, T. (2020) *Capital and Ideology*, England: Belknap Bress of Harvard University Press.

Sayoni (2018) *Violence and Discrimination Against LGBT Women in Singapore: Documentation of Human Rights Violations*, Singapore: Sayoni.

Sum, N.-L. and Jessop, B. (2013) *Towards a Cultural Political Economy: Putting Culture in its Place in Political Economy*, UK: Edward Elgar Publishing.

Sum, N.-L. and Jessop, B. (2015) 'Cultural political economy and critical policy studies: developing a critique of domination', in Fischer, F., Torgerson, D., Durnová, A. and Orsini, M. (eds) *Handbook of Critical Policy Studies*, Edward Elgar Publishing, pp 128–50.

Treas, J., Scott, J. and Richards, M. (2017) *The Wiley Blackwell Companion to the Sociology of Families*, UK: John Wiley & Sons.

Tremewan, C. (1994) *The Political Economy of Social Control in Singapore*, London: Macmillan Press.

Vasoo, S. and Lee, J. (2001) 'Singapore: social development, housing and the Central Provident Fund', *International Journal of Social Welfare*, 10(4): 276–83.

Ye, J. (2016) *Class Inequality in the Global City: Migrants, Workers and Cosmopolitanism in Singapore,* UK: Palgrave Macmillan.

12

Unmet need, epistemic injustice and early death: how social policy for Autistic adults in England and Wales fails to slay Beveridge's Five Giants

Aimee Grant, Gemma Williams, Kathryn Williams and Richard Woods

Introduction

Social policies are not neutral, and their impacts vary. Many social policies meet the needs of the majority at the expense of minority groups: a form of *epistemic injustice* (Fricker, 2007). For example, minority groups are often excluded or silenced by the policy-making process (*testimonial injustice*). Their contributions, such as to government consultations, are distorted or misrepresented due to policy makers' discriminatory beliefs and reliance on incorrect or outdated stereotypes (Chapman and Carel, 2022). Furthermore, a lack of resources available to explain problems faced by minorities, due to their exclusion from collective, social meaning-making practices by the powerful majority (*hermeneutical injustice*), compounds structural prejudice (Fricker, 2007). While all groups are impacted by hermeneutical resources, the powerful majority benefits, while minority groups are unjustly disadvantaged. Remi Yergeau illustrates this point in relation to Autistic people: 'Despite autistic people's increased visibility and, indeed, increased participation in public policy and political advocacy, autistic stories are not the autism stories that circulate, dominate or permeate' (Yergeau, 2017: 4).

Autism is a normal part of cognitive diversity, affecting around 2% of the population, although variation in diagnosis by gender and ethnicity occurs (Centre for Disease Control (CDC) 2022). Being Autistic, however, is often experienced as a challenging disability in the UK and beyond, due to policies being based on outdated medical (deficit-focused) models of Autism which downplay societal impacts (Woods et al, 2018). Autistic people die between 16 and 30 years before our neurotypical peers and the suicide rate for Autistic people is nine times that of other adults (Mandell, 2018). However, over 80% of Autistic people would not accept a 'cure' for Autism if it existed (Bonnello, 2022). There has been growing recognition of neurotype being a core demographic attribute, for example through being included in the 2011 Scottish Census. However, to date, the impact of being Autistic on social policy has not been explored. Furthermore, in general, neurodivergent people's ability to speak for themselves and to advocate for policies and services which meet their needs has not been widely recognised in the UK or elsewhere due to the privileging of parent voices (for example, in Italy: Sicilia et al, 2016), aiming to 'cure' our neurotype (for example, the USA *Combating* Autism Act 2006) and the adoption of tokenistic gestures such as 'Autism Awareness Day'. Catala et al, (2021) identify these types of epistemic injustice as disabling for Autistic people. This chapter is written by four Autistic academics, who have lived experience of inaccessible services arising from social policy, including benefits (Grant, 2023), employment (Grant and Kara, 2021) and healthcare (Williams, 2022).

The Autism Act 2009 (as revised by the *Think Autism Strategy*, 2014), required governments to develop and implement strategies to provide services for Autistic adults, with Local Authorities obliged to deliver these services. The current strategies, in the context of devolution are the English *National Strategy for Autistic Children, Young People and Adults: 2021–2026* (*'Strategy'*) (Department of Health and Social Care (DHSC) and Department for Education, (DfE) 2021), and the Welsh *Autism Delivery Plan 2021–2022* (*'Code of Practice'*) (Welsh Government, 2021a). The *Strategy* acknowledges that there is a lack of understanding and acceptance of Autistic people, and that significant change is required. It identifies six priorities for improving support, access, and addressing inequalities faced by Autistic people which include education, health, employment and criminal justice. *The Code of Practice* provides guidance to ensure that service requirements written into existing legislation placed on statutory services are met. That these additional policies are required indicates that existing social policy did not sufficiently address the needs of Autistic people.

One of the central pillars of the Autism Act 2009 was to improve the diagnostic pathway, which is echoed in the Welsh *Code of Practice*. However, Welsh diagnosis statistics show that only 0.5% of people are diagnosed as Autistic (Underwood et al, 2021), thus around three-quarters of Autistic people are not diagnosed (CDC, 2022) which hides their needs. Diagnostic pathways are not expected to significantly improve according to the Royal College of Psychiatrists (2020). Moreover, the Westminster Commission on Autism (2021) identified significant and growing dissatisfaction regarding diagnostic services, including long delays, lack of clarity about diagnostic pathways, insufficient time with health professionals and not feeling listened to. With significant barriers to obtaining a diagnosis, some of which particularly impact Autistic people's needs (Howard and Sedgewick, 2021), some Autistic people will remain undiagnosed indefinitely. Furthermore, misdiagnosis is common for Autistic people, with many English diagnostic services providing broad diagnoses like 'personality disorder' rather than using more specific diagnoses included in diagnostic manuals, such as Autism (Allsop and Kinderman, 2021). However, many public services aimed at Autistic people cannot be accessed until a diagnosis is received (Westminster Commission, 2016).

Should an Autistic adult secure a diagnosis, there is no automatic service provision for them. Generic barriers to accessing public services can negatively affect Autistic people seeking public services. For example, public service staff often have inadequate resources to match demand, resulting in them using discretion when deciding who to help (Lipsky, 2010). Autistic people experience widespread stigmatisation and discrimination, in part due to dehumanising misinterpretations of differing communication styles (Williams, G. 2021) despite a lack of *neurotypical* empathy being central to mutual misunderstanding (Milton, 2012). Furthermore, public service staff are often subjected to targets and intensive monitoring, which can lead to those with more complex needs failing to benefit from the system (Lipsky, 2010). In this multiply challenging context, it is likely that Autistic people – and particularly those who are also marginalised in other ways, such as by their ethnicity (Jones and Mandell, 2020) – will have lesser access to public services than neurotypical peers. Moreover, access to public services in the UK is often via telephone, which is known to be so challenging for Autistic people to navigate that they are unable to access services intended for them (Grant et al, in preparation).

Having considered barriers around diagnosis and widespread systemic barriers to accessing public services, this chapter moves on to consider how UK social policy is experienced by Autistic people. We utilise a modern iteration of Beveridge's (1942) Five Giants: health (disease), education (ignorance), employment (idleness), poverty (want) and housing (squalor).

Health

Health services in the UK are highly bureaucratic, prone to significant delays and are confusing for patients – even more so for marginalised groups (Robards et al, 2018). The National Health Service (NHS) long-term plan specifically includes access to healthcare for Autistic people as a priority, as well as social prescribing (NHS, 2019). However, without appropriate diagnoses, as described in the introduction, this aim cannot be realised. In addition to delayed diagnosis, 76% of diagnosed Autistic people have noted that their General Practitioner (GP) does not make any reasonable adjustments for them, despite the value of small accommodations such as additional processing time during appointments (Westminster Commission, 2016). Moreover, GP records may not be updated to show a diagnosis (Williams, K., 2022), and many Autistic people do not proactively disclose being Autistic during appointments due to fear of stigma, receiving worse treatment, and even their children being taken into social care. Lack of clinician understanding of Autistic presentations of pain and distress are a further barrier to adequate care (Grant et al, in preparation). These findings are echoed in research with health professionals including a lack of knowledge and confidence in supporting Autistic patients (Corden et al, 2022). Furthermore, during COVID-19, Autistic people were involuntarily subjected to Do Not Resuscitate orders, showing dehumanisation in healthcare (Mladenov and Brennan, 2021).

Within England, Oliver McGowan Mandatory Training in learning disability and Autism will be introduced in 2022 for health and social care staff with the aim of increasing 'understanding of people's needs, resulting in better services and improved health and wellbeing' (Health Education England, 2022: 1). The development of training materials was not Autistic-led, and this training is based on outdated understandings of Autism, such as the impaired theory-of-mind hypothesis which has a questionable evidence base (Williams, 2021). Additionally, an evaluation by the National Development Team for inclusion (NDTi, 2022) found that two of the three training packages presented for review had insufficient and low-quality evidence. Furthermore, while we agree that providing education in understanding Autism could lead to better care, such training can be viewed as shifting responsibility for inaccessible care to individual clinicians, rather than addressing structural and material factors (such as consistent underfunding) which make individualised care almost impossible to deliver in the NHS.

One of the greatest barriers reported by Autistic people to accessing healthcare is the challenges to using the telephone for booking appointments or talking to service providers, with nearly two thirds of Autistic adults (62%) reporting significant difficulties booking a GP appointment by telephone, compared to only 16% of non-Autistic respondents (Doherty et al, 2022). Furthermore, Doherty and colleagues identified that difficulties using the telephone to book an appointment were found to be significantly associated with almost all adverse health outcomes for Autistic people. An additional barrier to accessing healthcare is the sensory environment of clinical spaces, which can be too bright, too busy, and too loud while staff restrict the use of Autistic coping strategies (NDTi, 2020); digital healthcare could remove many of these barriers, although early evidence suggests it is not currently meeting Autistic needs (Williams, 2022).

A low-cost, largely tokenistic attempt to make healthcare more accessible to Autistic people, including by making changes to the sensory environment, is the use of Autism Health Passports, a short digital or paper-based record, containing individual Autistic people's needs relating to communication and sensory environments. These are recommended by the UK National Institute for Health and Care Excellence (NICE, 2021). However, health passport tools and wider interventions, such as training and electronic prompts, are almost all inadequately theorised, under evaluated and operating in a hostile context, so the passports do not seem to benefit Autistic patients (Ellis et al, forthcoming).

Education

Being Autistic has known impacts on accessing education, including deficits in executive function, working memory and the need for additional processing time; all of which may become more disabling in an inhospitable sensory environment. Additionally, in a society where Autistic experiences are denied legitimacy, communication barriers and stigma may result in Autistic people being considered 'troublemakers' rather than Disabled. Neurodivergences are known to cluster, and around one third of Autistic people have co-occurring learning disabilities (CDC, 2022). These educational barriers impact Autistic children, who make up most children with Special Educational Needs in England, and account for 80% of children in alternative educational provision (formerly Pupil Referral Units). Only one fifth reach expected standards in writing and maths (HM Government, 2022). This failure has dramatic impacts on post-16 education opportunities available to Autistic adults, and Holmes (2022) notes that only 8% of students with a statement of special educational needs or an Education, Health and Care Plan (EHCP) progress to university compared to almost 50% of students without an identified additional need. The difference is even more stark for prestigious universities. Unsurprisingly, only 4% of Autistic people report feeling supported in education (DfE and DHSC, 2021).

Disabled Students Allowances (DSA) have been available since 1974 as a non-means-tested grant to assist with the disability related costs of higher education study. It is open to all Disabled students, including those who are Autistic. However, multiple systemic barriers have been identified by Lord Holmes' (2022) review which have led to less than one third of students who declared that they were Disabled accessing the allowance, not to mention those who did not declare their disability. These barriers included a challenging application process, significant delays in processing applications (preventing support being in place at the beginning of study), the requirement for Disabled students to coordinate their own support – which has been described as akin to a 'full time job' – and inconsistent quality in provided support (Holmes, 2022: 6). These barriers would be challenging to any Disabled student, but particularly so to Autistic people, who often struggle with the executive functioning necessary to drive an application for DSA forward. When UK universities were initially required to implement support packages for Autistic people, they provided the minimum acceptable level of support (Madriaga and Goodley, 2010). More recently, EHCPs were designed to be used for those living in England with additional support needs, including those linked to being Autistic, until the age of 25 years. In Wales, the Additional Learning Needs Code for Wales 2021 (Welsh Government, 2021b) has introduced a similar policy. However, both policies stipulate that this support is for those entering further education rather than higher education. Therefore, universities are not legally obliged to offer these, and students must apply for DSA instead.

Autistic students within UK higher education have reported numerous barriers to equal participation including navigating group work without adequate support, assessment accommodations marking them out as 'other', and being excluded from social activities (Madriaga and Goodley, 2010). This may be related to staff believing that they *are* accommodating Autistic students, when their actions while teaching show unconscious resistance to inclusive practices, partially in response to inadequate Autism training (von Below et al, 2021) or a hidden curriculum that disadvantages Autistic people (Byrne, 2022). Such exclusion from peers and teachers disadvantages students both at university and in their professional lives (Byrne, 2022), and relatively little mental health support is available for Autistic students (Mulder and Cashin, 2014) who are known to intensely feel the impact of such exclusion.

Employment

Autistic adults who are unemployed have a lower quality of life than those in work (Mason et al, 2018). The Autism Act 2009 emphasises that Autistic people should be able to access employment. However, Autistic people are under-employed compared to neurotypical people, with 22% of Autistic people in paid work compared to 81% of non-Disabled people (ONS, 2021), although this figure is unreliable due to underdiagnosis. Autistic people face barriers to employment at every step of the employment journey, beginning with inaccessible recruitment practices, not having their communication and sensory needs met within the workplace (leading to challenges in completing work), feeling the need to 'mask' Autistic traits during interaction with colleagues, managers who do not understand Autistic needs, and bullying, harassment and discrimination (Booth, 2016). Additionally, senior managers may be prejudiced, discrimination may be justified on the grounds of it being best for the business, and Autistic strengths may go unrecognised (Djela, 2021). In this context it is unsurprising that only 18% of Autistic people report that they have good accommodations at work (Bonnello, 2022). The COVID-19 global pandemic made work more accessible for some Autistic people due to the use of remote working, which allowed the use of sensory strategies not possible to use within workplaces (Autistic UK, unpublished data). However, during the pandemic, Disabled employees were more likely to be made redundant (Citizens Advice, 2020), and politicians and employers alike have pushed for a return to the office which would have a disproportionately negative impact for Autistic employees.

A range of government initiatives can be found within the UK with the prima facie aim of supporting Disabled people into work. There are no specific policies aimed solely at Autistic people, although some resources have been developed by the DWP and partner organisations run by neurotypical people, using outdated stigmatising language; these are yet to be evaluated (House of Commons, 2018). Within JobCentre Plus, the UK version of a 'welfare office', Disability Employment Advisors are intended to support Disabled people into work, using a 'menu' of support options that include advice regarding job seeking, training and various government initiatives such as referrals to for-profit job coaches. However, just 4% of Autistic adults considered the Autism knowledge of Jobcentre Plus staff to be 'good' (NAS, 2019).

For Autistic people who have made it into employment, Access to Work is an initiative to pay for the additional disability-related costs of being employed. For Autistic employees, a support worker may be provided, as well as training for managers and colleagues (to reduce discrimination) and coaching for the Autistic person to help them identify strategies to cope with barriers in the workplace. However, like DSA, it is difficult to access and bureaucratic in a way that is particularly challenging for Autistic people to navigate. This means that while 42% of Autistic adults feel that they require support to access employment, only 12% are in receipt of such support (NAS, 2019).

The Equality Act 2010 strengthened anti-discrimination legislation in the workplace, making it illegal for employers to refuse 'reasonable adjustments' relating to recruitment, promotion, pay and terms of employment. If Autistic employees feel that reasonable adjustments have not been made for them or they have been terminated due to discriminatory reasons, they can take their complaint to an Employment Tribunal. Employment Tribunals were initially intended to be a fast, cheap, and informal way of resolving employment disputes, but the system has become more cumbersome over time, relying on complex legal tests and restrictive judicial decisions, making the system inaccessible to unrepresented Disabled employees (William et al, 2019). Furthermore, Citizens Advice (2020) note that, in response to the COVID-19 pandemic, already significant delays have been exacerbated at a time when demand has increased, and the Employment Tribunal system is now in crisis.

Poverty

Data on the prevalence on poverty among Autistic people is largely absent. However, in 2009 one third of Autistic people did not have access to benefits or paid work (UK Parliament, 2009), and 82% who had applied for benefits said they needed support to apply (Left Brain Right Brain, 2009). Unsurprisingly, an international survey of Autistic people found that 63% have financial concerns, and concerns were higher among those aged under 50 years (Bonnello, 2022). Among Autistic adults in Australia, the mode income level was around one quarter of the mean income for full time employed adults (Cai et al, 2022), showing significant disadvantage. Furthermore, one third of Autistic children in America live in poverty (Life Course Outcomes Program, 2020). Evidence related to Disability more generally shows a 12% point difference in poverty rates between those who are Disabled and those who are not, which is linked to under-employment (Joseph Rowntree Foundation, 2022). Accordingly, we conclude that Autistic people, who are less likely to be employed than Disabled people overall (ONS, 2021), are more likely to live in poverty than their neurotypical peers.

Within the English National Autism *Strategy*, there is no content related to poverty or housing. Poverty relief is controlled by the Westminster government, not devolved, and this lack of focus impacts Autistic people in Wales as well as England. Overall, poverty relief for Disabled people is founded on Victorian values that assume claimants are undeserving (Grant, 2023). As Autism is a largely hidden Disability, and Autistic accounts of pain and distress are minimised as part of epistemic injustice, these narratives of undeservingness can play a larger role for Autistic claimants.

For Autistic people who attempt to claim benefits, there are likely to be many challenges. The major forms of out of work income maintenance, Employment and Support Allowance (ESA) and Universal Credit, have been identified as problematic for all users due to delays, low rates of benefits that are not uprated in line with inflation, sanctions, and bureaucratic processes (see Grant, 2023). ESA prioritises work ('Employment') and is aggressively conditional on the claimants' behaviour ('Allowance'). Access to ESA is based on the Work Capability Test, which has been identified as unfit for purpose, due to its focus on being able to do any job, not just those that are available to the claimant, and outsourcing testing to private for-profit companies (Warren et al, 2014). Assessors are required to have Autism training and 'points', demonstrating eligibility for the Allowance, can be awarded for Autistic impairments related to claimants' responses to change and communication (House of Commons, 2018). However, access to ESA and Universal Credit is particularly challenging for Autistic people because of the confusing bureaucratic process. At the time of writing, the results of an inaccessible and underfunded benefits system were exacerbated by the cost-of-living crisis, which particularly impacts the cost of food and fuel.

In addition to income maintenance policies, Personal Independence Payment (PIP), is designed to meet the additional disability-related costs of living related to personal care and mobility (including journeys outside of the home). However, from its outset, PIP had the aim of reducing spending on disability living costs (Gray, 2017). The application process requires telephoning to obtain a form and then providing hand-written answers before a one-to-one interview where everything the person does can be used as evidence that they are not sufficiently Disabled (Grant, 2023). Claimant trust in PIP reaching correct and fair decisions is low due to lack of specialist assessors, lack of accuracy in recording interview contents and lack of transparency; the majority of appeals are awarded showing this lack of trust is evidence-based (Gray, 2017). Furthermore, within the reporting statistics, Autism is incorrectly classed as a psychiatric disorder, which as a category is the highest proportion of all claims, totalling 38%. However, this group is least likely to get an award following assessment, most likely to receive a short duration of award and least likely to have the award renewed (DWP, 2022). In addition, those who experience distress during journeys have been awarded less support than those with physical impairments (House of Commons, 2018), negatively impacting Autistic claimants who may find the sensory environment on public transport distressing.

Housing

Securing adequate housing is often problematic for Autistic people, with around 12% being homeless (Garratt and Flaherty, 2021). Within the UK, Housing Benefit (HB), or the housing component of Universal Credit, contributes towards rent for those on a low income or who are out of work. However, Autistic people have identified that staff administering social housing and benefits are unlikely to understand Autism (DfE and DHSC), 2021), which is likely to result in worse outcomes for Autistic people (Lipsky, 2010). Further challenges include the *bedroom tax*, where the cost of additional bedrooms is not included within HB, disproportionately affecting people who live alone, due to a dearth of one-bedroom properties. As Autistic people's sensory needs mean living with others can be challenging, they are particularly likely to be penalised by the *bedroom tax*. This is of more concern for those under the age of 35 who are likely to be in receipt of the Shared Accommodation Rate (Clair, 2022). Furthermore, the amounts covered by these benefits for those who rent in the private sector are based on the Local Housing Allowance (LHA) Rate – the 30th percentile of rent costs in the Broad Rental Market Area – rather than the actual cost of rent, and many private landlords refuse to accept tenants in receipt of welfare (Bailey, 2020; Clair, 2022). Furthermore, annual increases to LHA do not track rental price increases, disproportionately affecting Disabled people (Clair, 2022). As discussed in the previous sections, Autistic people are less likely to be in employment *or* be in receipt of appropriate benefits, for example, PIP, exacerbating their difficulty in meeting increasing housing costs.

Autistic people can experience joy in response to pleasant sensory experiences, however a challenging sensory environment in the home can cause severe distress. Due to lack of choice, many Autistic people will live in housing that does not meet their sensory needs and may be uncomfortably loud, too bright, visually cluttered, or have unpleasant textures or smells. Unpleasant sensory experiences can add to the 'sensory load' an Autistic person experiences; too high a sensory load can be overwhelming, and result in delayed processing, meltdowns (explosive reactions) or shutdowns (retreating inside one's self and becoming non-speaking). This can also lead to burnout in the long term, where skills – such as talking – can be lost for months, years or never be regained (NDTi, 2020: 19). This in turn negatively affects physical health, executive function and one's ability to engage in work or study.

Social care can range from organising ones' own support in their own home, to being placed in incarceration-like residential units, where personal freedoms are severely limited. Within England, when Disabled – including Autistic – people are awarded social care funds they receive a Personal Budget and are required to organise their own care. This is paradoxical as only the most severely Disabled Autistic people will be awarded a budget and are likely to find organising their care particularly challenging (NAO, 2018). Furthermore, a lack of appropriate housing for Autistic people has been identified as increasing the likelihood of secure residential care (Joint Committee on Human Rights, 2019). Widespread abuse of institutionally housed Autistic people was identified in the Winterbourne View report a decade ago and in the more recent Mendip House review, both of which also identified that many of the residents should never have been living there (DHSC, 2012; Flynn, 2018).

Residential care for Autistic people is often inappropriately based on the principles of Applied Behaviour Analysis and its sister-approach Positive Behavioural Support, despite strong evidence that Autistic people experience Post-Traumatic Stress Disorder as a response to this approach and subsequent guidance that it should not be used in the UK (Gore et al, 2022). The Care Quality Commission (2020) have reported inappropriate use of restraint and the use of incarceration, including solitary confinement like conditions, which are not in the person's best interest; both are associated with the death of Autistic people. To date there is a dearth of high-quality evidence for how Autistic adults should be supported by social care (DHSC, 2022). However, the DHSC (2022) recommended that social care for Autistic people should be based on a principle of autonomy, with the least possible intervention used, and that specialist social workers should be established to facilitate appropriate social care.

Discussion: What would good social policy for Autistic people look like?

Our analysis shows that social policies in England and Wales consistently fail to meet Autistic needs in relation to all five of Beveridge's Giants. Overall, bureaucracy is rife throughout all areas of social policy, which is particularly difficult for Autistic people to navigate. This affects those seeking accommodations related to health, education (DSA), income maintenance (ESA and UC), disability-related costs of living (PIP), in work disability accommodations (Access to Work) and housing (HB). Policies are also largely created without sufficient input from Autistic people, and place responsibility on individual Autistic people and/or public servants, meaning that widespread systemic barriers prevent policies from meeting their stated aims. A lack of staff time and resources are a common barrier across the Giants, as has been understood for almost half a century (Lipsky, 2010). When this is accompanied by misunderstandings of Autism and the incorrect problematisation and stigmatisation of Autistic people (Milton, 2012), it is no wonder that these policies fail to support Autistic people. We believe that this systematic failure of social policy plays a part in the extremely high suicide rate of Autistic people compared to neurotypical peers (Mandell, 2018).

When we consider these social policies together, the knock-on impacts from one policy area to the next are clear. Starting with a lack of diagnosis, delays and the requirement that Autistic people navigate bureaucratic mazes mean that many fail to receive recognition of their impairments. Although a diagnosis is not a golden ticket that automatically guarantees support, often without it no other support can be received. Diagnoses are not always added to primary care records and do not guarantee that any accommodations will be made, so Autistic people are more likely to have unmet healthcare needs. Regarding education, Autistic children are failed by the system which leads to Autistic adults being less likely to attend further and higher education. Without qualifications that match abilities, Autistic people are underemployed. This impacts income significantly, with one third of Autistic people who are not working also not claiming benefits, resulting in significant poverty. With insufficient income, Autistic people have a high risk of becoming homeless. This may result in institutionalisation, which restricts our liberties and is known to negatively impact on our health, thus further exacerbating our disadvantage.

We propose that this systematic failure is rooted in epistemic injustice. Government consultations and policies are written from non-Autistic perspectives, providing limited opportunities for Autistic people to talk about the discrimination and barriers we face every day (Fricker, 2007). At times it can feel as though these are grounded in understandings which aim to privilege our abilities – and lack of reliance on government support – without accepting the disabling nature of contemporary society and our inability to access said support. For instance, all four authors have succeeded in *some* academic environments, where barriers to participation have been removed. However, while we can excel at this work, we could not work (for example) as a bartender, due to the overwhelming sensory environment. There is currently no meaningful inclusion of these lived experiences within UK social policy, which is a form of hermeneutical injustice. In addition, when Autistic people try to explain these lived experiences, non-Autistic policy makers find it unbelievable or minimise the extent of the issue, because it is so far from their own lived experiences – an example of testimonial injustice. The construction of Autism as a medical condition and a mental illness by the Department for Work and Pensions can invalidate our experiences further.

For UK social policy to effectively address the Five Giants for Autistic people, first and foremost Autistic people need to be accepted and afforded the same epistemic validity as non-Autistic people. This process can be started through co-producing social policy as per the Welsh Government model (for example, see Welsh Government, 2021c). This should not be limited solely to Autism policy. As we have outlined, Autistic people do not exist in a silo. All social policy affects Autistic people; therefore, Autistic people's experiences and knowledge need to be included in the shaping of these wider policies. Should UK policy makers wish to be more inclusive of Autistic people when designing their policies, some *easy wins* are available. First, access to all public services should be available via email for everybody, instead of lengthy waits on hold followed by a telephone call, which is known to be *painful* to Autistic people (Howard and Sedgewick, 2021). The application process for DSA, ESA, PIP and Access to Work, all of which attract Disabled claimants, seems to have been deliberately designed to limit access. Requiring PIP application forms to be completed by hand is archaic and punishing to neurodivergent people who may otherwise use software to write for them. Second, as Autistic people's trust in the knowledge of public servants is low (and staff themselves report a lack of knowledge and confidence), widespread training in Autism should be delivered. Unlike the Oliver McGowan Mandatory Training, it should be designed and delivered by Autistic people, to ensure that those staff can reliably *understand* our needs. If our needs were better met in educational settings, our employment trajectories would improve, reducing poverty and homelessness as well as improving Autistic people's mental health. Third, a policy that would benefit many Disabled people in addition to Autistic people, would be to ensure the right to flexible studying and working including working from home whenever the type of study or work allows. Fourth, Autistic people should never be denied an advocate to speak on their behalf when accessing public services.

The popular understanding of Autism still centres around young, cis-gendered white men and boys. However, we know that many kinds of people are Autistic. Accordingly, an intersectional approach is essential to reduce disadvantage in government policy (Crenshaw, 1989). For example, one survey of Autistic adults found that half identified as lesbian, gay, bisexual and transgender (LGBT+), 19% as transgender and 56% as Disabled (Bonnello, 2022). For those Autistic people with additional marginalised identities – including being female, Black, Brown, or from another other minoritised ethnicity (Jones and Mandell, 2020), Disabled, or otherwise marginalised – there will be additional and cascading disadvantage. For example, the death of Esther Eketi-Mulo and her four-year-old son Chadrack show how a Black, refugee, Autistic and epileptic woman died alone in her home, with her son starving to death two weeks later. Multiple public service failures, embedded in systematic racism, ableism and bureaucracy led to these entirely preventable deaths (Kourti, 2022). In addition, to date there has been a dearth of research on the experiences of older Autistic people and this has yet to clearly focus on their *needs* (Happé and Charlton, 2012). Almost a decade ago, the National Autistic Society (2013) produced a report on the challenges facing older Autistic people and their families, making suggestions for policy-based changes. However, the English Autism *Strategy* does not mention Autistic older people or their specific needs, and references in the Welsh *Code of Practice* are extremely limited and lack specificity.

Conclusion

Epistemic injustice has meant that social policies impacting the lives of Autistic people are currently based on deficit narratives about us, which have been outdated since the introduction of the 1960's Social Model of Disability. There is now an urgent imperative for all areas of social policy to comprehensively consider the needs of Autistic people through every level of policy making – not simply in Autism-specific policies. This should be actualised through meaningful co-production of policy with Autistic adults, using an assets-based approach that understands Autism as a neuro-difference, not a neuro-deficit. This should replace the use of tokenistic consultations which are often inaccessible to Autistic people, and particularly Autistic people with learning disabilities. It is especially important for an intersectional lens to be used, to ensure that the needs of Autistic people who are multifariously marginalised are met, and to ensure that the needs of older Autistic people are met. When social policy better meets the needs of Autistic people, we theorise that our early mortality rate and extremely high suicide rate will become closer to those of the general population.

Acknowledgements: we acknowledge editorial support of Carol McIntyre and Libby Foot, and the Access to Work funding which paid for their time.

Grant's role was funded by the Higher Education Funding Council for Wales. G. Williams and K. Williams receive support from the Economic and Social Research Council, and K. Williams is a Director of Autistic UK. Woods earns income from Autism and Pathological Demand Avoidance related training events.

References

Allsop, K. and Kinderman, P. (2021) 'The use of diagnoses in mental health service eligibility and exclusion criteria', *Journal of Mental Health*, 30(1): 97–103.

Bonnello, C. (2022) 'Autism survey'. Available from: *https://autisticnotweird. com/autismsurvey/#autisticpeople* [Accessed 7.9.22].

Bailey, N. (2020) 'Poverty and the re-growth of private renting in the UK, 1994–2018', Mourshed, M. (ed.) *PLOS ONE* 15(2): e0228273. Available from: Doi: 10.1371/journal.pone.0228273

Beveridge, W. (1942) *Social Insurance and Allied Services*, London: HMSO.

Booth, J. (2016) *Autism Equality in the Workplace*, London: Jessica Kingsley.

Byrne, J.P. (2022) 'Perceiving the social unknown: how the hidden curriculum affects the learning of autistic students in higher education', *Innovations in Education and Teaching International*, 59(2): 142–9.

Cai, R.Y., Gallagher, E., Haas, K., Love, A., Gibbs. (2022) 'Exploring the income, savings and debt levels of autistic adults living in Australia', *Advances in Autism*. Available from: https://doi.org/10.1108/AIA-01-2022-0004

Care Quality Commission. (2020) 'Out of sight – who cares? A review of restraint, seclusion and segregation for autistic people, and people with a learning disability and/or mental health condition', [online], Care quality Commission. Available from: https://www.cqc.org.uk/sites/default/files/20201218_rssreview_report.pdf

Catala, A., Faucher, L. and Poirier, P. (2021) 'Autism, epistemic injustice, and epistemic disablement: a relational account of epistemic agency', *Synthese: 199: 9013-9039*. Doi:10.1007/s11229-021-03192-7 – Available from: https://link.springer.com/article/10.1007/s11229-021-03192-7

Centers for Disease Control and Prevention (CDC). (2022) *Autism Data*. Available from: https://www.cdc.gov/ncbddd/autism/data.html [Accessed 8.8.22].

Chapman, R. and Carel, H. (2022) 'Neurodiversity, epistemic injustice, and the good human life', *Journal of Social Philosophy: 53(4)*: 614–631. Available from: https://doi.org/10.1111/josp.12456

Citizens Advice. (2020) *Tribunal Trouble*. Available from: https://www.cit izensadvice.org.uk/about-us/our-work/policy/policy-research-topics/work-policy-research-surveys-and-consultation-responses/work-policy-research/tribunal-trouble-how-a-backlogged-tribunal-system-is-stopp ing-people-enforcing-their-rights/ [Accessed 23.8.22].

Clair, A. (2022) 'The effect of local housing allowance reductions on overcrowding in the private rented sector in England', *International Journal of Housing Policy*, 22(1): 119–37.

Corden, K., Brewer, R. and Cage, E.A (2022) 'Systematic review of healthcare professionals' knowledge, self-efficacy and attitudes towards working with Autistic people', *Journal of Autism and Developmental Disorders*, 9: 386–99

Crenshaw, K. Demarginaliszing the intersection of race and sex: aa black feminist critique of antidiscrimination doctrine, feminish theory and antiracist politics. *University of Chicago Legal Forum*, 1: 139–167.

DfE and DHSC. (2021) *Summary of findings from the government's review of the National Autism Strategy 'Think Autism': Call for evidence.* Available from: https://www.gov.uk/government/consultations/review-of-the-natio nal-autism-strategy-think-autism-call-for-evidence/outcome/summary-of-findings-from-the-governments-review-of-the-national-autism-strat egy-think-autism-call-for-evidence [Accessed: 2.12.21]

DHSC. (2012) 'Winterbourne View Hospital: Department of Health Review and Response'. Available from: https://www.gov.uk/governm ent/publications/winterbourne-view-hospital-department-of-health-rev iew-and-response [Accessed 8.9.22].

DHSC. (2022) 'A spectrum of opportunity'. Available at: https://www.gov. uk/government/publications/social-work-and-autistic-young-people-an-exploratory-study/a-spectrum-of-opportunity-an-exploratory-study-of-social-work-practice-with-autistic-young-adults-and-their-families#reco mmendations [Accessed 24.8.22].

DHSC and DfE (2021). National Strategy for autistic children, young people and adults: 2021 to 2026. Available form: https://www.gov.uk/governm ent/publications/national-strategy-for-autistic-children-young-people-and-adults-2021-to-2026 [Accesses 2.3.23]

Djela, M. (2021) 'Change of autism narrative is required to improve employment of autistic people', *Advances in Autism*, 7(1): 86–100.

Doherty, M., Neilson, S., O'Sullivan, J., Carravallah, L., Johnson, M., Cullen, W., et al (2022) 'Barriers to healthcare and self-reported adverse outcomes for autistic adults', *BMJ Open*, 12(2): e056904.

DWP. (2022) 'Personal Independence Payment: Official Statistics'. Available from: https://www.gov.uk/government/statistics/personal-independence-payment-statistics-to-april-2022/personal-independence-payment-offic ial-statistics-to-april-2022#pip-statistics-by-disabling-condition [Accessed 24.8.22].

Ellis, R., Williams, K., Brown, A., Healer, E., Grant. A. (forthcoming) 'A hostile context, very limited intervention theory and almost no change in outcomes: findings from a systematic realist review of health passports for Autistic adults'

Flynn, M. (2018) 'Safeguarding Adults Board: Mendip House'. Available from: https://ssab.safeguardingsomerset.org.uk/wp-content/uploads/2018 0206_Mendip-House_SAR_FOR_PUBLICATION.pdf Accessed 23.9.22

Fricker, M. (2007) *Epistemic Injustice*, Oxford: Oxford University Press.

Garratt, E. and Flaherty, J. (2021) '"There's nothing I can do to stop it": homelessness among autistic people in a British city', *Disability & Society*, Available from: Doi: 10.1080/09687599.2021.2004881

Gore, N., Sapiets, S., Denne, L., Hastings, R., Toogood, S., MacDonald., et al (2022) 'Positive Behavioural Support in the UK: A State of the Nation Report' *International Journal of Positive Behavioural Support* 12(1): i–46 Available from: https://www.ingentaconnect.com/contentone/bild/ijpbs/2022/00000012/a00101s1/art00001?crawler=true&mimetype=applicat ion/pdf [Accessed 24.8.22]

Grant, A., et al (forthcoming) 'Use of Health Passports for Autistic people in UK maternity care: A survey of Autistic adults'

Grant, A. (2023) 'Scroungers, shirkers and the sick: disability and welfare in the 21st Century', in Gregory, L. and Iafrati, S. *Diversity and Welfare Provision,* Bristol: Policy Press.

Grant, A. and Kara, H. (2021) 'Considering the autistic advantage in qualitative research: autistic researchers and qualitative data collection and analysis', *Contemporary Social Science* 16(5): 589–603, Available from: Doi: 10.1080/21582041.2021.1998589

Gray, P. (2017) *The Second Independent Review of Personal Independence Payments.* London: Department for Work and Pensions. Available from: https://ass ets.publishing.service.gov.uk/government/uploads/system/uploads/atta chment_data/file/604097/pip-assessment-second-independent-review. pdf. [Accessed 24.8.22].

Happé F, Charlton R, A: Aging in Autism Spectrum Disorders: A Mini-Review. Gerontology 2012;58:70–78. doi: 10.1159/000329720

Health Education England. (2022) *The Oliver McGowan Mandatory Training in Learning Disability and Autism.* Available from: https://www.hee.nhs.uk/ our-work/learning-disability/oliver-mcgowan-mandatory-training-learn ing-disability-autism. [Accessed 8.8.22].

HM Government. (2022) *SEND Review.* Available from: https://www.gov. uk/government/consultations/send-review-right-support-right-place-right-time. [Accessed 7.9.22].

Holmes, C. (2022) 'Report into Disabled Students Allowance'. Available from: https://lordchrisholmes.com/report-disabled-students-allowance-dsa/. [Accessed 22.8.22].

House of Commons. (2018) *Autism – Overview of UK Policy and Services.* Available from: https://www.base-uk.org/sites/default/files/knowledgeb ase/CBP-7172.pdf [Accessed 24.8.22].

Howard, P. L., & Sedgewick, F. (2021). "'Anything but the phone!":
Communication mode preferences in the autism community', *Autism*,
25(8): 2265–2278. https://doi.org/10.1177/13623613211014995

Joint Committee on Human Rights. (2019) *The Detention of Young People with
Learning Disabilities and/or Autism*. Available from: https://publications.par
liament.uk/pa/jt201919/jtselect/jtrights/121/121.pdf. [Accessed 24.8.22].

Jones, D.R. and Mandell, D.S. (2020) 'To address racial disparities in autism
research, we must think globally, act locally', *Autism*, 24(7): 1587–e9.

Joseph Rowntree Foundation. (2022) *UK Poverty 2022*. Available
from: https://www.jrf.org.uk/report/uk-poverty-2022 [Accessed 24.8.22].

Kourti, M. (2022) Autism, race and ethnicity, *Autscape, The Hayes, Derbyshire*.
9.8.22

Left Brain Right Brain. (2009) *Don't Write Me Off*. Available from: https://
leftbrainrightbrain.co.uk/2009/10/13/3322/. [Accessed 7.9.22].

Life Course Outcomes Program (2020). *National Autism Indicators
Report: children on the autism spectrum and family financial hardship*. Available
from: https://drexel.edu/~/media/Files/autismoutcomes/publications/
2020%20Nair%20report.ashx [Accessed 2.3.23]

Lipsky, M. (2010) *Street-Level Bureaucracy*, New York City: Russell
Sage Foundation.

Madriaga, M. and Goodley, D. (2010) 'Moving beyond the minimum: socially
just pedagogies and Asperger's syndrome in UK higher education',
International Journal of Inclusive Education, 14(2): 115–31.

Mandell, D. (2018) 'Dying before their time: addressing premature mortality
among autistic people', *Autism*, 22(3): 234–5.

Mason, D., McConachie, H., Garland, D., Petrou, A., Rodger, J., Parr, J.
(2018) 'Predictors of quality of life for autistic adults', *Autism Research*,
11(8): 1138–47.

Milton, D. (2012) 'On the ontological status of autism: the "'double empathy
problem'", *Disability & Society*, 27(6): 883–7.

Mladenov, T. and Brennan, C.S. (2021) 'Social vulnerability and the impact
of policy responses to COVID-19 on disabled people', *Sociology of Health
& Illness*, 43(9): 2049–65.

Mulder, A.M. and Cashin, A (2014) 'The need to support students with
Autism at university', *Issues in Mental Health Nursing*, 35(9): 664–71.

National Audit Office (NAO). (2018) *Adult Social Care at a Glance*,
London: National Audit Office. Available from: https://www.nao.org.
uk/wp-content/uploads/2018/07/Adult-social-care-at-a-glance.pdf.
[Accessed 23.9.22].

National Autistic Society. (2013) Getting on? Growing Older with Autism: A
Policy Report. Available from: https://www.basw.co.uk/system/files/
resources/basw_21807-10_0.pdf. [Accessed 12.12.21].

National Autistic Society. (2019) *The Autism Act, 10 Years On*. Available from: https://s4.chorus-mk.thirdlight.com/file/1573224908/61601577 629/width=-1/height=-1/format=-1/fit=scale/t=443899/e=never/k= a402a7d4/nas_appga_report.pdf. [Accessed 7.9.22].

NDTi. (2020) *Supporting Autistic Flourishing at Home and Beyond*. Available from: https://www.ndti.org.uk/assets/files/Housing-paper-final-format ted-v2.pdf. [Accessed 9.8.22].

NDTi. (2022) *Evaluation of the Oliver McGowan Mandatory Training Trial in Learning Disability and Autism*. Available from: https://healtheducationengl and.sharepoint.com/:w:/g/Comms/Digital/EfplaksIV79FiLeFHJT798c BWDB9ePLKuWRPnbr8aferwg?rtime=LsJifceQ2kg. [Accessed 7.9.22].

NHS. (2019) *NHS Long Term Plan*. Available from: https://www.longtermp lan.nhs.uk/wp-content/uploads/2019/08/nhs-long-term-plan-version-1.2.pdf [Accessed: 31 May 2022].

NICE. (2021) *Autism Spectrum Disorder in Adults: Diagnosis And Management*. Available from: https://www-nice-org-uk.abc.cardiff.ac.uk/guidance/ cg142/chapter/Recommendations.

ONS. (2021) *Outcomes for Disabled People in the UK: 2020*. Available from: https://www.ons.gov.uk/peoplepopulationandcommunity/healthandsoc ialcare/Disability/articles/outcomesforDisabledpeopleintheuk/2020#emp loyment. [Accessed: 6.8.21].

Robards, F. Kang, M., Usherwood, T. and Sanci, L. (2018) 'How marginalized young people access, engage with, and navigate health-care systems in the digital age: systematic review', *Journal of Adolescent Health*, 62(4): 365–81.

Royal College of Psychiatry. (2020) *The Psychiatric Management of Autism in Adults*. Available from: https://www.rcpsych.ac.uk/improving-care/ campaigning-for-better-mental-health-policy/college-reports/2020-coll ege-reports/cr228. [Accessed 12.8.22].

Sicilia, M., Guarini, E., Sancino, A., Andreani, M., Ruffini, R. (2016) 'Public services management and co-production in multi-level governance settings', *International Review of Administrative Sciences*, 82(1): 8–27.

UK Parliament. (2009) *Don't Write Me Off Campaign*. Available from: https:// edm.parliament.uk/early-day-motion/39649/dont-write-me-off-campa ign [Accessed 7.9.22].

US Government (2006) *USA Combating Austim Act 2006*. Available from: https://www.govinfo.gov/app/details/PLAW-109publ416

Underwood, J.F.G., DelPozo-Banos, M., Frizzato, A., John, A., Hall, J. (2021) 'Evidence of increasing recorded diagnosis of autism spectrum disorders in Wales, UK', *Autism*, 26(6): 1499–508.

von Below, R. Spaeth, E. and Horlin, C. (2021) 'Autism in higher education: dissonance between educators' perceived knowledge and reported teaching behaviour', *International Journal of Inclusive Education*, Doi: 10.1080/13603116.2021.1988159

Warren, J., Garthwaite, K. and Bambra, C. (2014) 'After Atos Healthcare: is the employment and support allowance fit for purpose and does the Work Capability Assessment have a future?', *Disability & Society*, 29(8): 1319–23.

Welsh Government. (2021a) *Code of Practice on the Delivery of Autism Services*. Available from: https://gov.wales/code-practice-delivery-autism-services-0 [Accessed 8.8.22].

Welsh Government. (2021b) *The Additional Learning Needs Code for Wales 2021*. Available at: https://gov.wales/sites/default/files/publications/2022-06/220622-the-additional-learning-needs-code-for-wales-2021.pdf [Accessed 12.8.22].

Welsh Government. (2021c) *Strategy for Unpaid Carers*. Available from: https://gov.wales/strategy-unpaid-carers [Accessed 14.04.22].

Westminster Commission on Autism. (2016) A *Spectrum* of *Obstacles*. Available from: https://westminsterautismcommission.files.wordpress.com/2016/03/ar1011_ncg-autism-report-july-2016.pdf [Accessed 8.8.22].

Westminster Commission on Autism. (2018) Support Surrounding Diagnosis. Available from: https://drive.google.com/file/d/12YS_OfUow 1GAXyfWTPv79UCZhOR6SFKZ/view [Accessed 8.8.22].

William, L., Pauksztat, B. and Corby, S. (2019) 'Justice obtained? How disabled claimants fare at employment tribunals, *Industrial Relations Journal*, 50: 314–30.

Williams, G. (2021) 'Theory of autistic mind: a refreshed relevance theoretic account of so-called autistic pragmatic "impairment"', *Journal of Pragmatics*, 180(1): 121–30.

Williams, K. (2022) '"Why Are You Causing Trouble?": Autistic Adults' Experiences of Ableism During Telehealth Appointments', MSc Dissertation, Cardiff University.

Woods, R. Milton, Arnold D. and Graby, S. (2018) 'Redefining critical Autism studies: a more inclusive interpretation', *Disability & Society*, 33(6): 974–9.

Yergeau, R. (2017) *Authoring Autism*, Durham, NC: Duke Press.

Index

References to endnotes show both the page number and the note number (164n4).